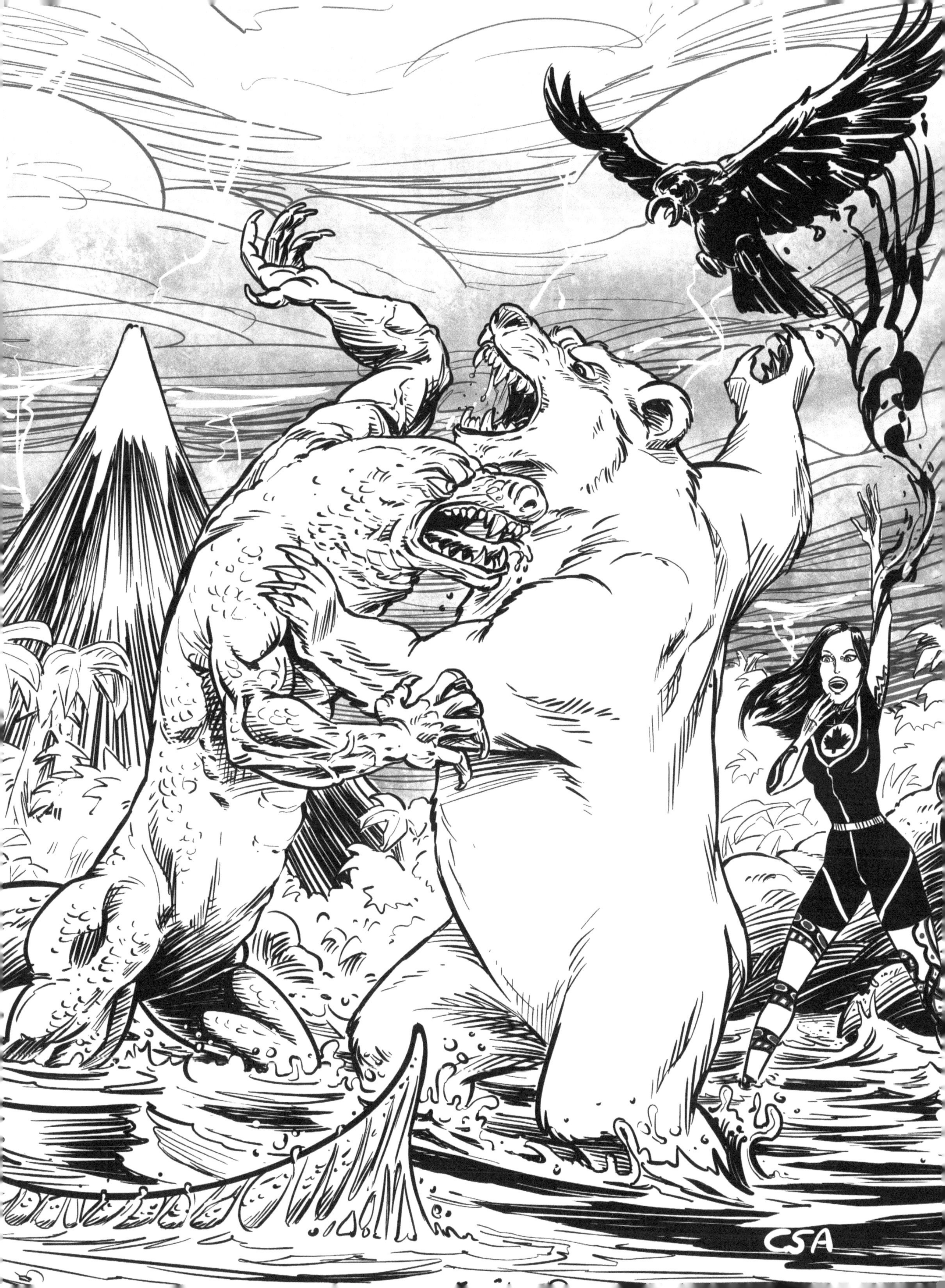

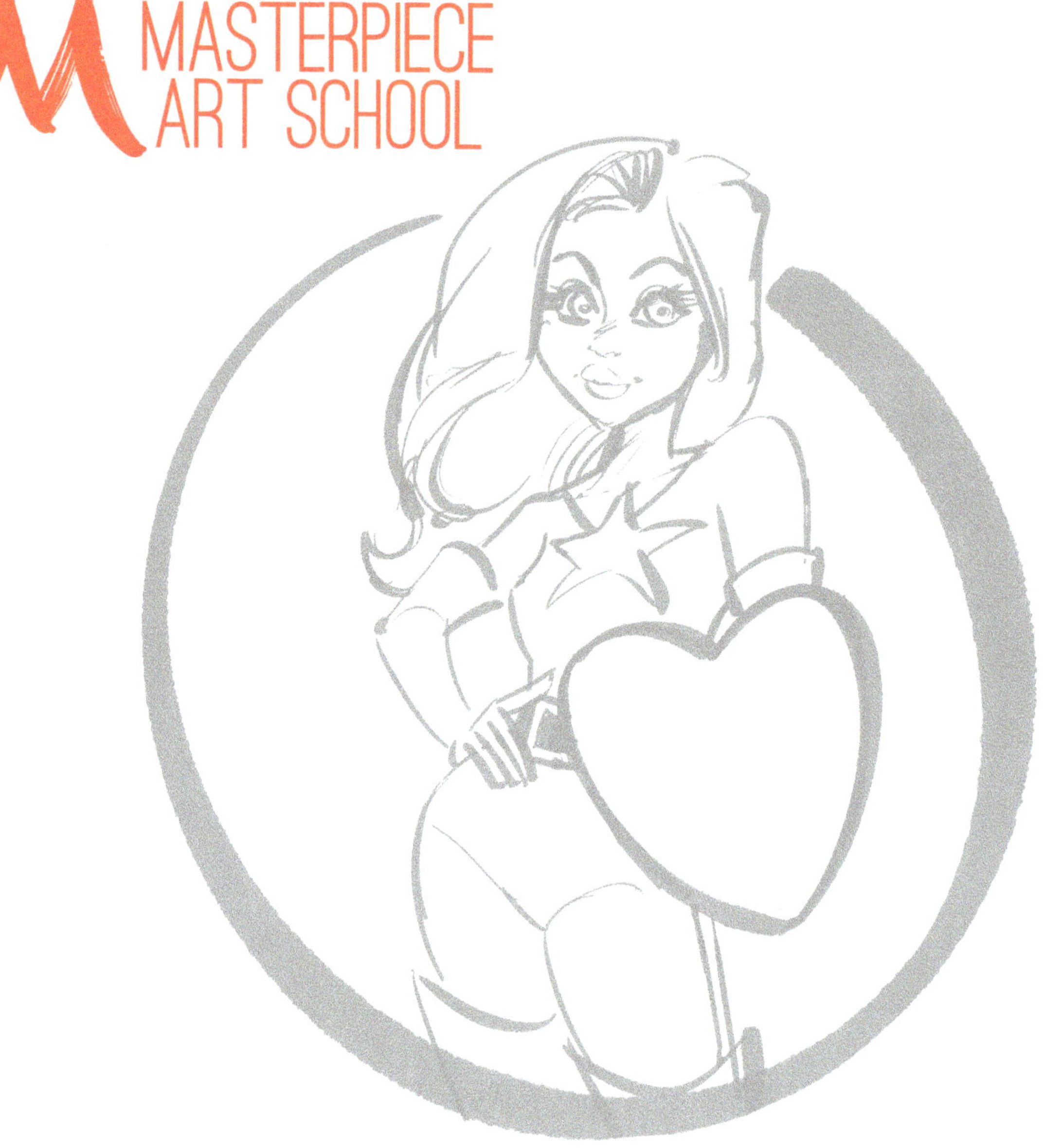

MasterpieceArtSchool.com

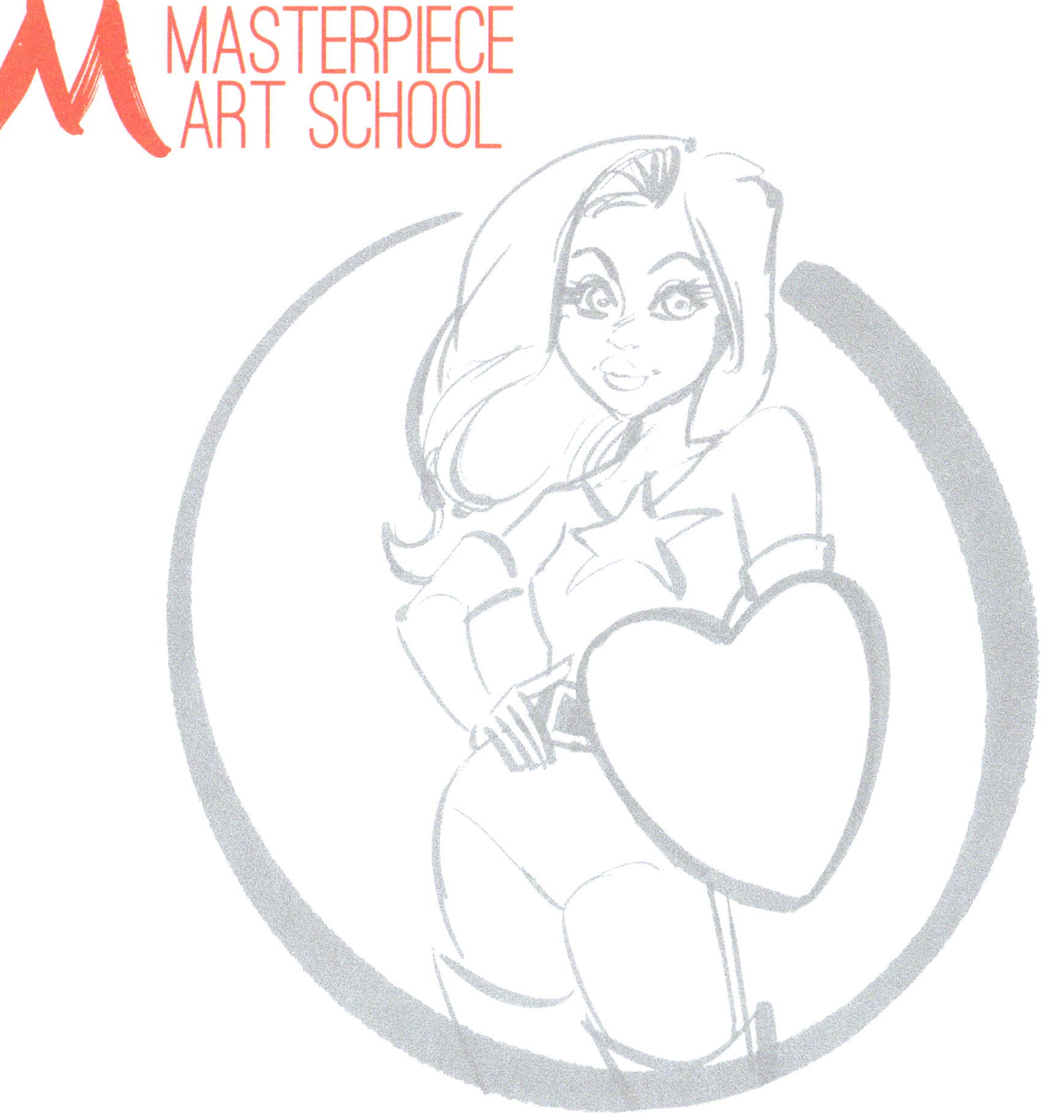

Cover Artwork by Cristian S. Aluas from the comic book titled "Camouflage"
Art and Graphic Design by Cristian S. Aluas

ISBN 979-8-218-03598-3

MasterpieceArtSchool.com

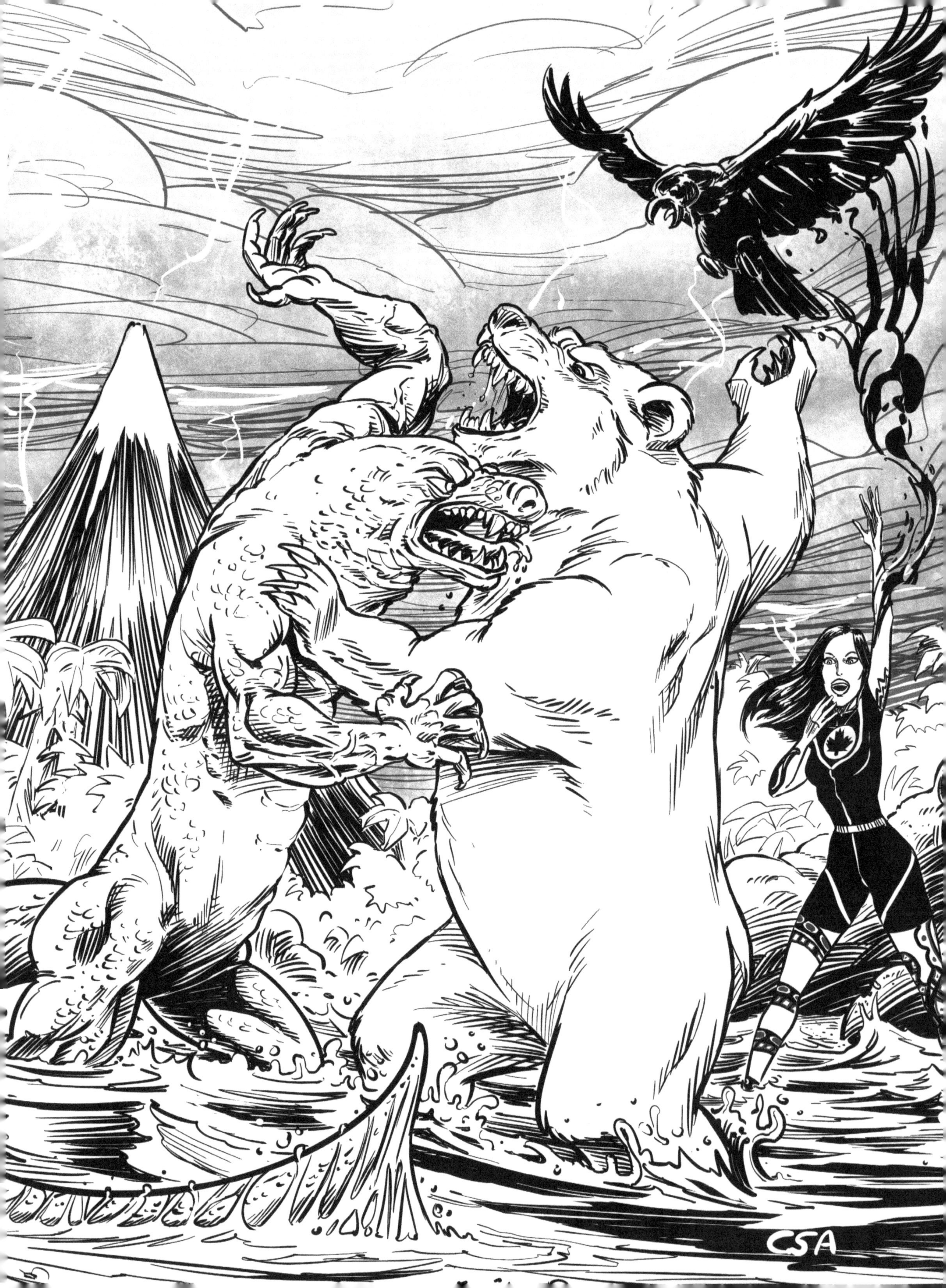

Table of Contents

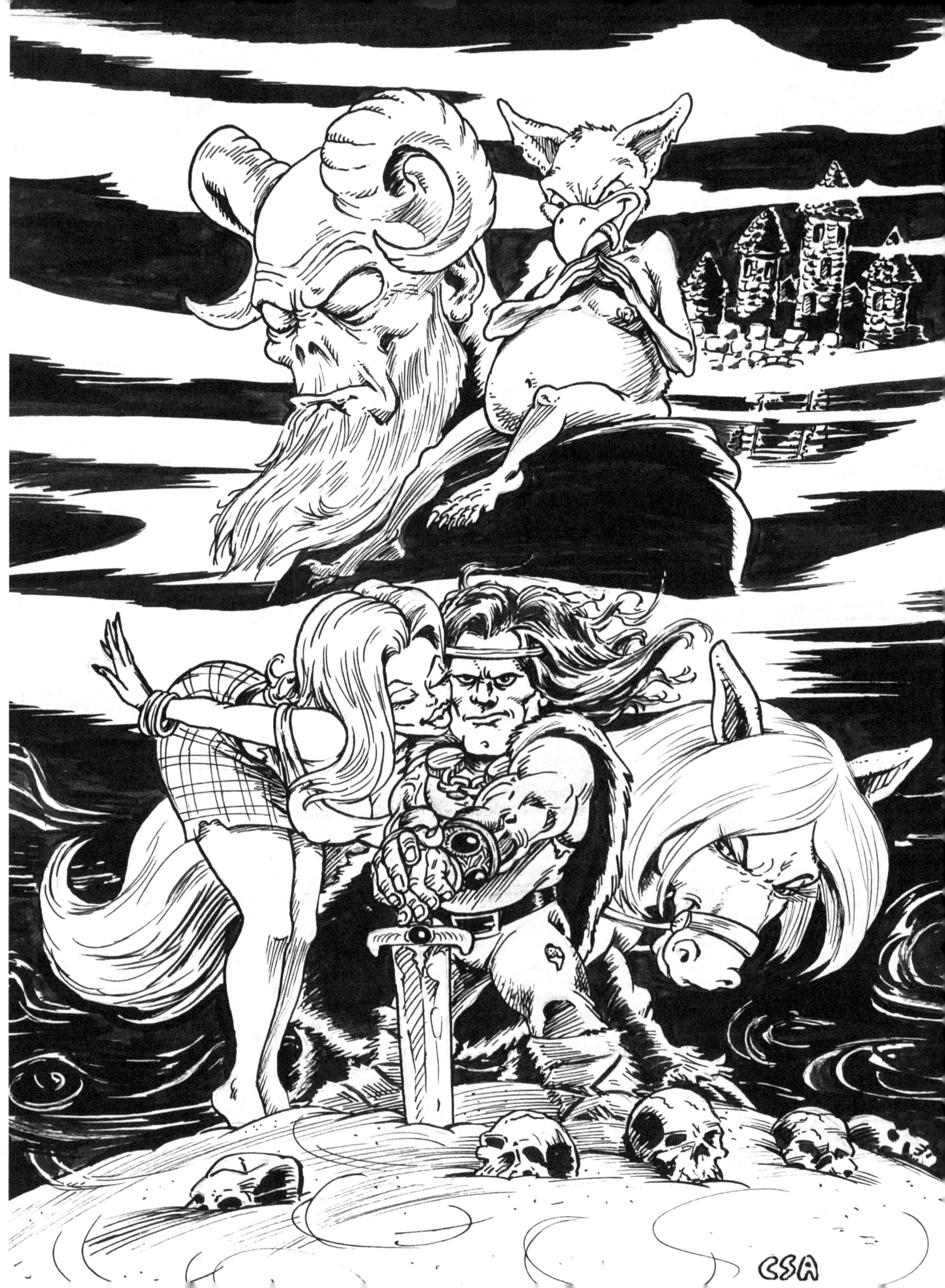

Introduction:

THIS BOOK IS A CULMINATION OF THE CARTOONING CLASSES THAT WERE TAUGHT AT MASTERPIECE ART SCHOOL. THE DRAWING THEORIES AND EXERCISES ARE COMPRISED OF THINGS I LEARNED WHILE STUDYING ANIMATION AT ALGONQUIN COLLEGE IN OTTAWA CANADA AND FIFTEEN YEARS OF TEACHING AT PRIVATE SCHOOLS, CITY-RUN SCHOOLS, AND AT MY BRICK AND MORTAR LOCATION. ALTHOUGH MANY OF THESE CARTOONING EXAMPLES ARE STILL AVAILABLE ONLINE AT MASTERPIECEARTSCHOOL.COM, I THOUGHT IT'D BE FUN AND USEFUL TO COMPILE THEM ALL IN ONE BOOK FOR STUDENTS TO ENJOY AND EASILY REFER BACK TO.

A BIT ABOUT MY BACKGROUND: I'M A BORN ARTIST. AT EIGHTEEN, I SELF-PUBLISHED MY VERY OWN COMIC BOOK. I WAS STILL IN HIGH SCHOOL AT THE TIME. IT WAS A GREAT FORMATIVE EXPERIENCE THAT I CHERISH AND FROM WHICH I LEARNED A LOT. ONE OF THE THINGS I LEARNED FROM THAT EARLY ENDEAVOR WAS THAT, ALTHOUGH I'M A PRETTY GOOD ARTIST (BEING SELF-TAUGHT UP UNTIL THAT POINT) THERE WAS A LOT THAT I DIDN'T KNOW. BESIDES THE PERSONAL FEAR OF BEING STUCK WORKING A MINIMUM WAGE JOB, I FELT FURTHERING MY EDUCATION WOULD BE A GREAT ADVANTAGE TO HELPING ME REALIZE MY PROFESSIONAL ASPIRATIONS. DRAWING WAS FUN AND I KNEW IT WOULD BE BETTER TO BE AN ARTIST AND DO WHAT I LOVE IN LIFE THAN TO TOIL FLIPPING BURGERS. I APPLIED TO THE ANIMATION PROGRAM IN MY LOCAL TOWN. IT WAS A GOOD PROGRAM AND ATTENDING A COMMUNITY COLLEGE GAVE ME THE TRAINING THAT WOULD LEAD TO A BETTER JOB IN A FIELD CATERED TO MY TALENTS AND INTERESTS. ADDITIONALLY, HAVING ATTENDED A SPECIALTY ARTS HIGH SCHOOL BEFORE THAT, I KNEW THAT TO BE A GREAT ARTIST YOU NEEDED TO HAVE A STRONG FOUNDATION. SMART ENOUGH TO KNOW THAT I COULD NOT IMPROVE ON MY OWN, I WENT TO COLLEGE.

IT WAS FUNNY; BEFORE COLLEGE, I THOUGHT CARTOONS WERE MADE BY MAGIC. I DREW A LOT ALL THROUGH MY CHILDHOOD BUT I NEVER IMAGINED IT WOULD LEAD TO ANYTHING. AT ALGONQUIN, IT WAS THE FIGURE DRAWING THAT APPEALED TO ME MOST. I HAD A LOT OF THAT IN HIGH SCHOOL AND I KNEW THAT IF I BECAME GOOD AT OBSERVATIONAL DRAWING FROM LIFE I'D BE GOOD AT DRAWING JUST ABOUT ANYTHING. BEYOND MY LOVE OF LIFE DRAWING, I BEGAN TO LOVE THE PEOPLE IN MY CLASSES AND THE RICH HISTORY OF ANIMATION AND CARTOONING. ALL THE CLASSES I TOOK WERE INDISPENSABLE AND WHAT I LEARNED ABOUT CARTOONING CHANGED MY LIFE FOR THE BETTER. I'VE HAD A TWENTY YEAR CAREER AS A FREELANCER UP UNTIL THIS POINT. AND STILL GOING STRONG.

A LOT OF THE EXERCISES THAT I'VE USED IN MY CLASSES I FIRST LEARNED IN COLLEGE, LIKE DESIGNING CHARACTERS WITH UNUSUAL SHAPES, EXAGGERATED POSING, THE THEORY OF STRETCH AND SQUASH, AND MY METHOD FOR DRAWING CARICATURES. A LOT OF THE OTHER TECHNIQUES I'VE DEVELOPED ON MY OWN OR FROM STUDYING VARIOUS COMIC BOOK ARTISTS. THEY ALSO GAVE US A SCREENWRITING CLASS. IT WAS VERY DRY BUT MORE RECENTLY I WROTE A COUPLE OF FEATURE-LENGTH SCREENPLAYS AND IN THAT PROCESS I REVISITED THE GENRE AND REINFORCED MY THEORIES ABOUT STORY ARCS AND DIRECTING. I'LL BE COVERING THE SUBJECT OF COMIC BOOK CARTOONING AND PANEL COMPOSITION TOO.

BY THE END OF THIS BOOK, YOU WILL HAVE A REALLY GREAT STARTER KIT FOR YOUR CARTOONING CAREER WITH MULTIPLE PATHWAYS TO FOLLOW. YOU'LL GET A PEEK INTO DRAWING REALISTIC CHARACTERS AND ALSO EXAGGERATING THOSE CHARACTERS FOR COMEDIC OR CREATIVE PURPOSES. YOU'LL GAIN TIPS FOR DRAWING SPECIFIC THINGS THAT ARE CONSIDERED DIFFICULT, SUCH AS HANDS, FEET, EARS, AND SO ON. YOU'LL LEARN HOW TO CONSTRUCT THE HUMAN BODY AND ANIMALS. YOU'LL LEARN HOW TO DRAW EXPRESSIONS, THROUGH THE FACE AND BODY. YOU'LL LEARN THE THEORIES OF ONE POINT, TWO POINT, AND THREE POINT PERSPECTIVE. AFTER ALL, WE HAVE TO PUT OUR CHARACTERS SOMEWHERE. BACKGROUNDS ARE IMPORTANT AND EXPRESSIVE TOO. THEN YOU'LL HAVE FUN DRAWING SINGLE PANEL COMICS AND MULTI-PANEL COMICS. IN THAT PROCESS, YOU'LL LEARN TO MERGE CHARACTERS WITH THEIR ENVIRONMENTS AND TELLING FUNNY OR COMPELLING STORIES WITH YOUR DRAWINGS.

THESE DETAILED YET SIMPLE LESSONS ARE MEANT TO BE INFORMATIVE AND FUN. PAGES ARE DESIGNED TO BE VISUALLY INTERESTING AND EASY TO FOLLOW. AS MENTIONED, MANY TOPICS WERE TAKEN FROM ACTUAL CLASSROOM HANDOUTS THAT WERE DISTRIBUTED AMONG STUDENTS. ANY OF THE PAGES CAN BE PRINTED OUT AND PINNED TO YOUR DESK, AS SIMPLE REMINDERS OR CHEAT SHEETS. KEEP IN MIND TOO THAT YOU SHOULD ALWAYS OBSERVE A LOT FROM LIFE. CARTOONING IS A SHORTHAND FOR QUICKLY RELAYING AMUSING IDEAS FROM OUR REAL-LIFE OBSERVATIONS. I BELIEVE THE BEST CARTOONISTS HOLD A MIRROR UP TO HUMANITY AND TRANSLATE OUR LIVES INTO CUTE AND SOMETIMES PIERCING CARICATURES. THE INDUSTRY IS WIDE OPEN FOR US TO BE AS CREATIVE AS POSSIBLE. THIS BOOK IS THE STARTER KIT TO YOUR IMAGINATION AND YOUR LIMITLESS POTENTIAL AS CARTOONISTS AND SEQUENTIAL ILLUSTRATORS. ENJOY!

SINCERELY, THANK YOU,

Cristian

NEW YORK, 2022

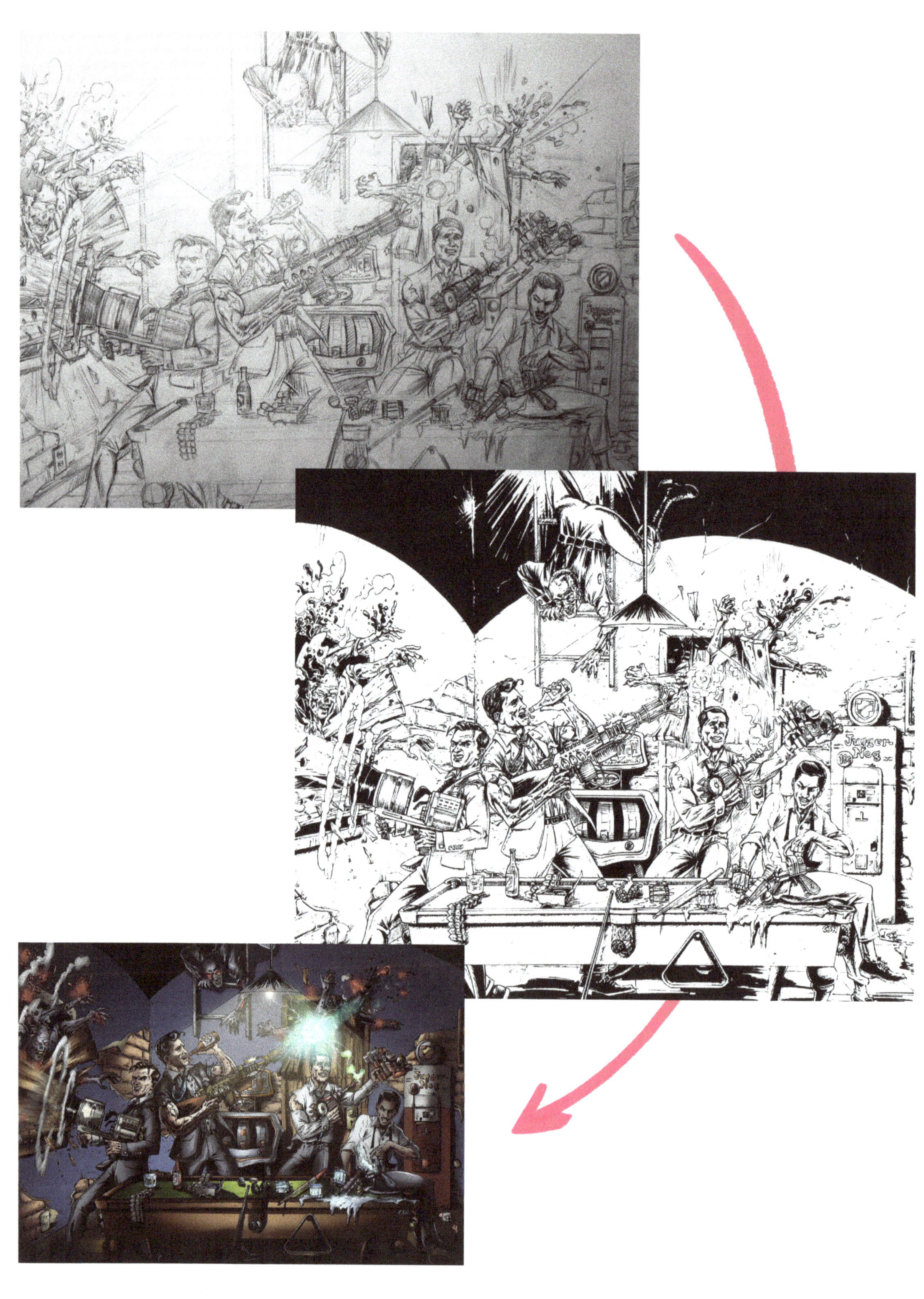

Supplies Needed

THEY SAY IT'S NOT THE SUPPLIES YOU HAVE BUT WHAT YOU DO WITH THEM. IT'S TRUE THAT SOME MATERIALS CAN MAKE YOUR LIFE EASIER. FOR MANY YEARS, I USED TO DRAW IN ADOBE PHOTOSHOP OR ILLUSTRATOR WITH A MOUSE ON A MOUSE PAD. IT WAS ALL I COULD AFFORD AT THE TIME AND, ALTHOUGH IT WASN'T AS EASY AS USING A HIGH-END TABLET NOW, IT DID THE JOB.

WHEN YOU'RE LEARNING, THE TOOLS DON'T MATTER MUCH. THE FACT THAT YOU'RE LEARNING MATTERS MOST.

THE TACTILE FEELING OF WORKING ON PAPER IS STILL ENJOYABLE AND CAN OFTEN BE EASIER THAN DIGITAL BECAUSE YOU DON'T NEED TO LEARN THE APPLICATION. YOU JUST DRAW. THIS BOOK WAS MADE DIGITALLY BUT MOST OF THE HANDOUTS THAT I HAD WERE DONE WITH PEN AND INK ON PAPER AND SCANNED.

FEEL FREE TO USE WHATEVER YOU HAVE AT YOUR DISPOSAL. SOMETIMES HAVING A FANCY SKETCHBOOK CAN BE INTIMIDATING AND DOESN'T ALLOW YOU THE FREEDOM TO FEEL THAT YOU CAN MAKE MISTAKES. WHEN YOU'RE STUDYING (AND TRUST ME, WE'RE ALL STUDYING), IT'S ALL ABOUT THE MISTAKES YOU MAKE AND LESSONS YOU LEARN FROM YOUR EXPLORATIONS, WHETHER IT BE WITH A PENCIL ON PAPER OR AN IPENCIL ON AN IPAD.

Materials & Supplies

Digital:

pressure-sensitive digital pencil

digital tablet that's fast and is best for handling graphics

- choose a good quality free or paid app for drawing

or Traditional:

- when you're learning, you need good quality supplies but just the basics

marker
pen
pencil & paper

ruler for perspective

BETTER SUPPLIES CAN'T MAKE YOU A BETTER ARTIST. PRACTICE AND STUDYING DOES.

AT THE BEGINNING, AN HB PENCIL AND ALMOST ANY PEN WILL DO THE JOB.

WITH PAPER QUALITY, JUST MAKE SURE IT'S SUITABLE FOR THE MEDIUMS YOU PLAN TO USE ON IT. TO START, YOU CAN DRAW ON PRINTING PAPER OR IN AN ECONOMICAL SKETCHBOOK.

IT'S AMAZING WHAT YOU CAN DO WITH BASIC ART SUPPLIES!

Drawing Heads

THERE'S A REASON EVERY ART CLASS YOU'VE EVER TAKEN STARTS OUT WITH DRAWING THE HEAD AND FACE. IT'S BECAUSE FACES ARE THE MOST RECOGNIZABLE. WE INTERACT WITH PEOPLE THE MOST AND, EVEN IF WE'RE SHY, EVERYONE CAN TELL IF A FACE OR HEAD IS DRAWN INCORRECTLY. FACES ARE ALSO A DRAWING SKILL THAT YOU WANT TO HAVE EARLY ON IN YOUR LIFE AS AN ARTIST, SO YOU CAN COPY PORTRAITS YOU ADMIRE OR DRAW YOUR FRIENDS AND FAMILY. MORE THAN THAT, A FACE HAS A LOT OF STORIES TO TELL. KNOWING HOW TO DRAW IT HELPS LATER ON WHEN YOU APPLY EXPRESSIONS TO IT.

STARTING WITH HEADS IS THE BEST FOUNDATION NEEDED TO BE ABLE TO TELL STORIES WITH YOUR DRAWINGS. COMICS AND MANGA ARE SHORT-HAND FOR A DEEPER SET OF DRAWING KNOWLEDGE. IF, AS AN ARTIST, YOU MASTER DRAWING THE FACE REALLY WELL AND CAN THEN CONVEY ITS EMOTIONS, THIS SKILL WILL BE A CRUTCH THAT YOU CAN ALWAYS LEAN ON. MASTERING THE PROPORTIONS OF THE FACE AND HEAD IS LIKE HAVING A RELIABLE MAP ON YOUR ARTIST JOURNEY.

IN THE COMING PAGES, PAY CLOSE ATTENTION TO THE AVERAGE PROPORTIONS OF THE FACE. COMMIT THEM TO MEMORY. ALWAYS MARK THE EYE LINE, NOSE LINE, MOUTH LINE, AND THE AXIS THROUGH THE CENTER OF THE FACE, NO MATTER HOW MANY TIMES YOU'VE DRAWN THE FACE. LINE UP THE FEATURES WHEN YOU PUT THEM ON THOSE AXIS AND DOUBLE-CHECK YOUR MEASUREMENTS BEFORE YOU MOVE ON. DRAW THESE LINES VERY LIGHTLY AND THEN THE FINAL FINISHED PENCILS WITH THE DETAILED FEATURES OF THE FACE OVER-TOP.

ONE LAST THING I'D LIKE TO EMPHASIZE HERE IS TO DRAW FROM LIFE. DRAW REAL PEOPLE. NOT JUST FROM PHOTOS. DRAW THEM FROM EVERY ANGLE. IMAGINE THE STRUCTURE THAT'S TAUGHT, OUTLINED UNDERNEATH THE SURFACE OF WHAT YOU SEE. APPLY SYMMETRY TO THEIR FACIAL FEATURES AND BASE EVERYTHING ON AVERAGE PROPORTIONS. THEN, BRING WHAT YOU'VE LEARNED BACK INTO YOUR CARTOONING FOR EVEN GREATER RESULTS!.

Drawing Heads

BEFORE WE GET INTO THE BODY, WE HAVE TO UNDERSTAND HOW TO DRAW HEADS. THERE ARE FOUR MAIN ANGLES TO CONSIDER: THE FRONT VIEW, THE PROFILE, THE THREE QUARTER VIEW, AND THE THREE QUARTER BACK VIEW. ONCE WE UNDERSTAND THE BASICS OF STRUCTURING THE HEAD, THEN WE CAN DRAW THE HEAD FROM OTHER ANGLES, LIKE UP SHOTS AND DOWN SHOTS.

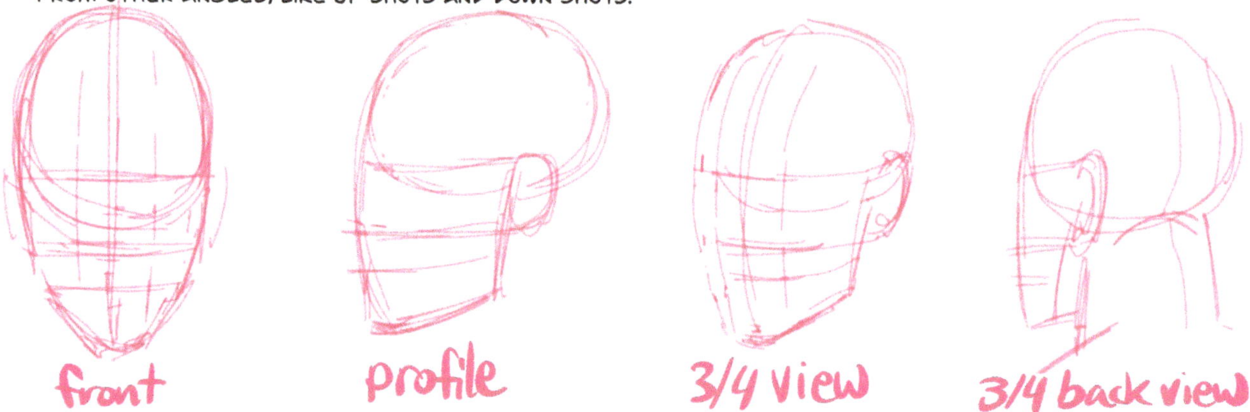

BELOW IS AN EXAMPLE OF A PORTRAIT I DID OF A FRIEND. IN DOING SO, I WANTED TO MAKE SURE THAT THE DRAWING WAS CONSIDERED BEAUTIFUL ON ITS OWN. TO ACHIEVE THAT, EVERYTHING MUST BE SYMMETRICAL. SYMMETRY EQUALS BEAUTY. JUST LOOK IN FASHION MAGAZINES. NOTICE THE SHAPE OF THE HEAD, THE AXIS OF THE CENTER LINE WITH THE OTHER LINES, AND THE DISTANCE BETWEEN FEATURES. ALSO, SEE WHERE THE EARS ARE, BETWEEN THE EYE LINE AND THE NOSE LINE. THE MOUTH IS HALF THE DISTANCE OF THE LENGTH OF THE NOSE AND IT'S NOT WIDER THAN THE PUPILS. THIS IS THE STRUCTURE OF A SYMMETRICAL HUMAN HEAD.

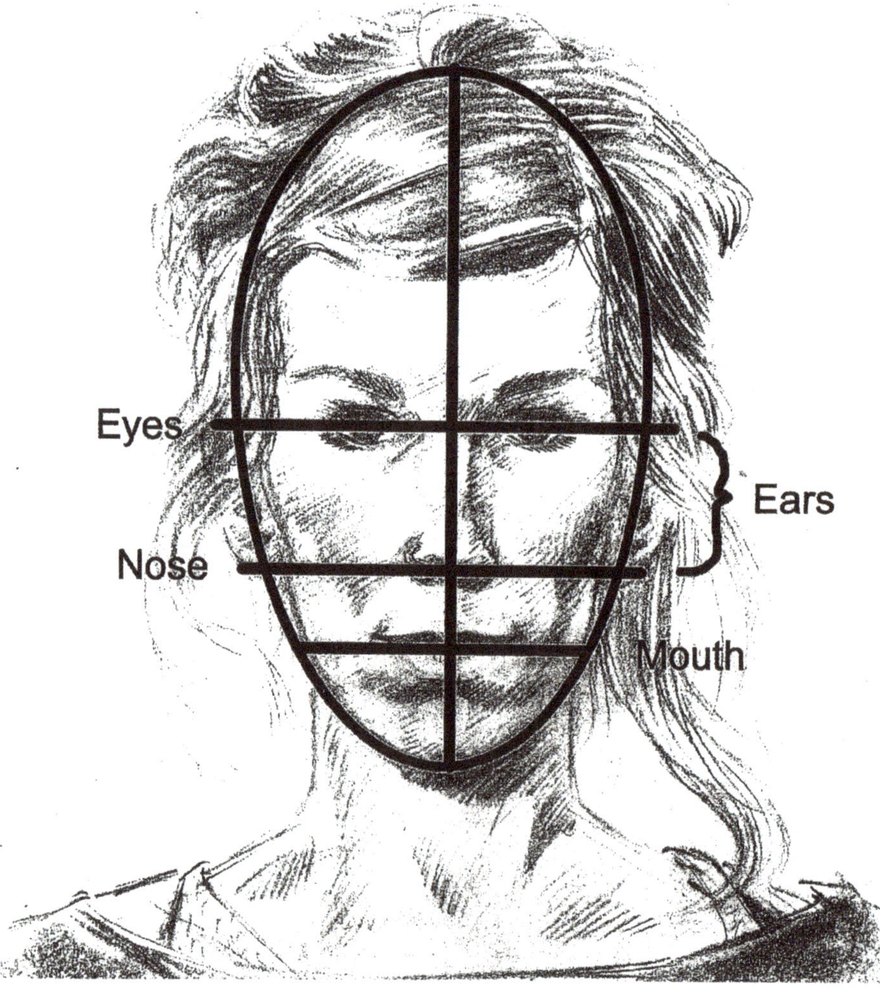

Front View Structure

START WITH AN EGG SHAPE, SLIGHTLY BIGGER AT THE TOP. THEN THE AXIS EXACTLY DOWN THE MIDDLE. THE EYE LINE SHOULD BE JUST ABOVE THE MIDWAY POINT FROM THE TOP TO THE CHIN. THE NOSE LINE A LITTLE ABOVE THE MIDWAY POINT FROM THE EYE LINE TO THE CHIN, AND THE MOUTH APPROXIMATELY A THIRD OF THE WAY DOWN FROM THE NOSE TO THE CHIN. THEN DRAW THE EYES FIRST. OLIVE SHAPED. THE ENDS REST ON THE AXIS. ONE EYE WIDTH APART AND ONE EYE WIDTH AWAY FROM THE EDGE OF THE FACE ON EITHER SIDE.

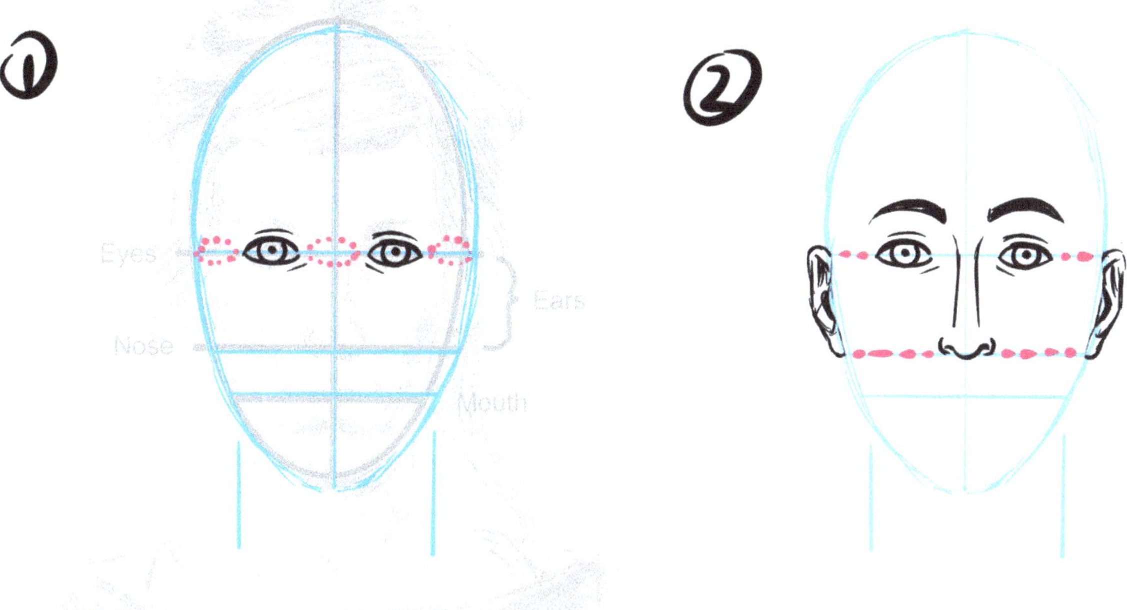

THE EYEBROWS FOLLOW THE CURVATURE OF THE EYES AND LEAD DOWN INTO THE NOSE. THE BRIDGE OF THE NOSE SHOULD BE THIN AND EQUAL ON BOTH SIDES OF THE AXIS. THE EARS LINE UP RIGHT BETWEEN THE EYE LINE AND THE NOSE LINE. THEY ARE THE SAME HEIGHT AS THE NOSE.

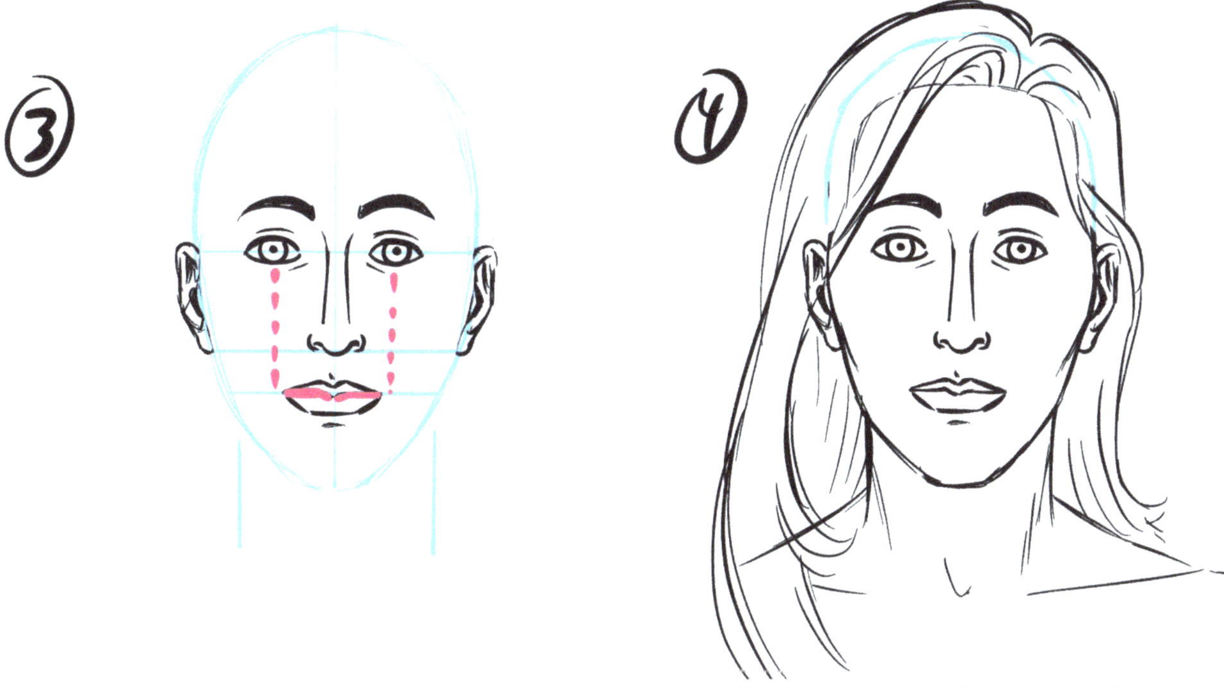

THE MIDDLE LINE OF THE MOUTH FITS RIGHT ALONG THE MOUTH AXIS AND THE MOUTH SHOULD NOT BE ANY WIDER THAN WHERE IT WOULD LINE UP WITH THE PUPILS. EVEN IN A SMILE, THE CORNERS OF THE MOUTH DO NOT WIDEN AS FAR AS WE THINK. LASTLY, THE HAIR IS ADDED ABOVE THE HEAD. HAIR IS ALWAYS AN EXTRA THING, LIKE A THICK HAT OR A HELMET.

3/4 View

back of head
These are the angles
①
add location of features (curved to show shape)
②
chin out
③
- overlap
- farthest half compressed
- back of head is larger
- ear behind jaw
invisible barrier
neck back

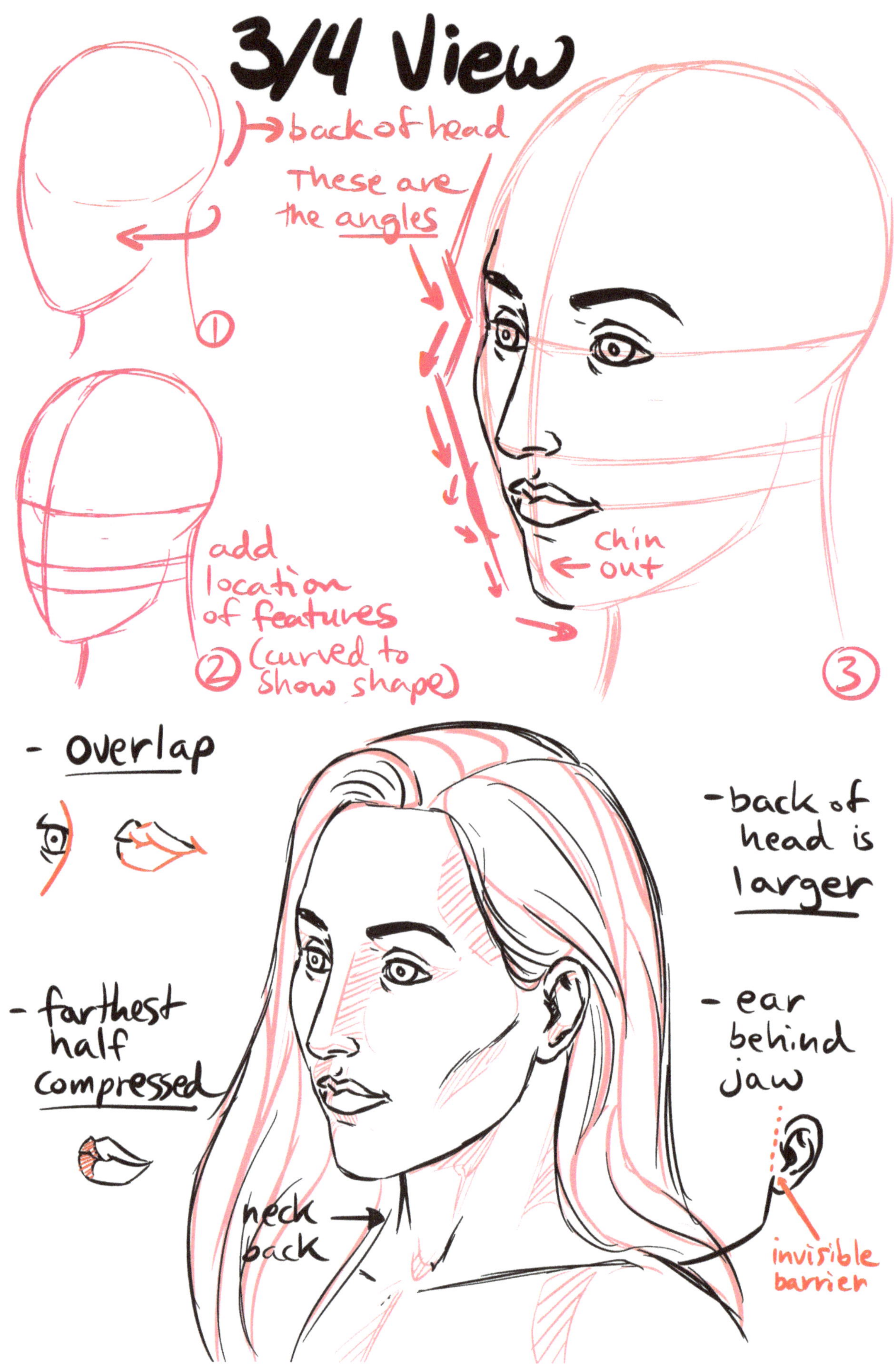

Facial Features

HERE'S A CONVENIENT AND EASY STEP-BY-STEP GUIDE TO DRAWING THE FEATURES OF THE FACE. INCLUDED ARE THE STEPS TO DRAWING EYES, THE NOSE, EARS, LIPS, AND EVEN DIFFERENT TYPES OF HAIR.

Eyes - put a lot of detail!

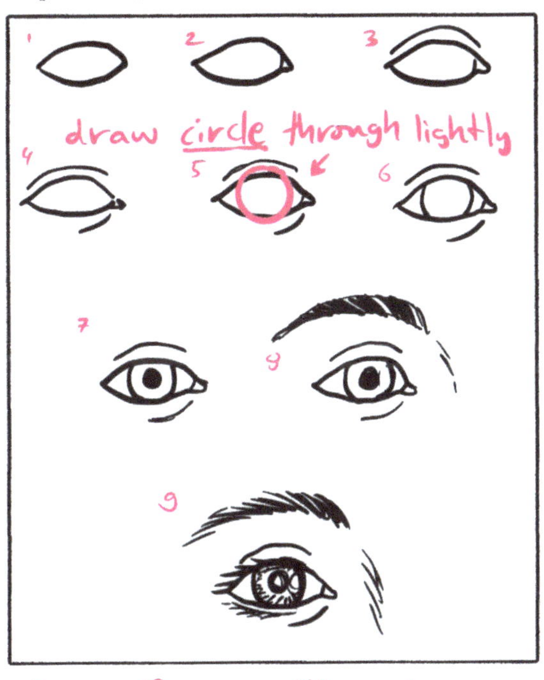

Nose - Remember that the nose comes from the eye brows!

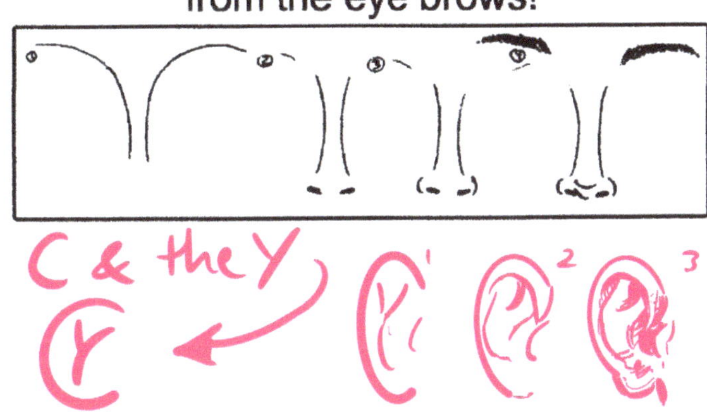

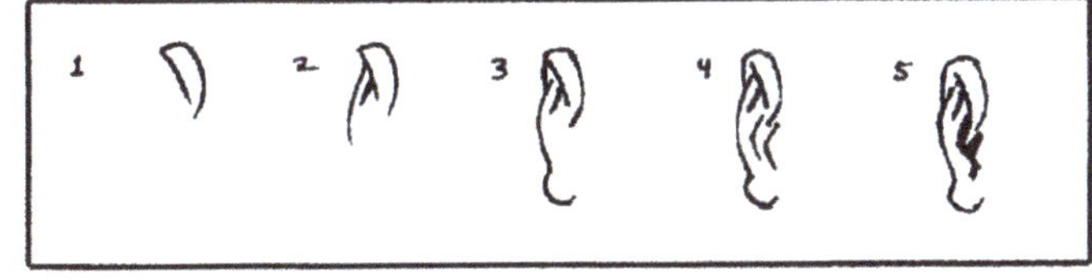

Ears - Step by step, yours are similar!

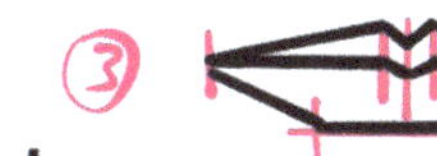

Lips: ① ② ③
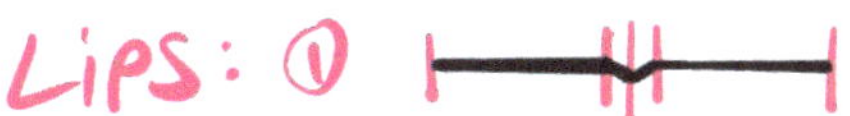

Hair - The less lines you put, the lighter the hair colour!

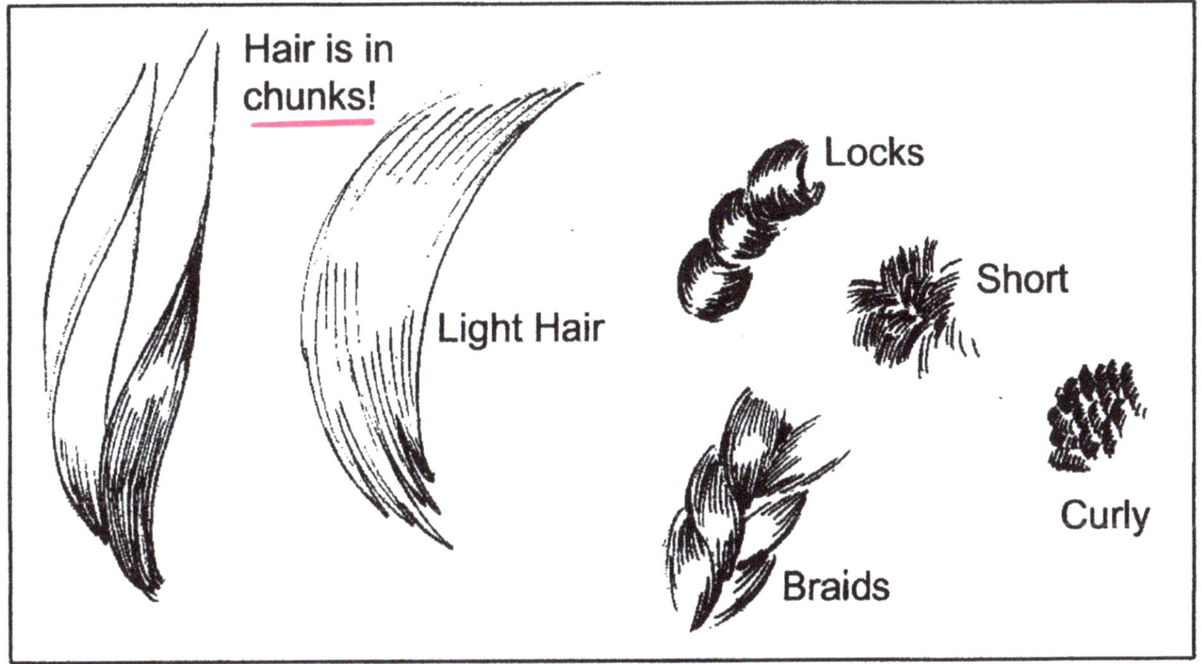

Noses and Mouths

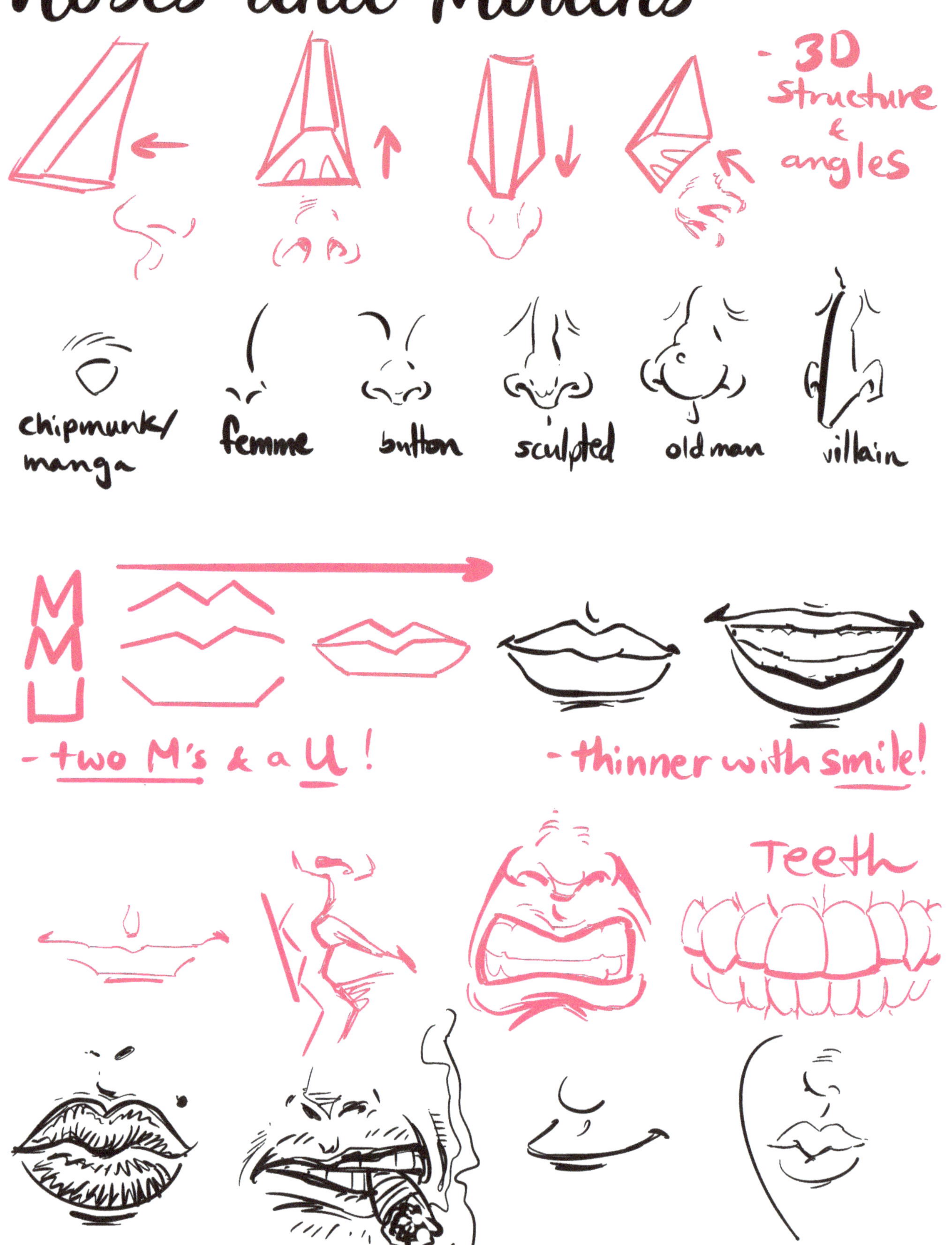

Drawing Eyes

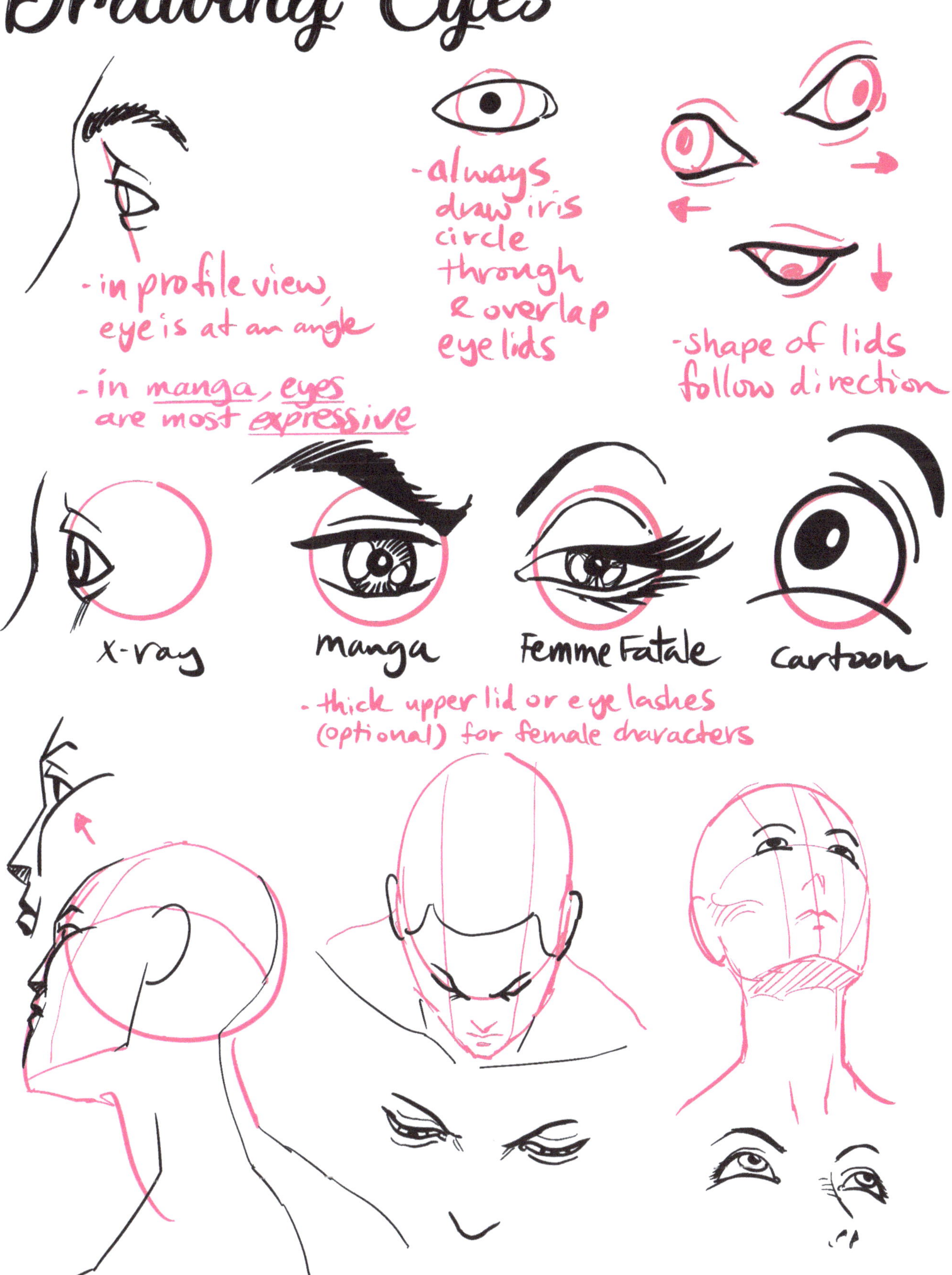

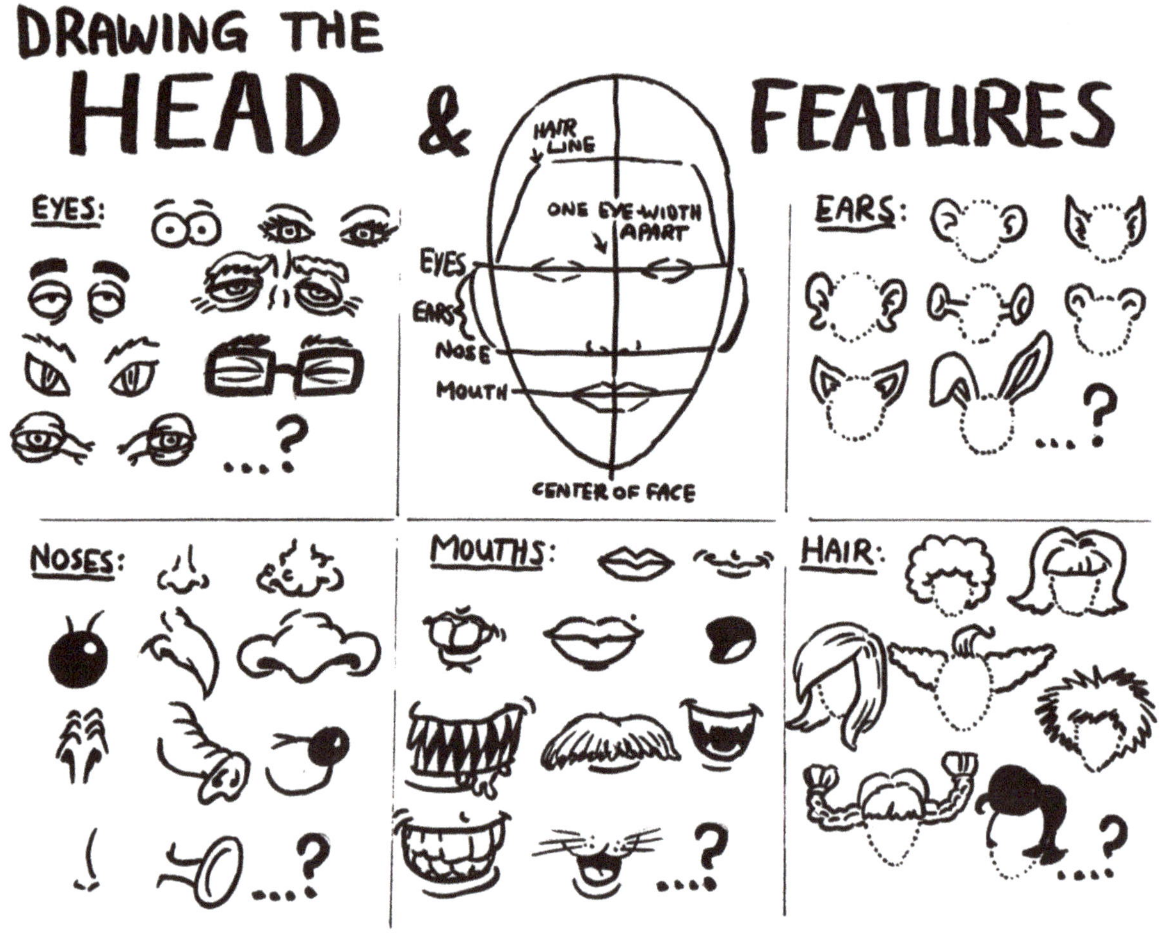

THIS IS A WORK-SHEET THAT RECAPS THE FEATURES OF THE HUMAN FACE, WITH A VARIETY OF EYES, EARS, NOSES, MOUTHS, AND HAIR STYLES TO INSPIRE ARTISTS WHEN CREATING THEIR OWN CHARACTERS. EVEN ANTHROPOMORPHIC CHARACTERS (ANIMALS WITH HUMAN ATTRIBUTES) START WITH THE HUMAN HEAD (AND LATER BODY) AS A BASIS. (REFER BACK TO SOME OF THESE FEATURES IN FUTURE CHARACTER DESIGN EXERCISES.)

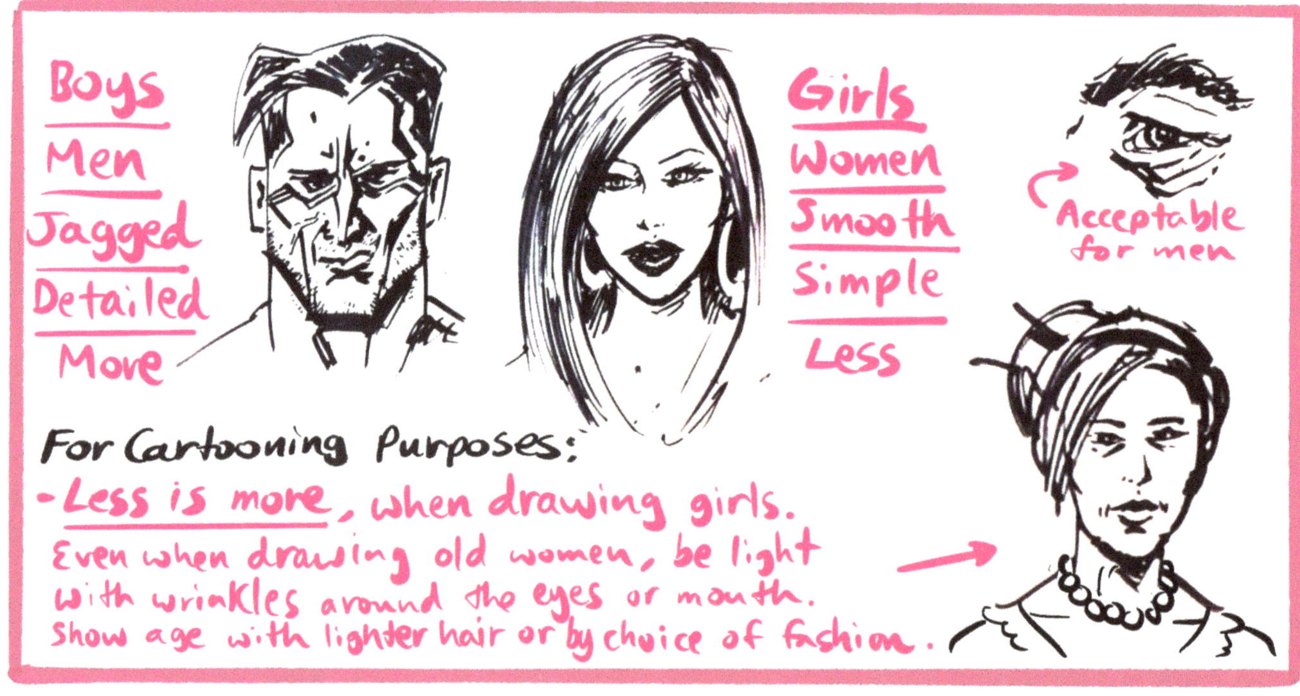

Cartoon Heads Exercise

THIS FUN EXERCISE WAS TAUGHT IN THE ALGONQUIN COLLEGE ANIMATION PROGRAM. IT LEFT A GREAT IMPRESSION FOR MANY REASONS AND TO THIS DAY IT'S STILL USED IN MY COURSES. SO, WHETHER YOU'RE A KID, A TEEN, OR AN ADULT, YOU'RE SURE TO HAVE FUN BEING CREATIVE WITH THESE HEAD DESIGN PROMPTS!

ONE OF THE BEST FEATURES OF THIS EXERCISE IS THAT THE MOST RECOGNIZABLE SHAPES CAN BE USED FOR CONSTRUCTING FULL BODIES LATER ON. YOU'LL SEE HOW THE "OVAL," THE "PYRAMID," THE "CUBE," AND THE "CYLINDER," WILL RECUR AGAIN AS USEFUL OBJECTS TO HELP US DEPICT VOLUME ON PEOPLE. IT'S ALSO USEFUL TO LOOK FOR THESE SHAPES IN MORE COMPLEX CHARACTERS, HELPING US DEMYSTIFY THE PROCESS OF CHARACTER DESIGN.

THIS UPCOMING EXERCISE IS GREAT TO DO SEVERAL TIMES, AS A WARM-UP, TO IGNITE YOUR IMAGINATION, AND TO JUST HAVE FUN!

Fun Exercise

USE THESE SHAPES AS STARTING POINTS TO CREATE YOUR OWN ORIGINAL CHARACTERS!

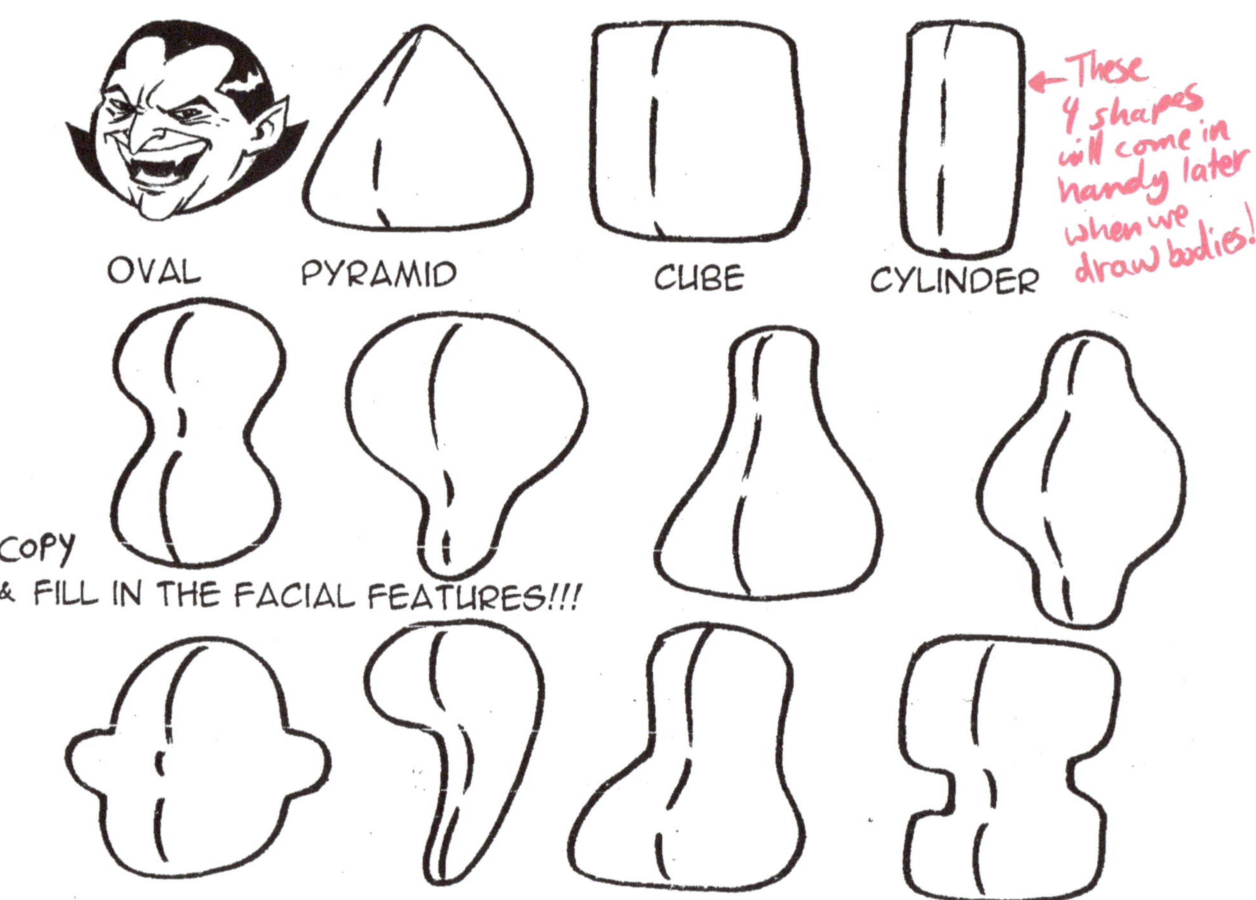

PUT THE EYE LINE, NOSE LINE, AND MOUTH LINE IN DIFFERENT LOCATIONS BUT KEEP THEM IN THE SAME ORDER —EYES ON TOP, THEN NOSE, THEN MOUTH. PLAY WITH THE STYLE OF FEATURES. YOU CAN GIVE THEM ALIEN EARS, TRUMPET NOSES, ETC. ✳

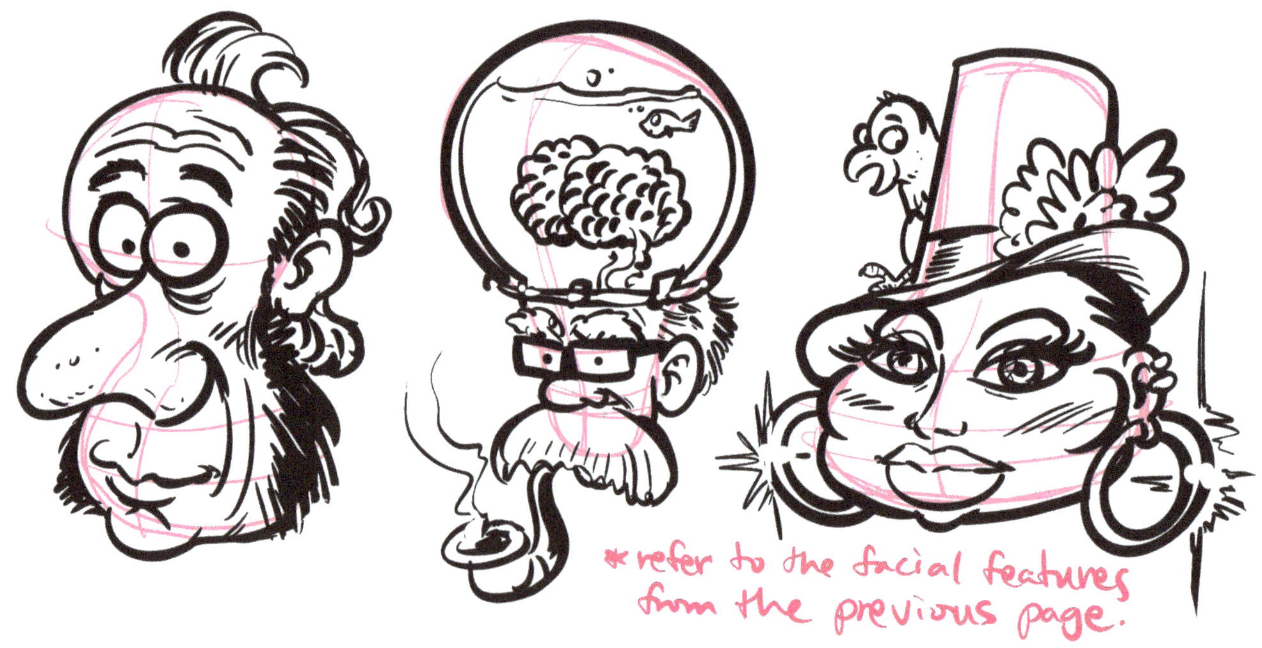

Drawing People

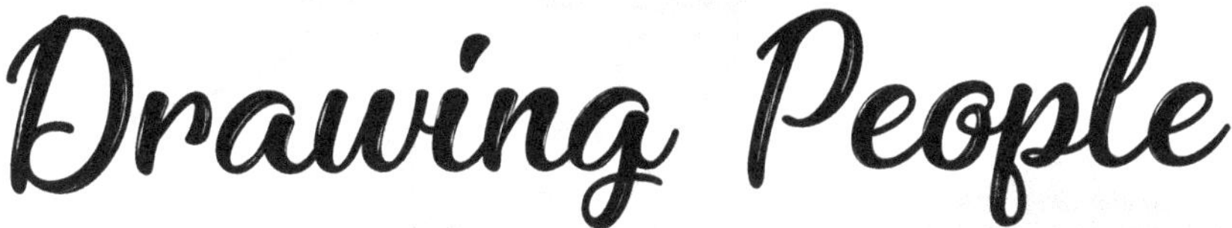

WHAT WAS MENTIONED ABOUT DRAWING HEADS, APPLIES HERE. IT'S HELPFUL TO STUDY FROM LIFE AS MUCH AS YOU INTERPRET THROUGH SHAPES AND CONSTRUCTION.

IF YOU HAVE A GOOD UNDERSTANDING OF ANATOMY FROM FIGURE DRAWING CLASSES, IT'S MORE CLEAR WHERE AND HOW TO APPLY THE CYLINDRICAL SHAPES TO BUILD A HUMAN BODY. HOWEVER, IF YOU HAVEN'T HAD AN OPPORTUNITY TO STUDY PEOPLE FROM REAL LIFE, THAT'S OKAY. BUT BE CONSCIOUS OF YOURSELF AND YOUR ANATOMY OR OBSERVE A FAMILY MEMBER NEAR-BY. WHEN YOU'RE BUILDING THESE SHAPES, REMEMBER THAT THEY'RE NOT INVENTED OUT OF THIN AIR. THE SHAPES ARE USED AS SHORT-HAND TO EXPLAIN WHAT WE'RE SEEING IN REAL LIFE. FROM THERE, THESE SHAPES CAN BE WARPED AND EXAGGERATED TO "CARTOONIFY" OUR CHARACTERS.

EVEN ABSTRACT ART IS ROOTED IN ACTION, SHAPES, COLOUR, AND IDEAS. SIMILARLY, CARTOONING IS ROOTED IN SOMETHING TANGIBLE: LIFE. IN THE END, IT'S THE COMEDY AND TRAGEDY OF LIFE THAT WE'RE TRANSCRIBING, AS CARTOONISTS, WITH THE QUICK-LINED GESTURES OF OUR PEN.

IT'S FUN TO DRAW PEOPLE. EVERY STORY IS ABOUT PEOPLE. WITHOUT PEOPLE, HISTORY DISSIPATES INTO ARCHEOLOGY ON OUR PAGE. KNOWING HOW TO DRAW PEOPLE REALLY WELL HELPS US AS CARTOONISTS TO EXPRESS OUR IDEAS. AND KNOWING HOW TO DRAW PEOPLE OF MANY DIFFERENT SHAPES AND BACKGROUNDS HELPS OUR STORYTELLING BECOME MORE DIVERSE AND INTERESTING.

WHETHER YOU'RE FASCINATED WITH ANATOMY, WITH CARTOONS, AMERICAN COMICS, OR JAPANESE MANGA, THERE'S MUCH IN THIS SECTION THAT WILL DEVELOP YOUR SKILLS AND GROW YOUR KNOWLEDGE-BASE.

Drawing the Full Body
with VOLUME !!!

IT'S IMPORTANT TO UNDERSTAND HOW TO DRAW STANDARD HUMAN PROPORTIONS, BEFORE EXAGGERATING BODY FEATURES. IT'S HELPFUL TO PICTURE THE BODY AS A SKELETON AND, FROM THAT SKELETON, CREATE A STICK PERSON. THE STICK PERSON HELPS WITH POSING LATER WHEN WE APPLY EXPRESSIONS AND PHYSICAL GESTURES.

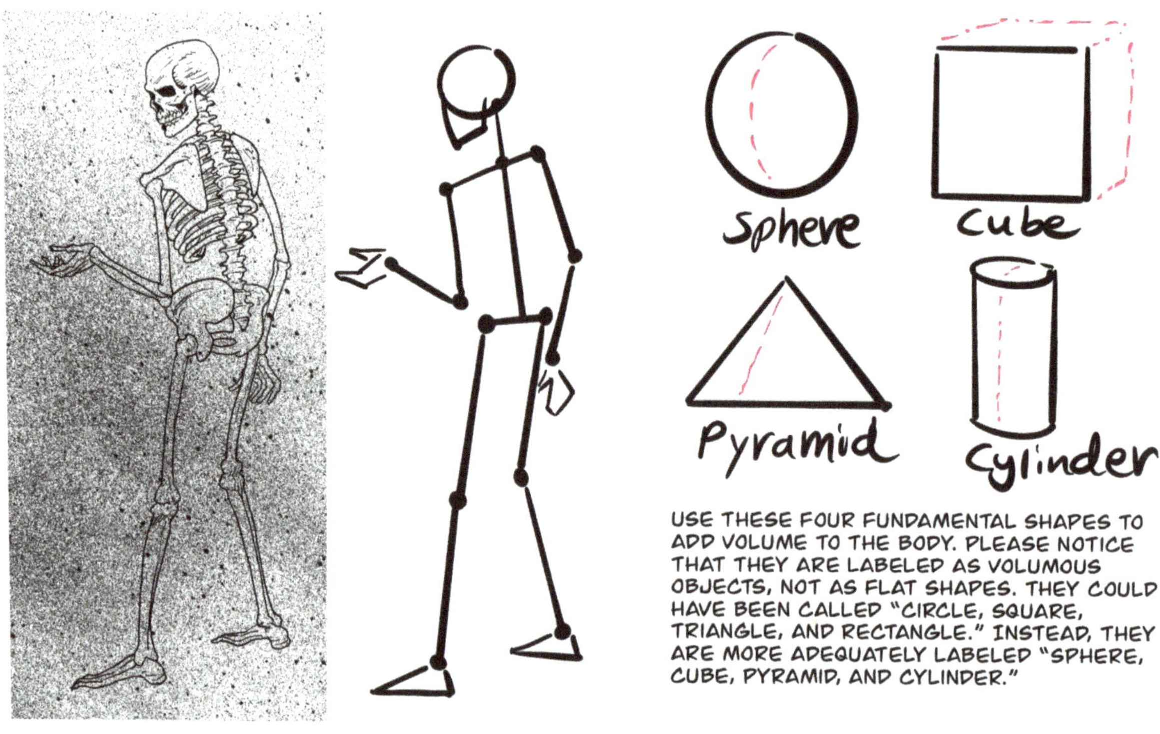

USE THESE FOUR FUNDAMENTAL SHAPES TO ADD VOLUME TO THE BODY. PLEASE NOTICE THAT THEY ARE LABELED AS VOLUMOUS OBJECTS, NOT AS FLAT SHAPES. THEY COULD HAVE BEEN CALLED "CIRCLE, SQUARE, TRIANGLE, AND RECTANGLE." INSTEAD, THEY ARE MORE ADEQUATELY LABELED "SPHERE, CUBE, PYRAMID, AND CYLINDER."

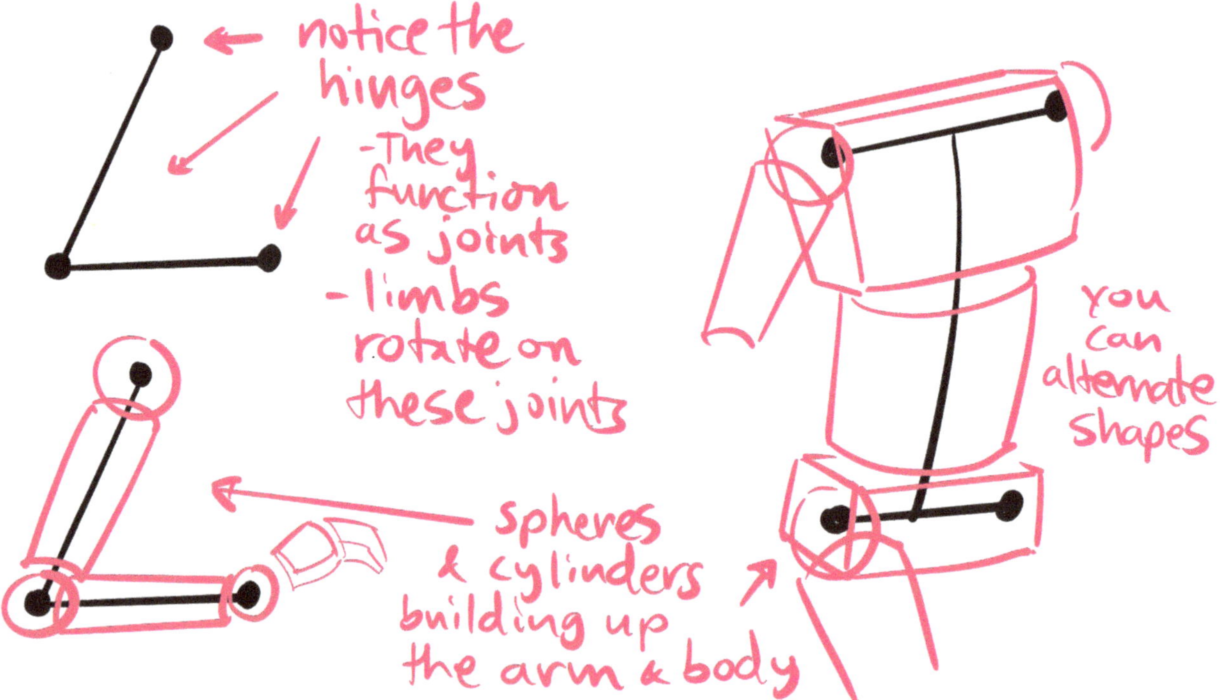

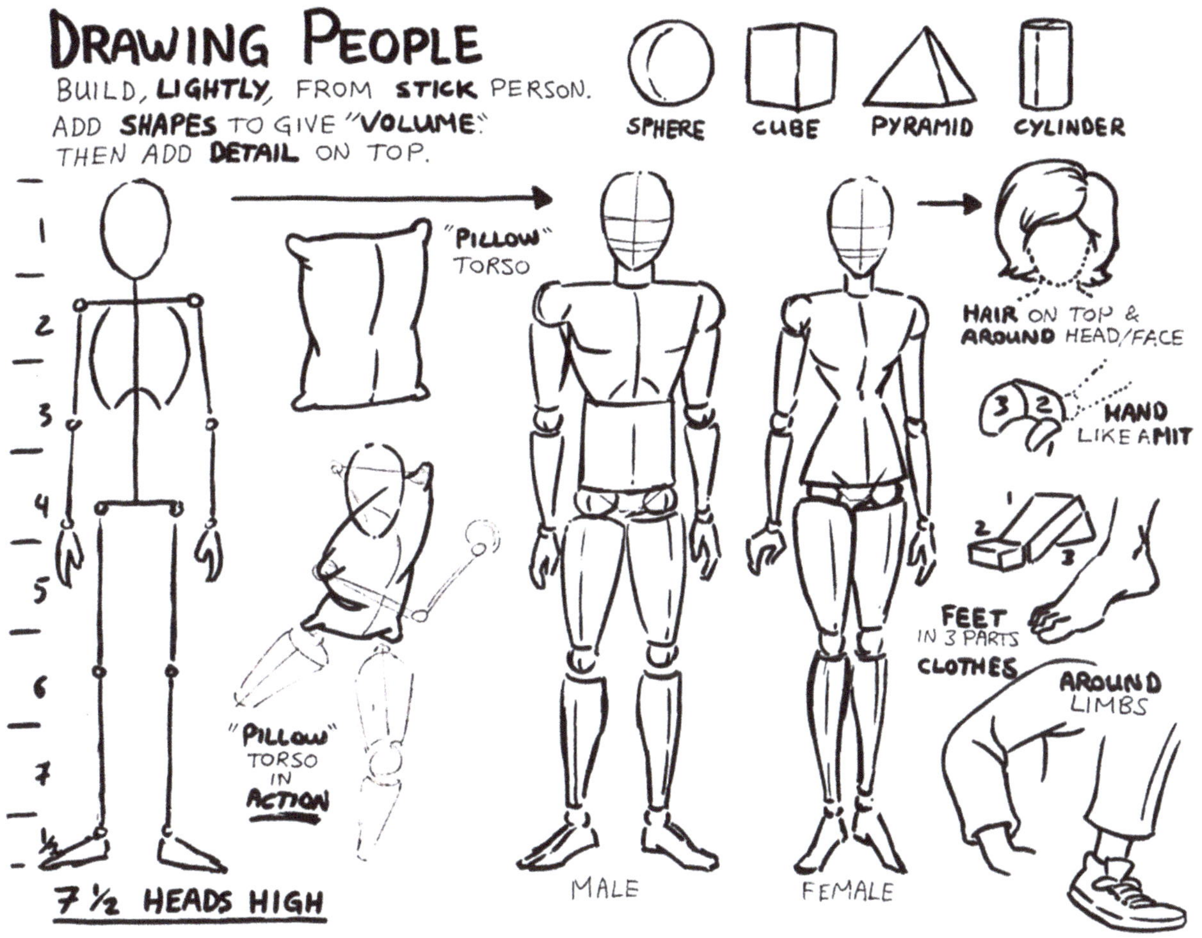

THIS IS AN ALL-ENCOMPASSING WORKSHEET THAT I USED IN MY ART CLASSES. IT POINTS OUT THAT THE AVERAGE PERSON IS ABOUT 7.5 HEADS HIGH. YOU CAN PLAY AROUND WITH THAT WHEN YOU'RE CREATING CARTOONS. THE "PILLOW" TORSO IS SOMETHING THAT I LEARNED IN ANIMATION COLLEGE. IT'S AN OLD DISNEY ANIMATION PRINCIPLE. WE'LL GET MORE INTO THAT WHEN WE DRAW EXAGGERATED POSES. THE THING TO NOTE NOW THOUGH IS THAT THE CORNERS OF THE PILLOW ARE THE JOINTS AND HINGES.

HAIR AND CLOTHING ARE SEPARATE LAYERS. THEY ARE EACH ELEMENTS THAT ARE ON TOP OF OUR CHARACTER FOUNDATION. THEY HAVE AN EXTRA THICKNESS.

HANDS AND FEET ARE BROKEN DOWN IN THREE STEPS, USING SIMPLE SHAPES. THE HAND I PICTURE LIKE A WINTER MIT. FEET ARE COMPRISED OF TWO CUBES AND A PYRAMID.

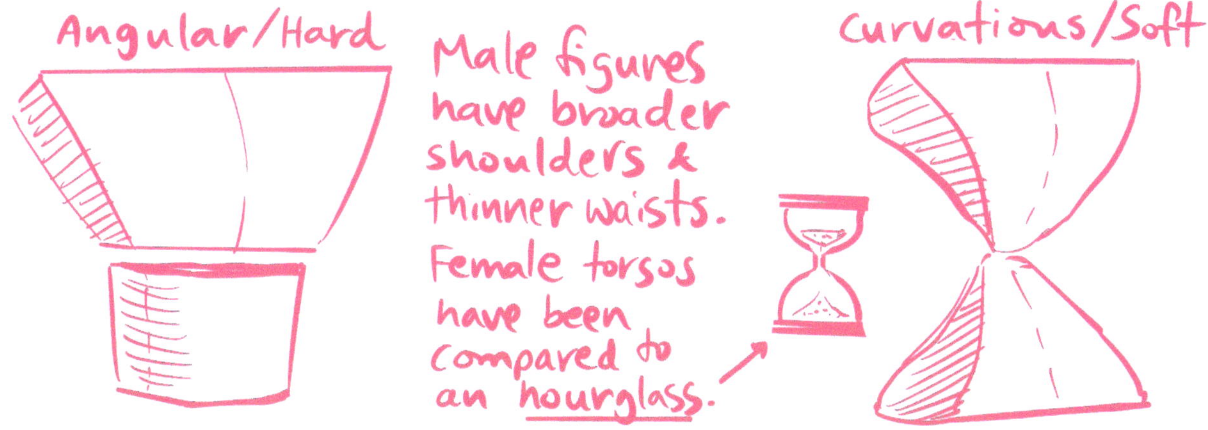

Anatomy & Muscles

THE DIRECTION OF THE MUSCLE STRANDS INDICATES THE DIRECTION BY WHICH THOSE MUSCLES EITHER COMPRESS OR EXPAND. THE ABS FOR EXAMPLE ARE UP AND DOWN BECAUSE FOR THE MOST PART WE BEND FORWARD OR BACKWARD. THEY ARE ALSO SPACED FOR THAT CONVENIENCE. THE OBLIQUES AT THE WAIST HELP USE TWIST SIDE TO SIDE. AND THE PECKS AND BACK MUSCLES HELP SUPPORT OUR SHOULDERS AND ARMS AND WEIGHTS THAT WE WOULD LIFT. OUR THIGH MUSCLES CARRY THE WEIGHT OF OUR TORSO AND HELP CUSHION THE IMPACT OF RUNNING OR LIFTING. FURTHERMORE, OUR FOREARMS AND OUR SHINS HAVE TWO BONES THAT HELP TURN THE WRISTS AND ANKLES, RESPECTIVELY. MUSCLES ALSO FOLLOW THE PATHS OF THE BONES.

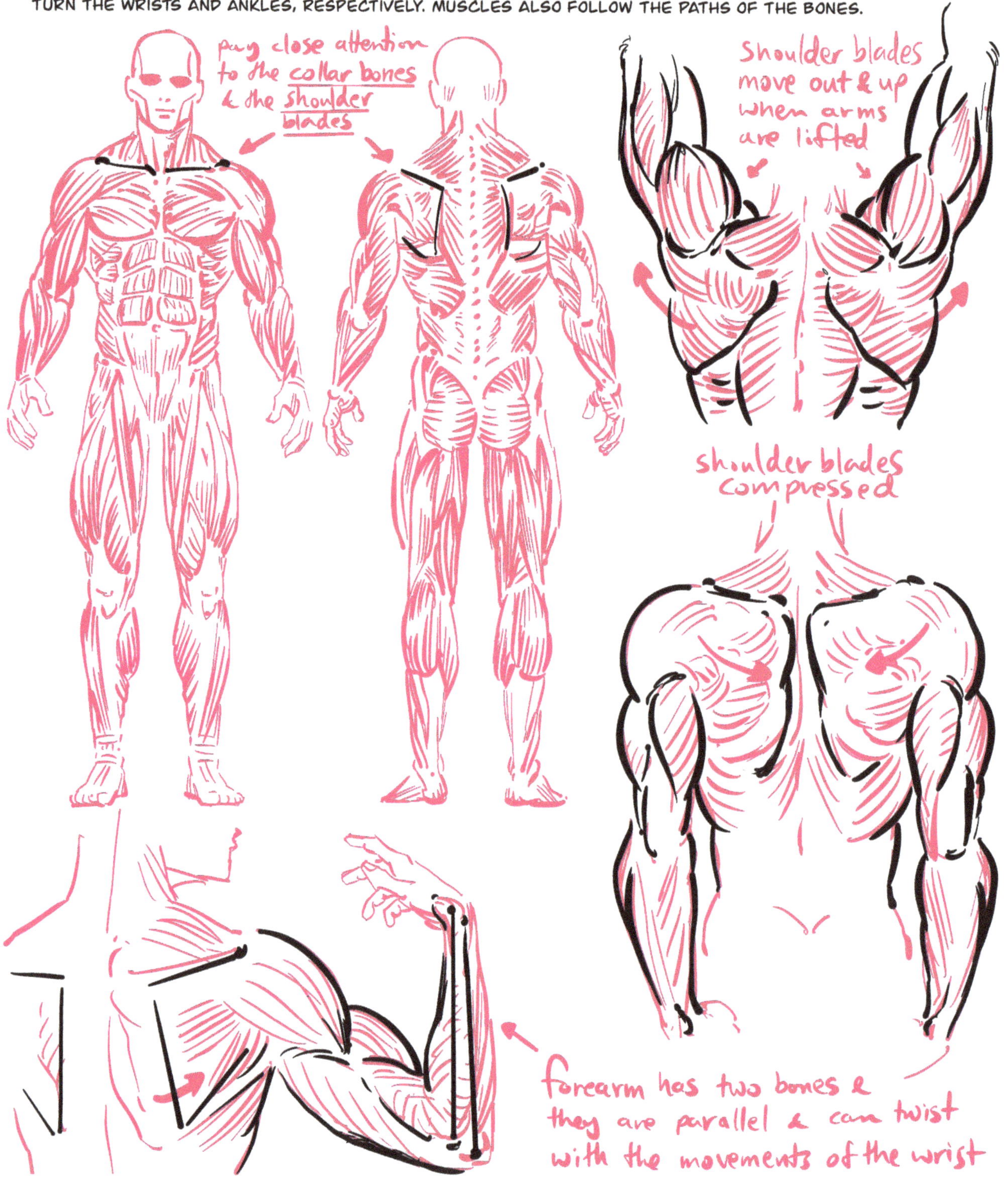

Muscle Shapes

A FEMALE'S FORM IS MORE SUBTLE THAN A MALE'S. THE MUSCLES ARE ALL THE SAME BUT LESS PRONOUNCED. HER SHOULDERS ARE MORE NARROW AND SHE HAS A THINNER WAISTLINE AND SHAPELIER HIPS.

WHEN DRAWING CHARACTERS THAT ARE ANATOMICALLY CORRECT, PLEASE NOTICE THAT THE ARMS AND LEGS LOOK AND FUNCTION THE SAME BUT BEND IN OPPOSITE DIRECTIONS. THE ARMS FLEX TOWARD THE CHEST WHILE THE LEGS CURL BEHIND US. THEIR SHAPES ARE VERY SIMILAR ONLY THE LEGS ARE ABOUT THREE TIMES THICKER THAN THE ARMS, FOR AN AVERAGE PERSON. LEG AND ARM MUSCLES ARE HELPFUL TO MASTER, ESPECIALLY TRICKY FEATURES LIKE THE QUADRICEPS, CALVES, AND ANKLES.

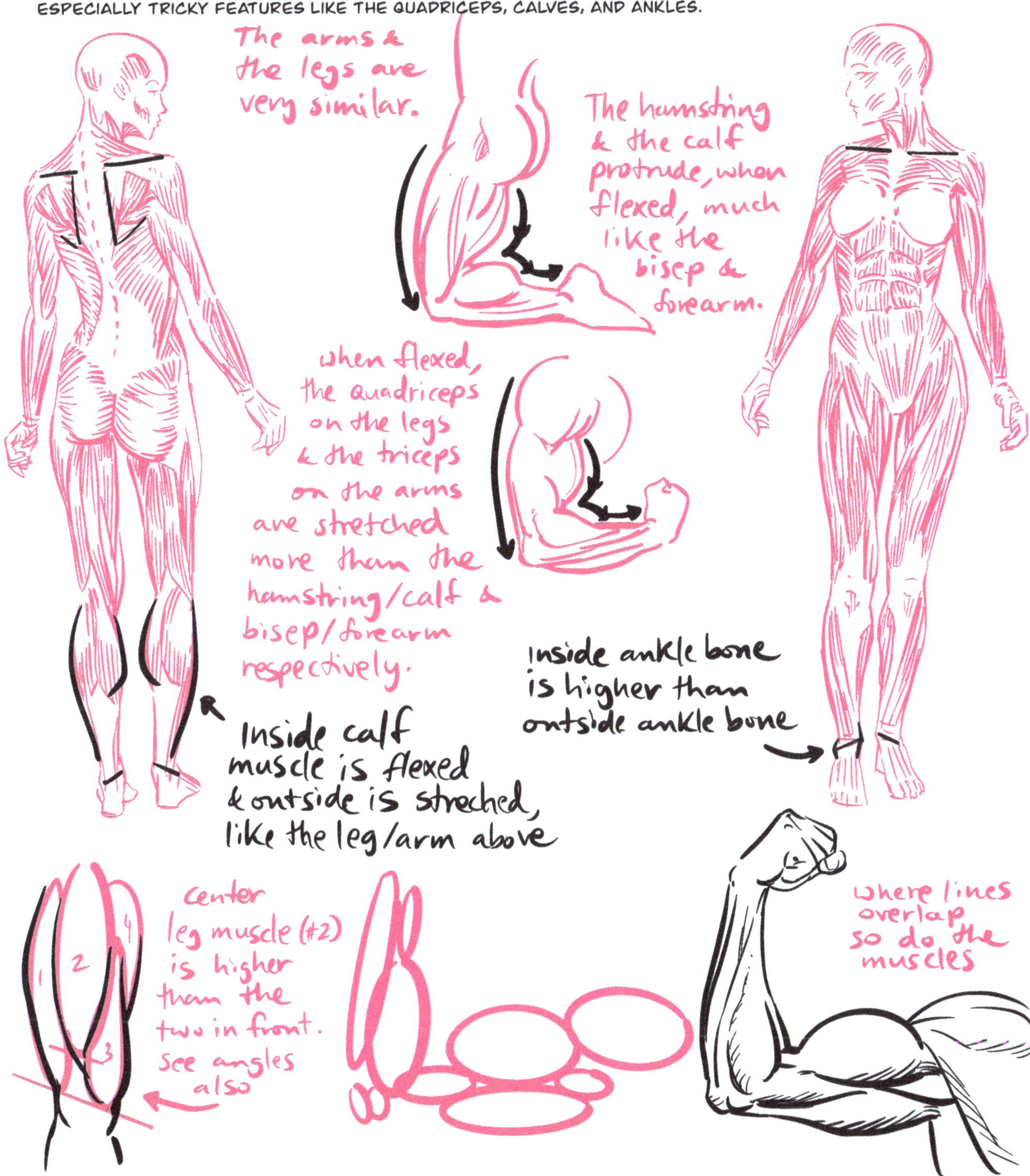

Body Types

TO SIMPLIFY OUR DRAWING PROCESS, IT'S CONVENIENT FOR US TO LOOK AT THREE DIFFERENT BODY TYPES: ECTOMORPH, MESOMORPH, AND ENDOMORPH. THESE TERMS WERE INVENTED BY AMERICAN PSYCHOLOGIST WILLIAM SHELDON. ALTHOUGH THESE STEREOTYPES ARE DEBATABLE, FOR THE PURPOSE OF CARTOONING, THEY SERVE US VERY WELL. WHAT YOU NEED TO KNOW IS THAT THE ECTOMORPH APPEARS SKINNY, THE MESOMORPH APPEARS ATHLETIC, AND THE ENDOMORPH APPEARS OVERWEIGHT. SHELDON ALSO ATTRIBUTED PERSONALITY CHARACTERISTICS WITH EACH BODY TYPE.

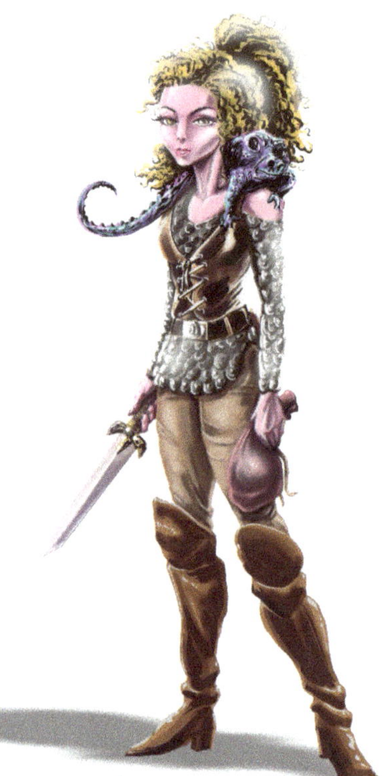 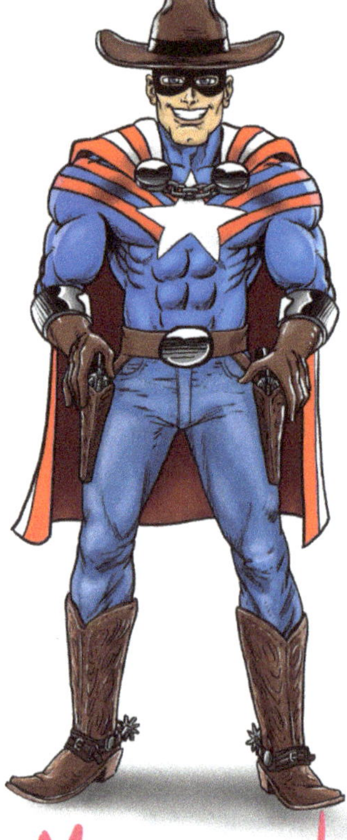 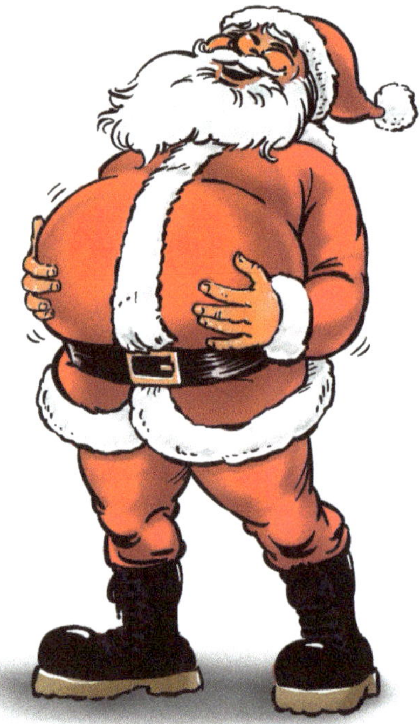

Ectomorph

- anxious
- self-conscious
- artistic
- thoughtful
- quiet
- private

Mesomorph

- adventurous
- assertive
- competetive
- fearless
- strong
- active

Endomorph

- relaxed
- comfortable
- good-humored
- even-tempered
- sociable
- tolerant

according to William Sheldon

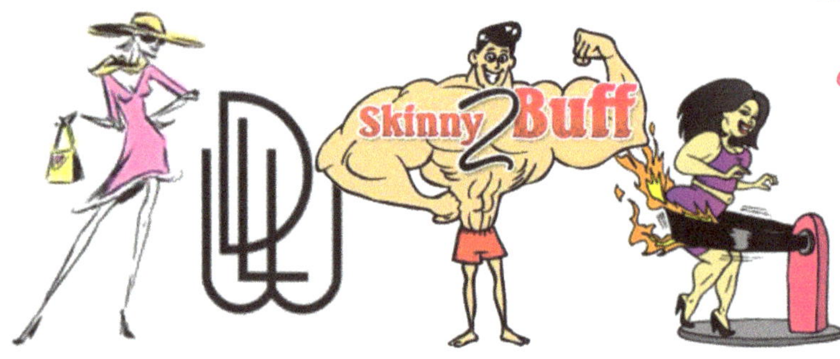

Full Body Character Designs

CREATE A REALISTIC BOY CHARACTER AND A GIRL CHARACTER, STANDING. USE THE STICK PERSON AND SHAPES TO CONSTRUCT THEM. THEN ADD FACIAL FEATURES AND CLOTHING.

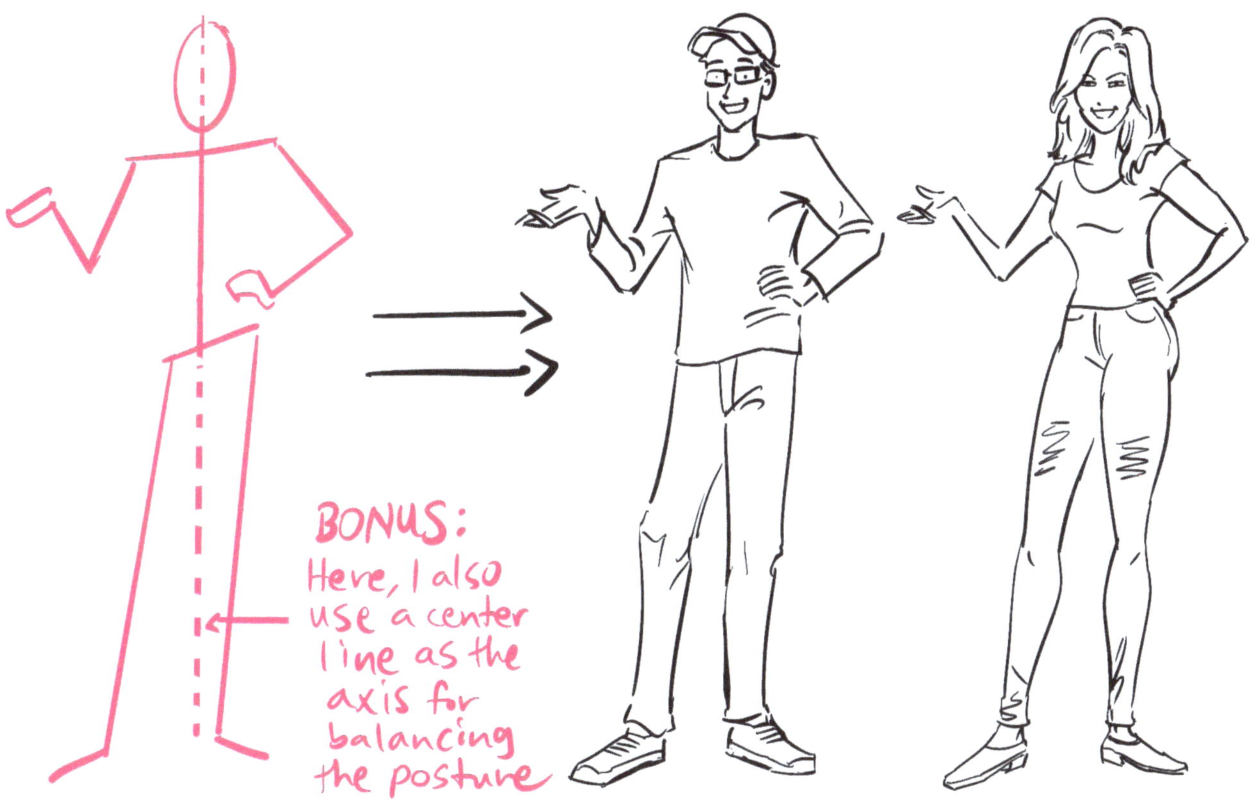

CREATE A STYLIZED BOY CHARACTER AND GIRL CHARACTER IN EXAGGERATED STYLES, USING THE VARIOUS SHAPES OF BODIES BELOW. DON'T STOP AT ONE CHARACTER EACH. HAVE FUN WITH IT. MAKE THEM QUICK SKETCHES AND KEEP EXPLORING. ADD ONE OF THE HEADS WE CREATED EARLIER TO THE BODIES.

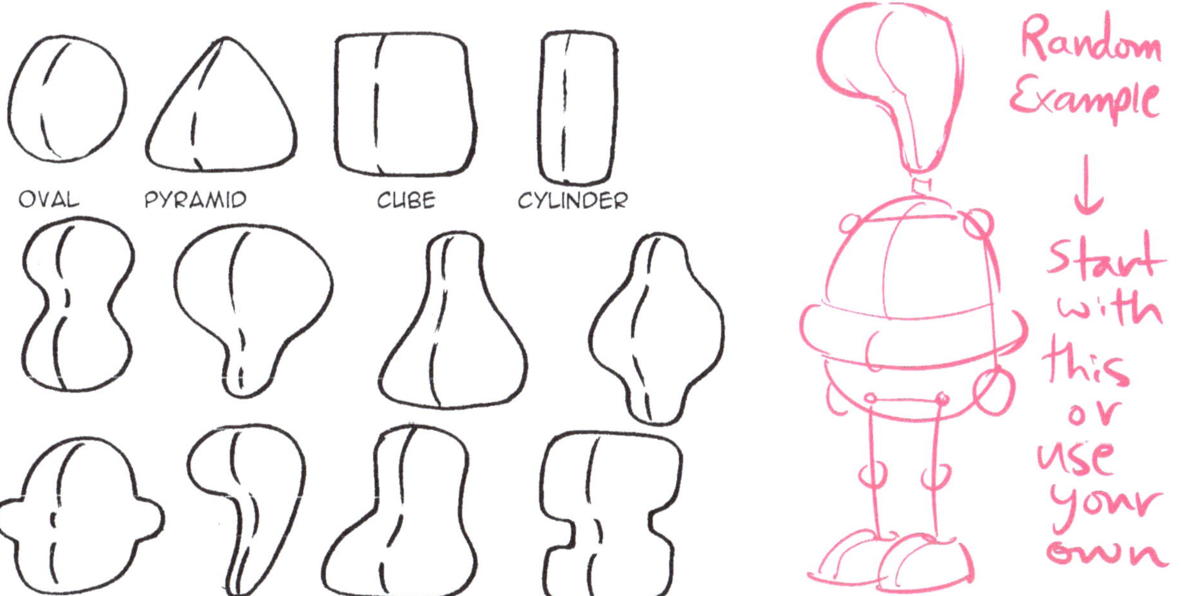

Manga Characters

MANGA CHARACTERS HAVE DISTINCT FEATURES APART FROM WESTERN COMIC BOOK CHARACTERS. FOR ONE, THEY HAVE BIG GLOSSY EYES. THEIR HAIR IS VERY JAGGED. THEIR NOSES ARE EITHER SMALL OR NON-EXISTENT. THEIR MOUTHS ARE NON-DESCRIPT AND EXAGGERATED, OFTEN BLANK WITHOUT SHOWING TEETH OR TONGUE. AND THEIR JAW-LINE IS OFTEN VERY ANGULAR.

EVEN WHEN MANGA CHARACTERS ARE DRAWN REALISTICALLY, WHEN THEY ARE CONVEYING EMOTIONS, THEIR FACIAL FEATURES ARE EXTREME AND CHILD-LIKE. THIS IS PART OF THEIR APPEAL AND DEMOGRAPHIC.

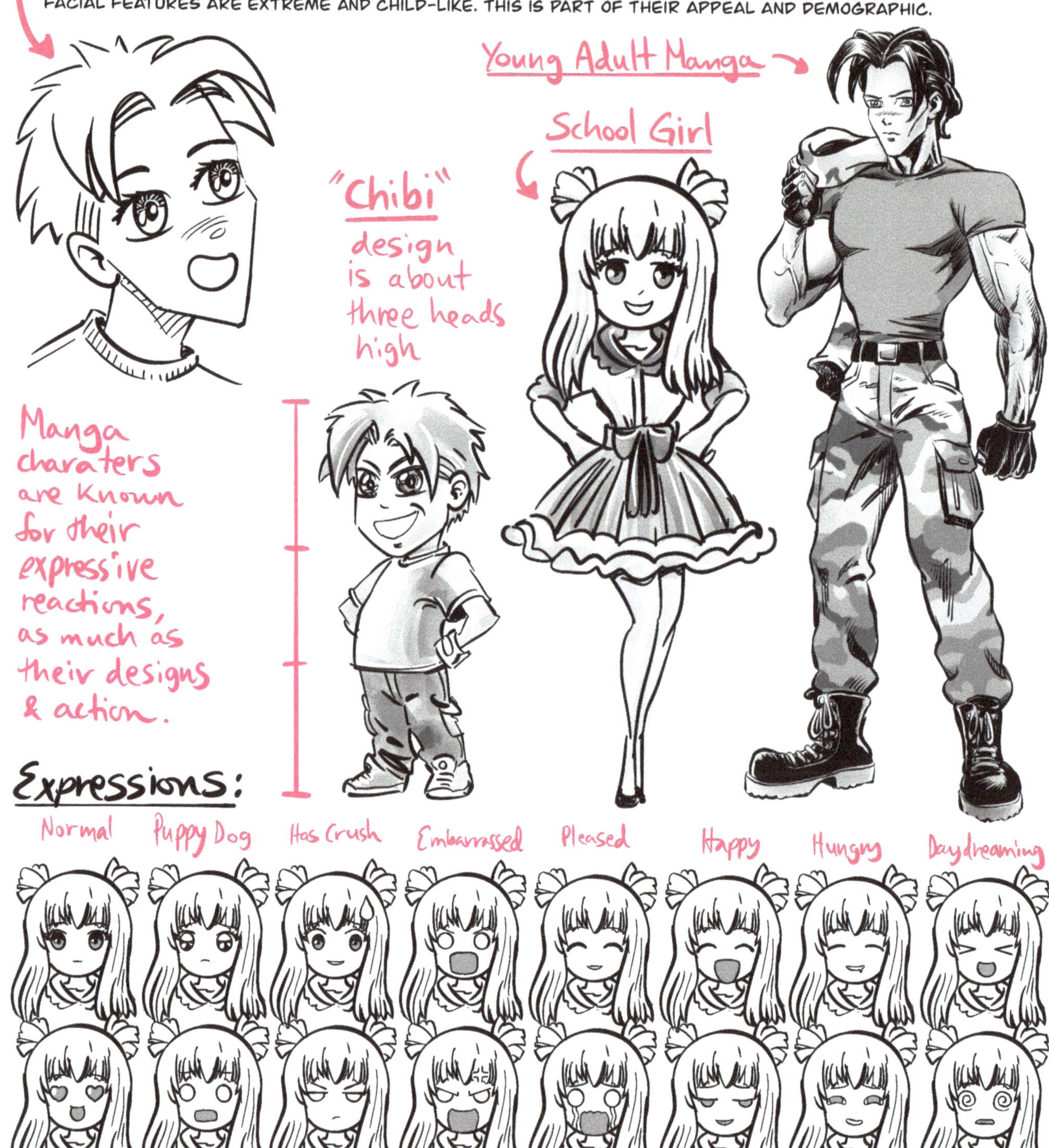

Drawing Super-Heroes

SUPER-HEROES ARE TYPICALLY TALLER THAN OTHER CARTOON CHARACTERS. THEY ARE AS MANY AS 10 HEADS HIGH. THE MALE FIGURES ARE MUCH MORE MUSCULAR AND THE FEMALES ARE DRAWN THIN YET ATHLETIC. LOOKING AT PHOTOS OF BODY BUILDERS AND SUPERMODELS WILL HELP TO UNDERSTAND THEIR PHYSIQUES. THEN EXAGGERATE!

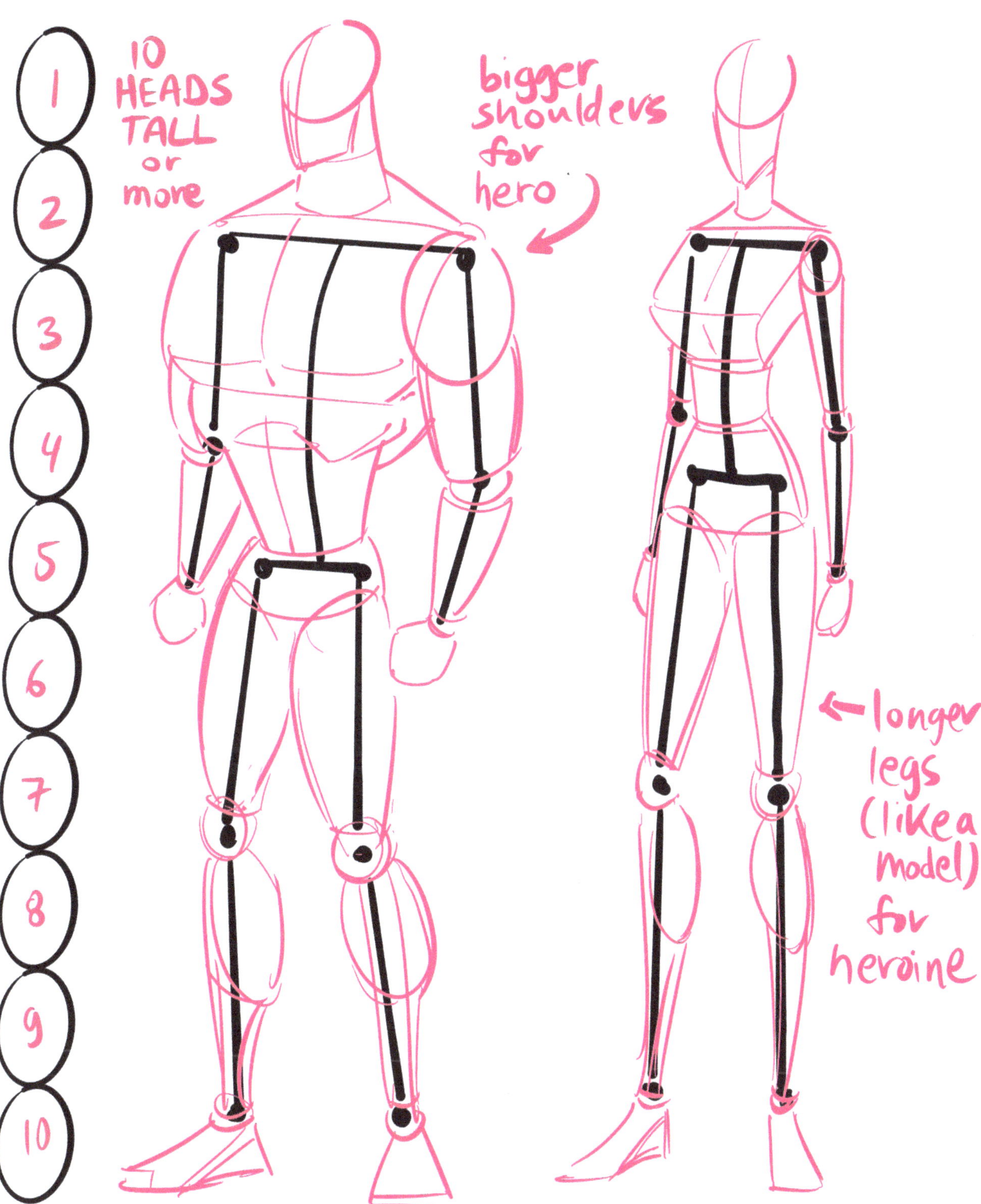

Fun Exercise

USING SHAPES, TO SHOW MUSCLE, DRAW YOUR OWN SUPER-HERO! *or villain*

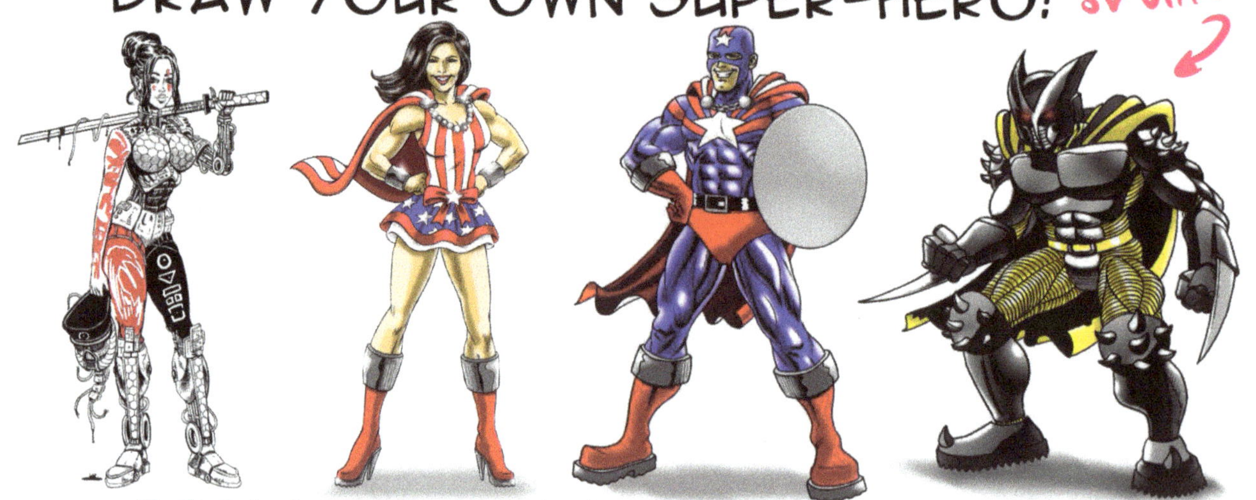

DRAW THEM IN AN EXCITING POSE!

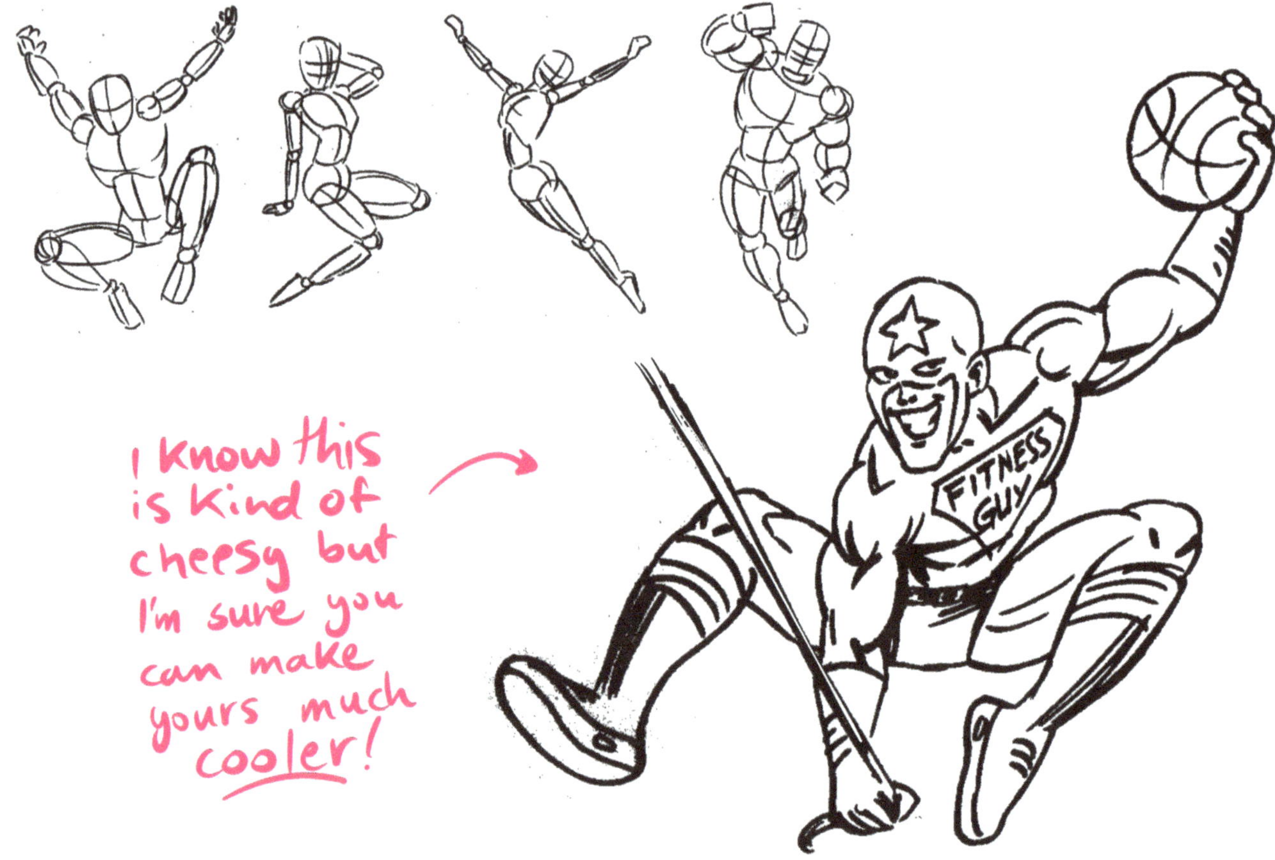

ADD A COSTUME AND DETAILS! BE CREATIVE AND HAVE FUN!

Hard Stuff Made Easy

WITH A RUSHED GLANCE, YOU CAN MESS UP A DRAWING OF A FACE AND IT MIGHT NOT BE NOTICEABLE AT FIRST. BUT HANDS AND FEET, EVEN BAD ARTISTS KNOW WHEN THEY'RE DRAWN WRONG.

EVEN BACK IN COLLEGE, ARTISTS USED TO HIDE THEIR HANDS AND FEET BY DRAWING CHARACTERS WITH HANDS IN THEIR POCKETS OR CHOPPING OFF THE COMPOSITION AT THEIR FEET. THE BEST PRACTICE IS TO JUST KEEP DRAWING THE THINGS YOU AREN'T GOOD AT, UNTIL THEY LOOK GOOD. IT HELPS TO HAVE SOME THEORY TO GO ALONG WITH THE PRACTICE.

THE SUMMER WHEN I WAS TWELVE YEARS OLD, I SPENT IN FRUSTRATION, TRYING TO UNDERSTAND HANDS ON MY OWN. ONE EXERCISE I RECALL WAS TRACING MY HAND ON A PIECE OF PAPER AND THEN OBSERVING IT AND ADDING ALL THE SHADING TO MY DRAWING. ANOTHER EXERCISE WAS MAKING A MAP OF ALL THE KNUCKLES AND WHERE THEY LINED UP ON EACH FINGER. THE MORE CHALLENGING EXERCISES WERE IN REDESIGNING HANDS IN DIFFERENT POSITIONS. AFTER ALL THAT, I WENT TO CONTORTING MY HAND IN THE MIRROR AND COPYING IT WITH THE OTHER. BY THE END OF THE SUMMER, I HAD MASTERED DRAWING ONE HAND POSITION REALLY WELL. EVERY CHARACTER, FROM THEN ON, HAD THAT HAND.

BEING ABLE TO DRAW FLYING SUPERHEROES IN COMICS, YOU HAVE TO KNOW THE SHAPES OF FEET. THEY OFTEN WEAR SKIN-TIGHT BOOTS AND THEY'RE KICKING AND MOVING AROUND. FEET IN ACTION ARE IN THE FOREFRONT. IT'S IMPORTANT TO NOTE THAT FEET ARE NEARLY AS EXPRESSIVE AS HANDS, ONLY WE DON'T PAY AS MUCH ATTENTION TO THEM. THEY KEEP US BALANCED AND, CERTAINLY WITH A LITTLE MOVEMENT, THEY CAN TELL STORIES TOO. FOR EXAMPLE, IMAGINE TRYING TO DRAW SOMEONE SHY BUT SHOWING ONLY THEIR FEET. ONE WAY WOULD BE TO COYLY HIDE ONE FOOT BEHIND THE OTHER.

BESIDES HANDS AND FEET, EARS GIVE MANY ARTISTS TROUBLE. AND A FEW OTHER PARTS OF ANATOMY STAND OUT AS CHALLENGING. HERE ARE SOME QUICK EXAMINATIONS OF THOSE.

Drawing Hands

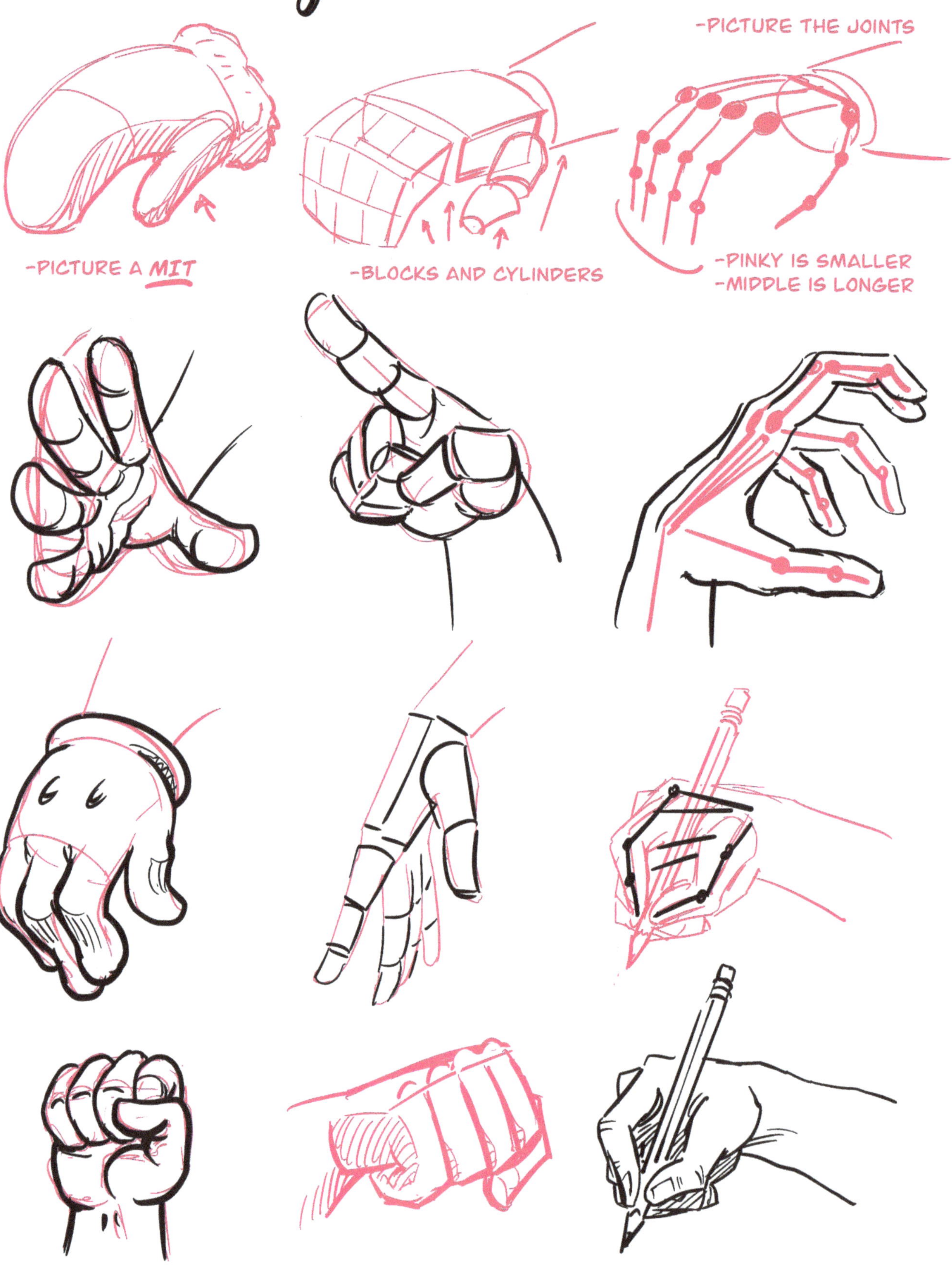

Drawing Feet

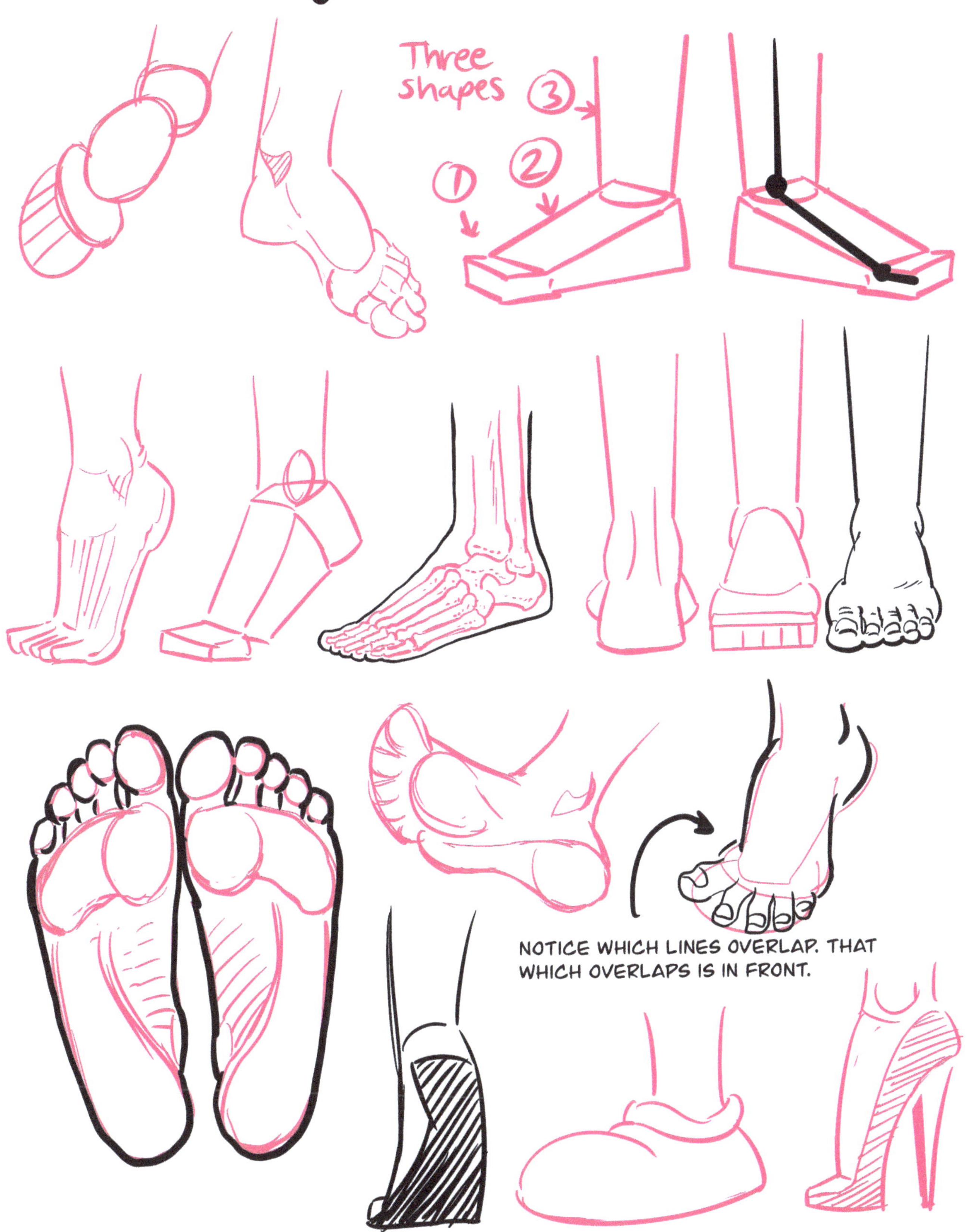

Miscellaneous Anatomy

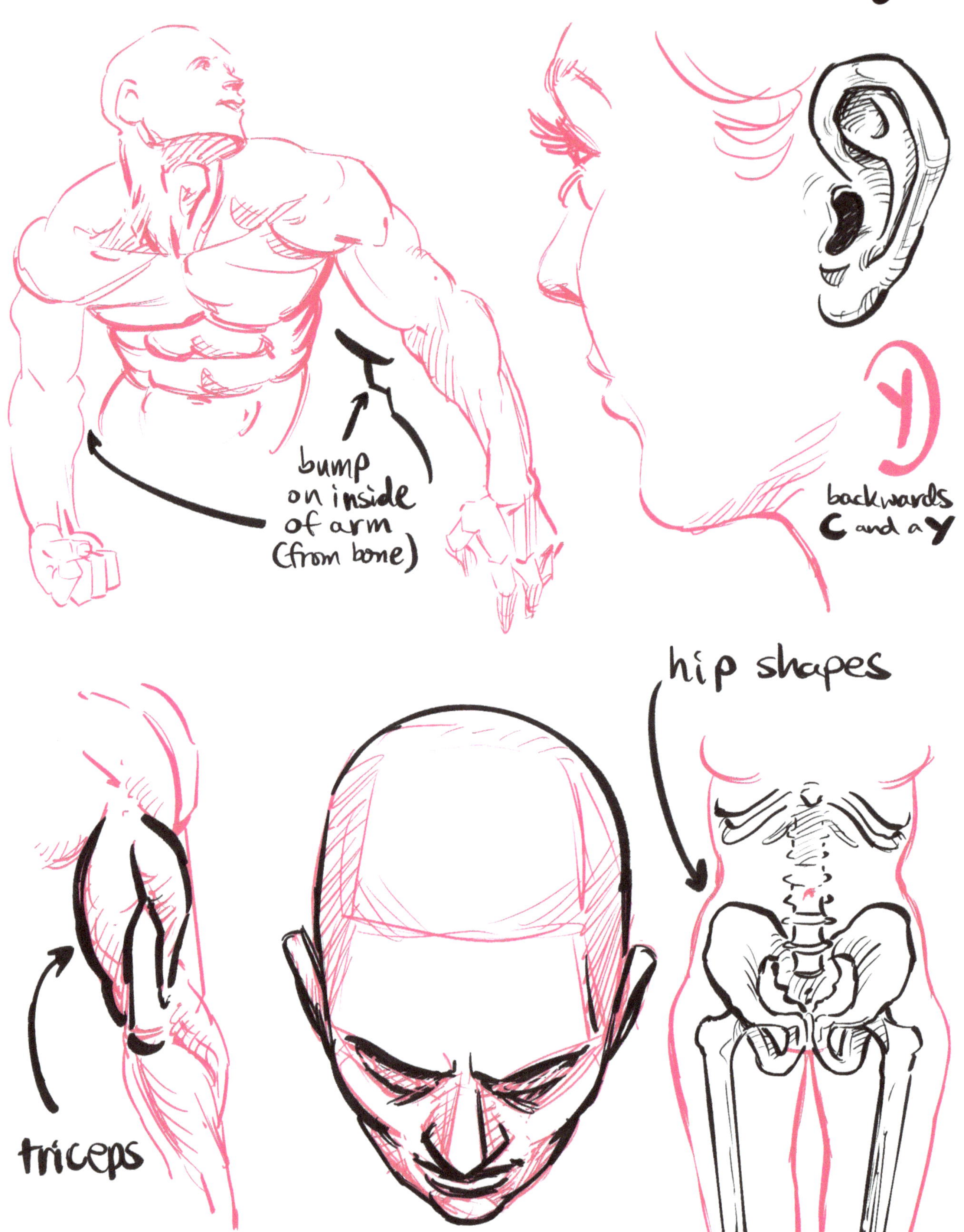

Caricatures

ONE OF THE SKILLS THAT I LEARNED IN LIFE DRAWING CLASS IN COLLEGE WAS HOW TO DRAW CARICATURES AND IT HAS HELPED ME OUT IMMENSELY THROUGHOUT MY CAREER.

THE WAY IT WAS TAUGHT IN CLASS WAS VERY SIMPLE. BIG HEAD AND SMALL BODY. EXAGGERATE AND INCORPORATE THE SITTER'S PERSONALITY INTO THE DRAWING. THAT'S BASICALLY IT. IN A NUTSHELL, IT'S THE SAME AS WHAT I TEACH.

MUCH LIKE MY TEACHER AT THE TIME, HOWEVER, I CARED MORE FOR THE CLASSICAL TRAINING. IT WAS ONLY A FEW YEARS LATER THAT THE SKILL CAME IN HANDY WHEN I LANDED A REALLY FUN SUMMER GIG DRAWING CARICATURES OF NURSES FOR "NATIONAL NURSES DAY" AT ST. MARY'S HOSPITAL IN MONTREAL. ONCE I BECAME A PROFESSIONAL, THIS SKILL WAS UTILIZED MANY TIMES OVER ONLINE AND WITH THE OCCASIONAL IN-PERSON GIG. IN LAS VEGAS, CARICATURE ARTIST BOOKINGS WERE PARTICULARLY POPULAR. I DREW AT BAR MITZVAHS, WEDDINGS, AND CORPORATE EVENTS. BEING AN ARTIST CAN BE LONELY, SITTING IN FRONT OF YOUR DESK, BUT THESE BOOKINGS BECAME A GREAT WAY TO MEET A WIDE ARRAY OF PEOPLE.

WITH THE EXCEPTION OF POLITICAL CARTOONS, THE BEST PART OF DRAWING CARICATURES IS THAT USUALLY THE SUBJECT AND THE OCCASION OF THE ARTWORK IS ALWAYS POSITIVE. IT'S ALWAYS SOME SORT OF CELEBRATION AND THE PEOPLE SITTING FOR YOUR FUNNY PORTRAIT ARE ALWAYS HAPPY AND SMILING. IN FACT, THE SMILE IS A REQUIREMENT! IT'S IMPORTANT TO REMEMBER THAT EVEN IF THE PHOTO REFERENCE OR THE PERSON IS NOT SMILING, MAKE THEM SMILE AND DRAW THEM SMILING. WHEN THEY LOOK BACK ON IT, THEY WILL SEE THEMSELVES SMILING AND IT WILL BRING A NEW SMILE TO THEIR FACE!

Drawing Caricatures

THE BEST ADVICE FOR DRAWING CARICATURES IS TO USE A SIMPLE BIG HEAD WITH SMALL BODY TECHNIQUE. CENTER YOUR DRAWING. HAVE A SUNNY BACKGROUND, IF POSSIBLE. GET TO KNOW YOUR SUBJECT AND ADD THE PERSON'S INTERESTS AND HOBBIES OR THE SPECIAL OCCASION DURING WHICH THE PICTURE WAS DRAWN. NOT ALL CARICATURE ARTISTS INCLUDE THESE EXTRA ITEMS BUT ADDING THEM WILL MAKE YOUR DRAWING MORE PERSONAL. CARICATURES ARE MEANT TO BE ENDEARING AND SHOULD FEATURE THE PERSON IN THE BEST LIGHT POSSIBLE. AND REMEMBER TO ALWAYS DRAW THE PERSON WITH A BIG SMILE ON THEIR HAPPY FACE!

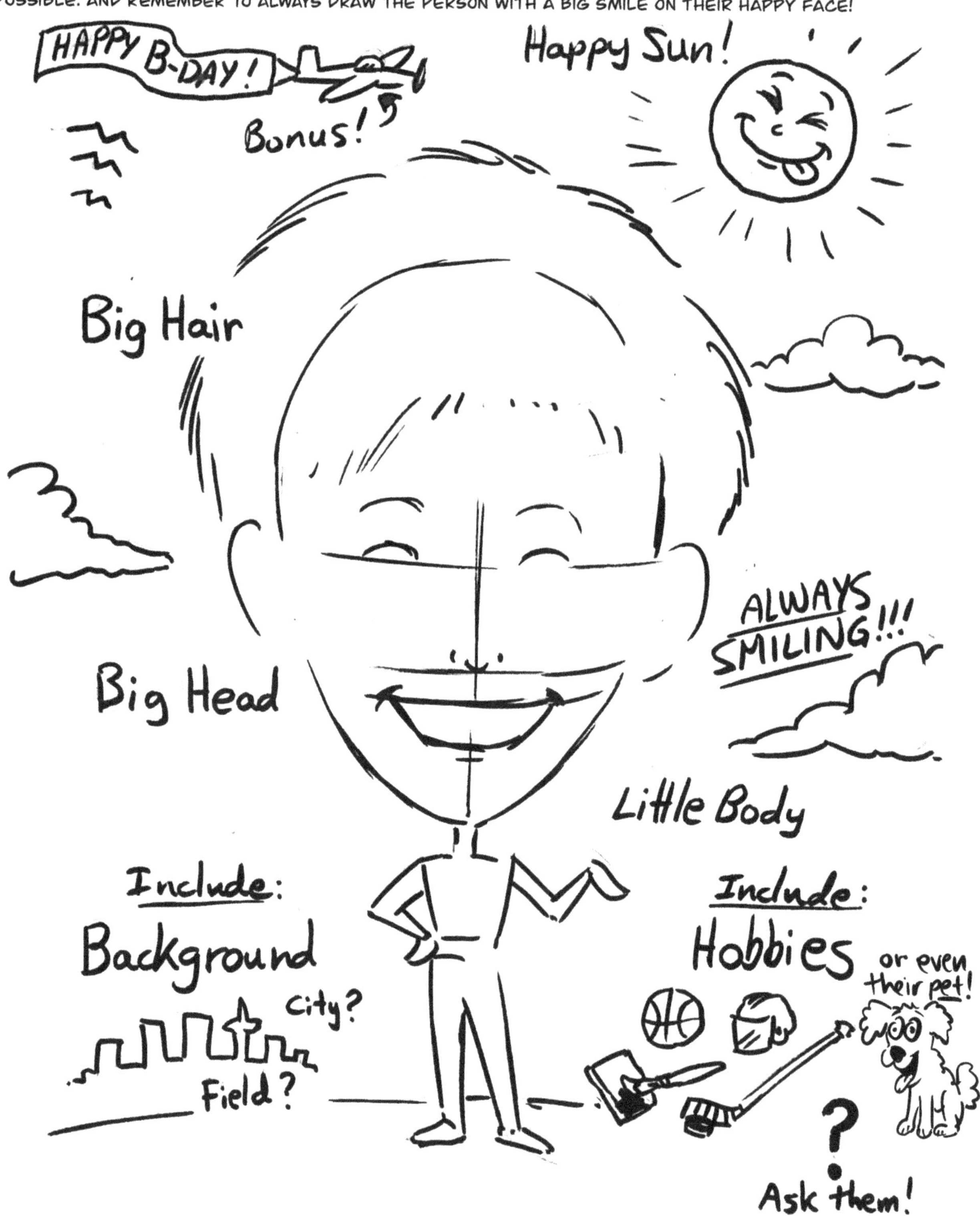

Caricature Examples

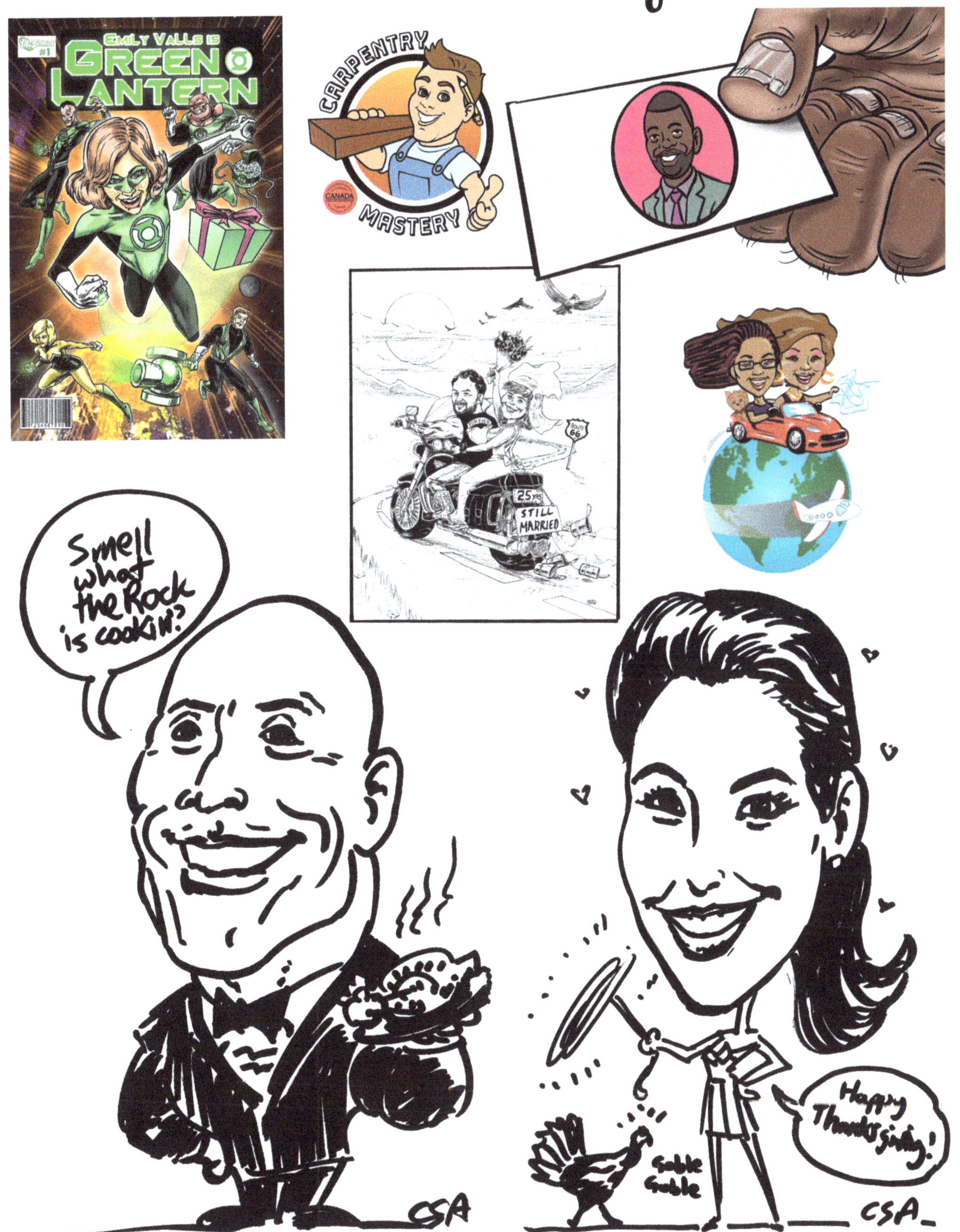

More Caricatures

WHETHER YOU'RE DRAWING QUICK FIVE TO TEN MINUTE SKETCHES AT PARTIES OR TO ENTERTAIN YOUR FRIENDS, OR DRAWING POLITICAL CARTOONS, KNOWING HOW TO DRAW CARICATURES IS A VALUED SKILL.

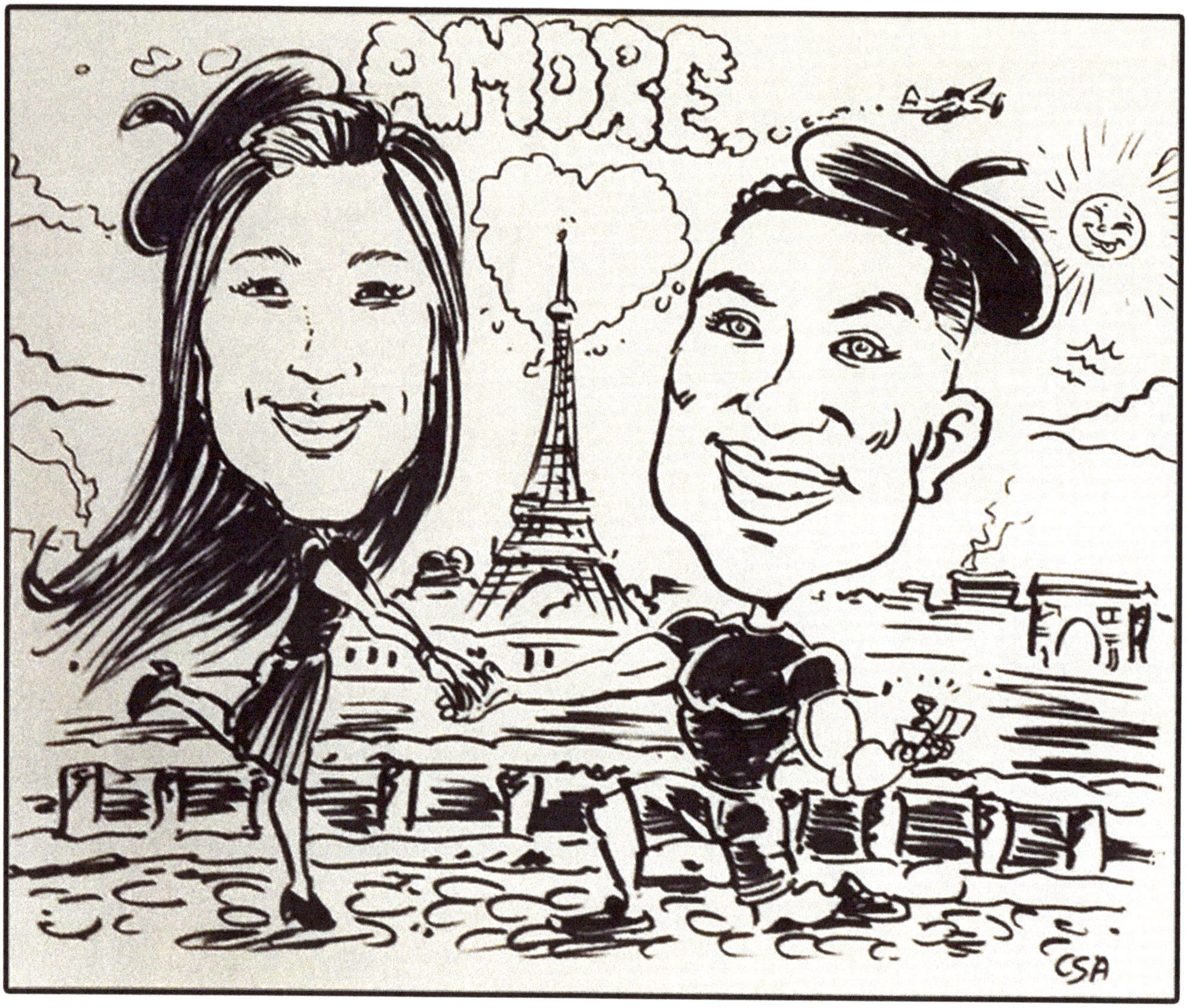

WITH COMMISSIONS, YOU CAN HAVE MORE TIME ON ILLUSTRATING AND COLOUR. MOST CARICATURES USE A BIG HEAD AND LITTLE BODY. THESE EXAMPLES BELOW ARE MORE TRADITIONALLY ILLUSTRATED BUT THE SUBJECTS ARE CARICATURED. THEY ARE OF THE SAME FAMILY, YEAR AFTER YEAR. IT SHOWS HOW CREATIVE YOU CAN BE.

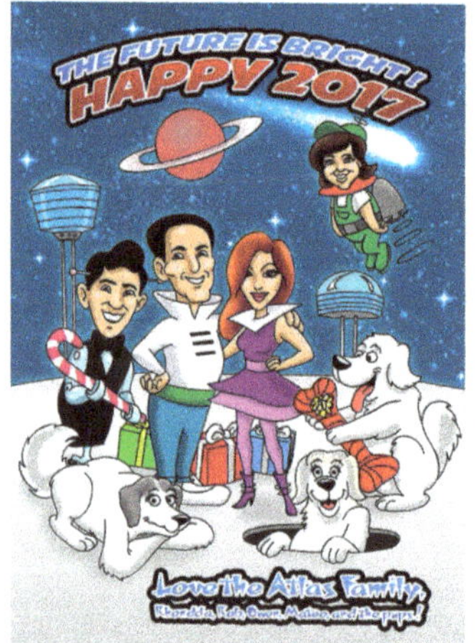

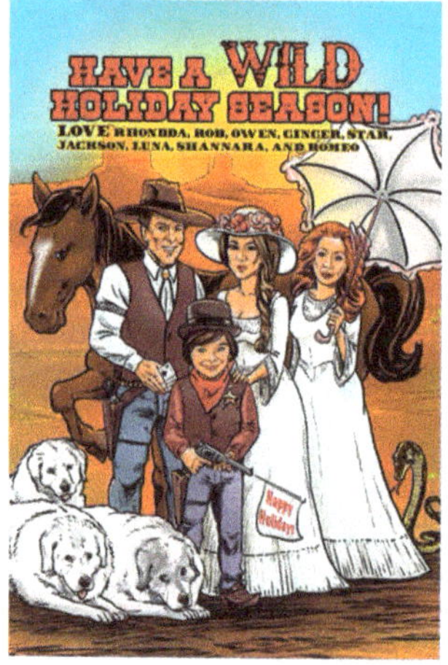

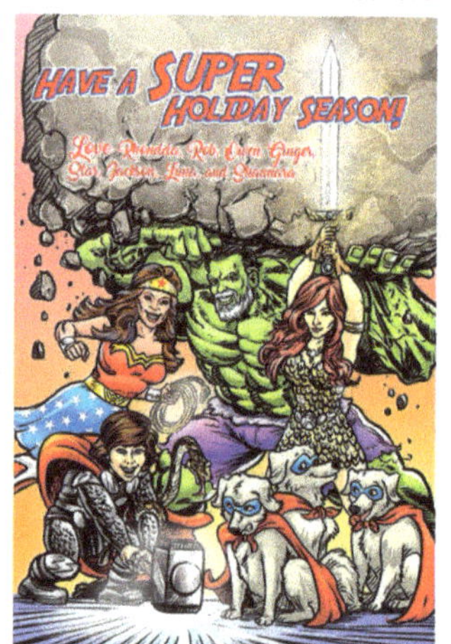

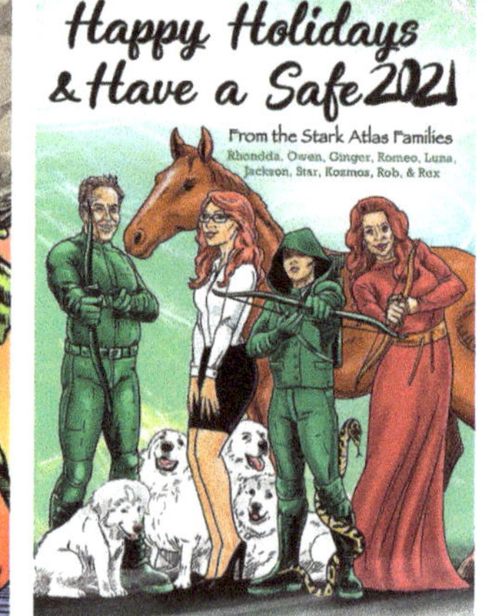

Designing Animals

ANTHROPOMORPHIC CHARACTERS ARE ANIMALS THAT WALK UPRIGHT OR TALK LIKE PEOPLE. MOST CARTOON ANIMAL DRAWINGS ARE ANTHROPOMORPHIC.

ANIMAL CARTOONS ARE A GREAT WAY TO INJECT CUTENESS AND HUMOUR INTO YOUR COMICS OR MANGA. AMERICAN COMIC STRIPS ARE KNOWN FOR HAVING A LOT OF FAMOUS CARTOON ANIMALS WHICH HAVE OFTEN BEEN CONVERTED TO ANIMATED FILMS. EVEN IF YOUR ANIMAL DOES NOT SPEAK, IT'S GOOD TO BE ABLE TO HUMANIZE THEIR EXPRESSIONS.

THE MOST COMMON PROJECT I USED TO WIN, EARLY ON IN MY FREELANCING CAREER, WAS "MASCOT LOGO DESIGN." FOR A PERIOD, ONLINE, MANY WEBSITES HAD SOME SORT OF MASCOT. GATORS WERE POPULAR, MANY TYPES OF DOGS, SOME CATS, AND MONSTERS. THE CHARACTERS WERE SOMETIMES LEANING ON THE LETTERS OF THE LOGO OR THEY'D STAND NEXT TO THE LETTERS OR INTERACT WITH THE LOGO IN SOME CREATIVE WAY. THIS PROVED THAT ANIMAL CARTOONS ARE A CUTE WAY TO ATTRACT CUSTOMERS TO A PRODUCT.

I BET IF YOU THINK OF SOME OF THE MOST ENDURING CARTOONS OF ALL TIME, MANY OF THEM ARE ANIMALS. ANIMALS HAVE ALSO FAMOUSLY BEEN USED AS METAPHORS, SUCH AS IN FABLES. SO AT FIRST GLANCE, IT CAN SEEM JUVENILE TO DRAW FUNNY ANIMALS BUT SURPRISINGLY IF YOU WISH TO CONVEY A MORAL STORY, ANTHROPOMORPHIC CHARACTERS ARE THE SMART WAY TO DO IT.

Animal Shapes

LEARNING HOW TO DRAW REALISTIC ANIMALS IS A GOOD BEGINNING, SINCE IN COMICS AND MANGA REALISTIC CHARACTERS MAY INTERACT WITH A VARIETY OF REAL ANIMALS.

YOU CAN USE THE SAME FOUR BASIC SHAPES TO DECIPHER AND CONSTRUCT ANIMALS.

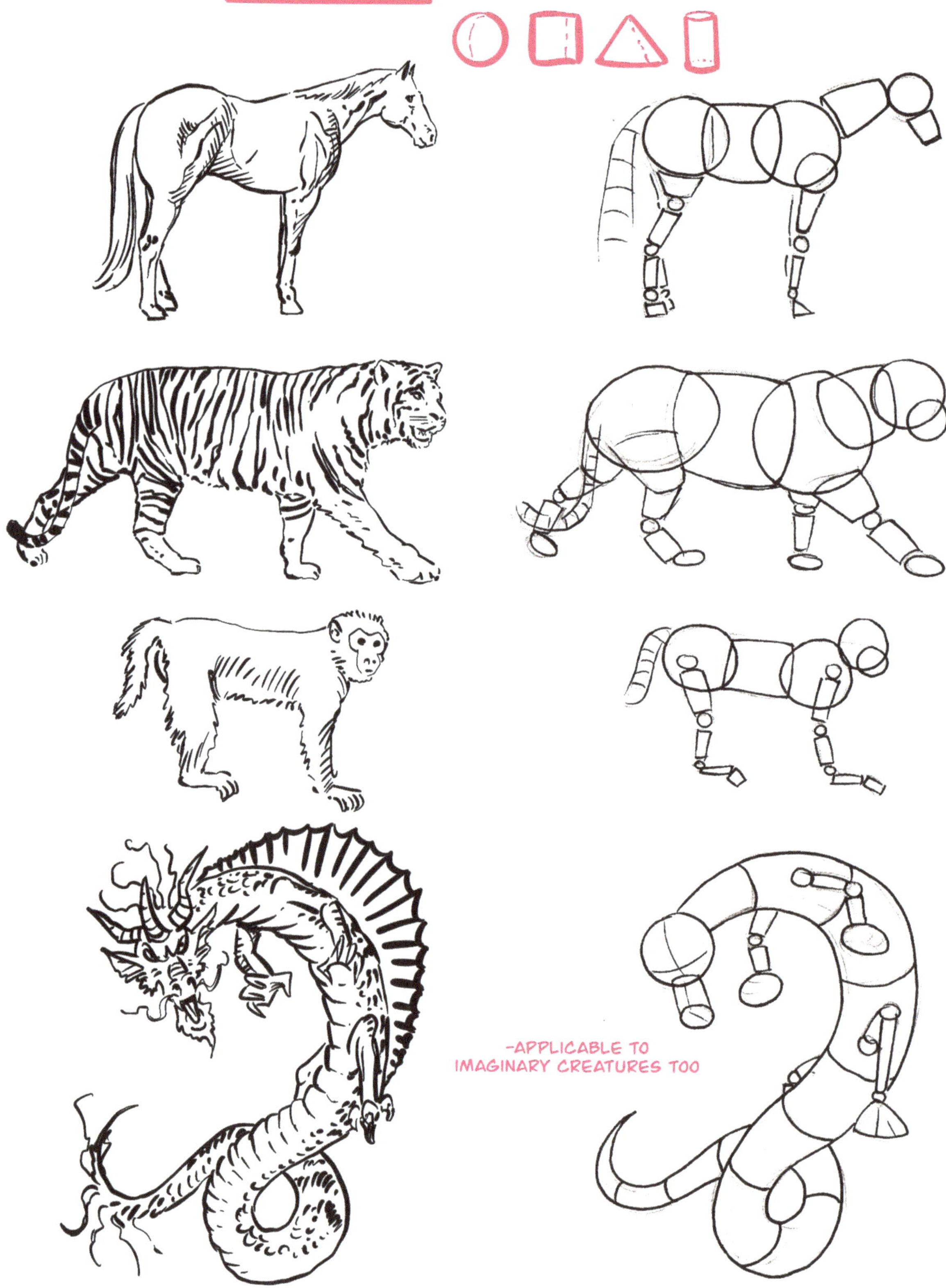

Drawing Horses

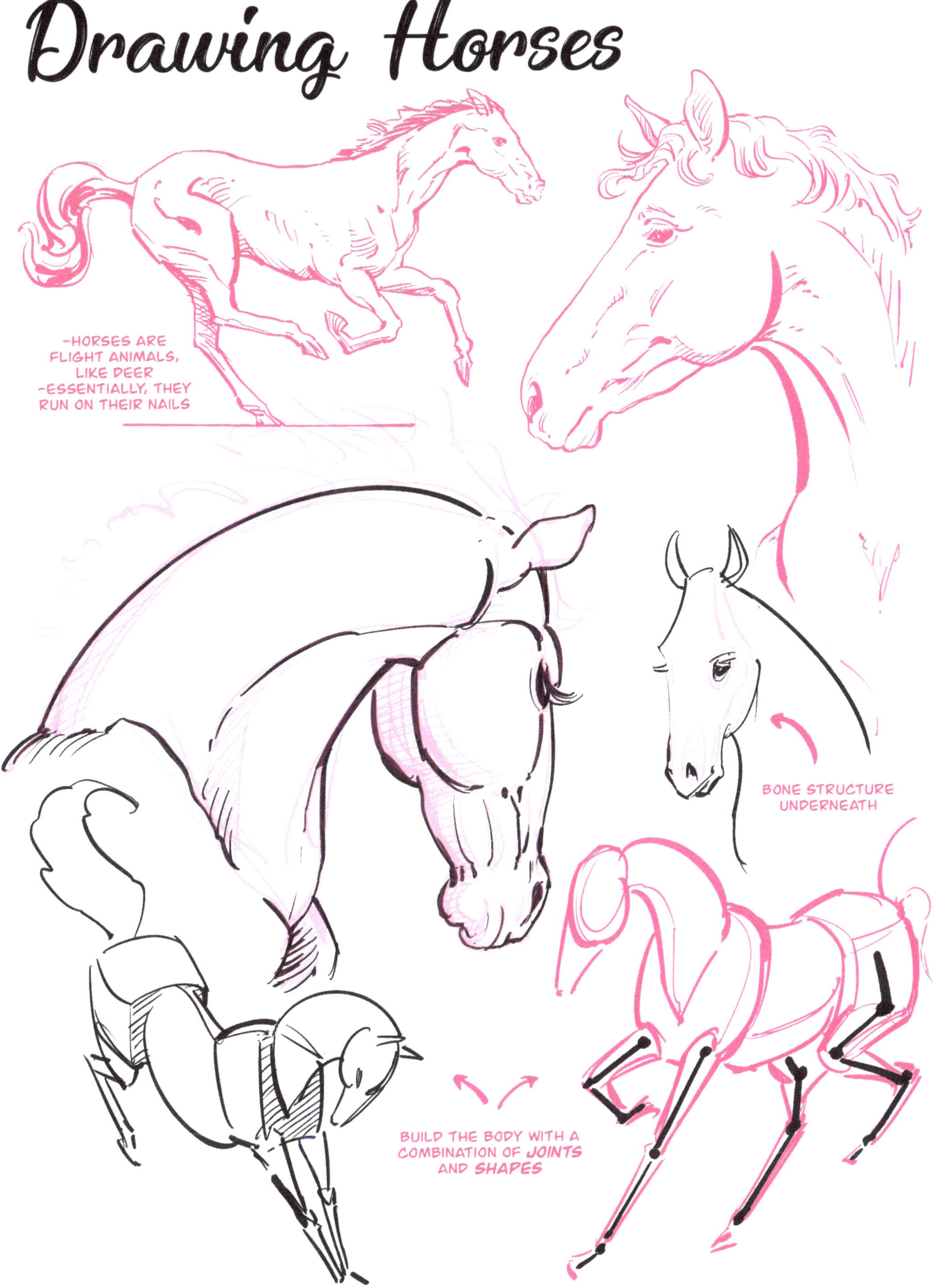

Anthropomorphic Characters

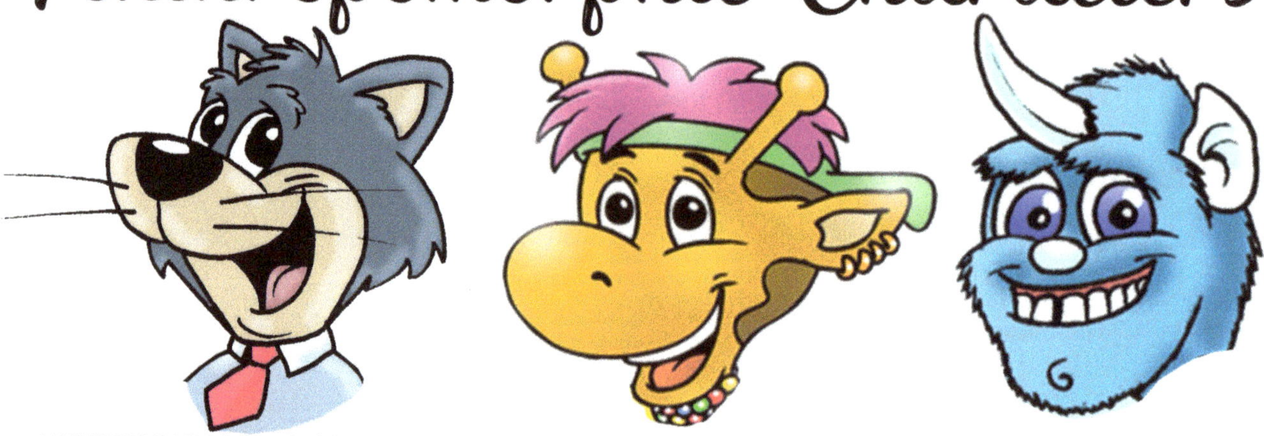

ANTHROPOMORHIC CHARACTERS OFTEN HAVE ANIMAL HEADS WITH HUMAN EXPRESSIONS, ANIMAL BODY COLORS AND TAILS, BUT ARE BIPEDS LIKE HUMANS AND OFTEN DRESS LIKE PEOPLE. BELOW IS A DESIGN EXAMPLE.

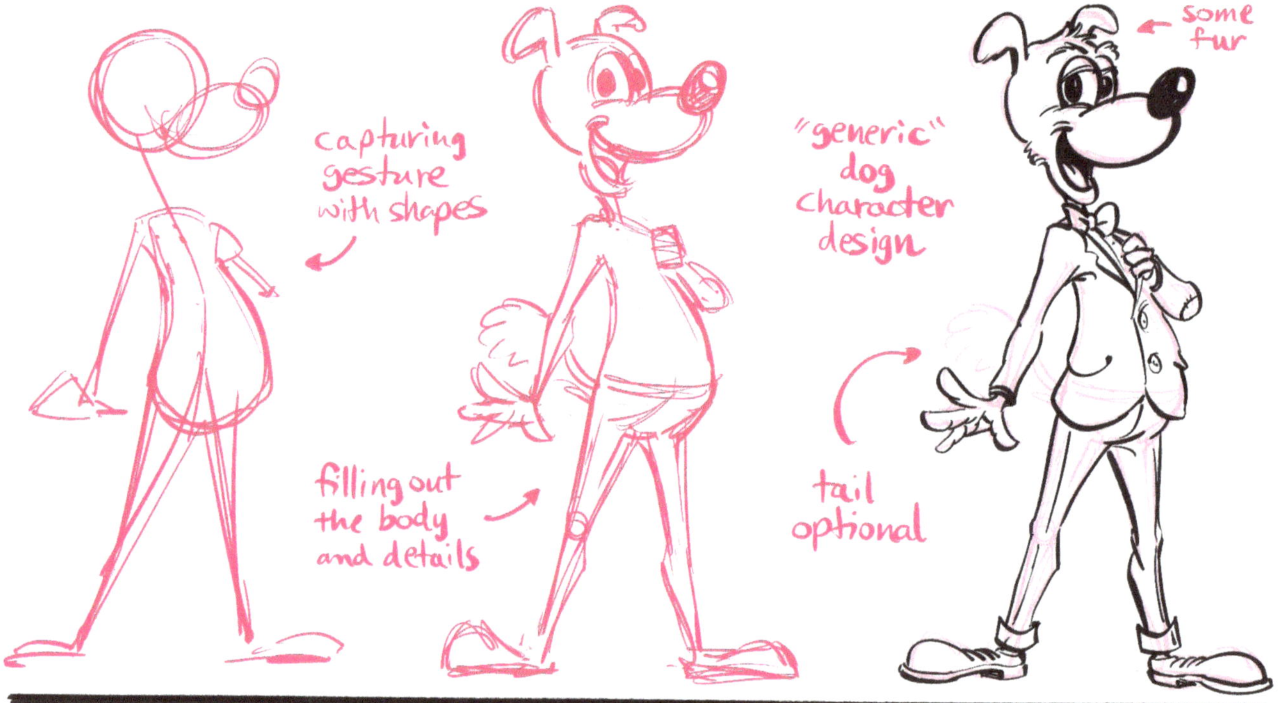

capturing gesture with shapes

filling out the body and details

"generic" dog character design

some fur

tail optional

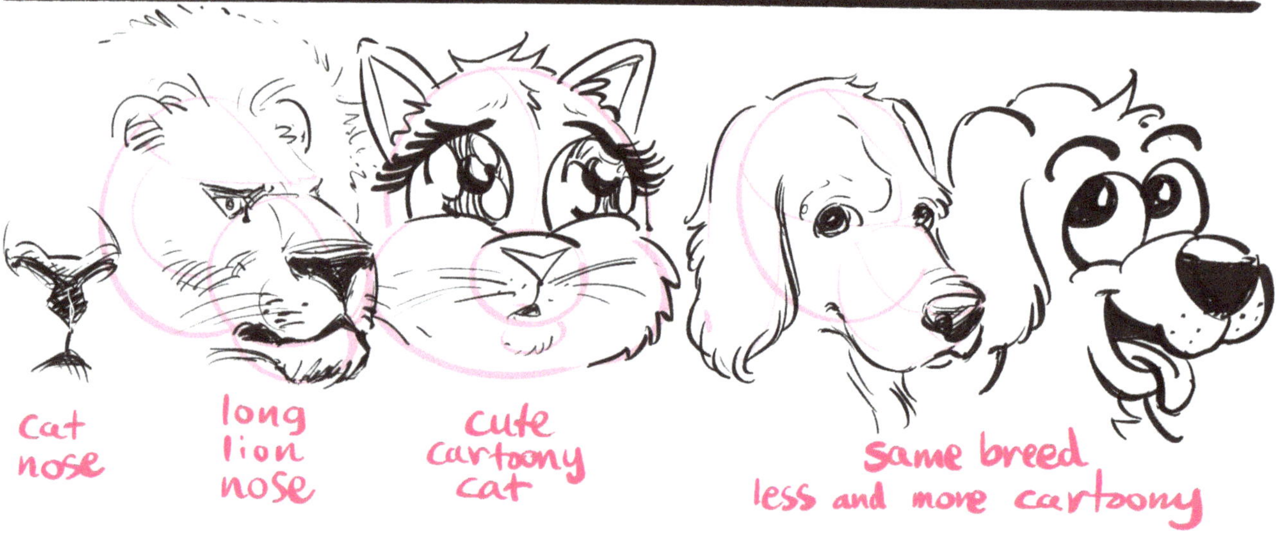

cat nose

long lion nose

cute cartoony cat

same breed less and more cartoony

www.MasterpieceArtSchool.com

EASY AND FUN CARTOONING TECHNIQUES FOR DRAWING COMICS AND MANGA

FUN EXAMPLES AND EXERCISE: HERE ARE SOME NOTES AND A COLLAGE OF MY OWN EXAMPLES FOR INSPIRATION. GIVE YOUR CHARACTER DESIGNS ANIMAL FEATURES.

CARTOON ANIMALS

WHEN DESIGNING A CARTOON ANIMAL, USE REFERENCE PHOTOS WHEN POSSIBLE

MAKE THEM CUTE, SMILING, AND IN A FUN ACTION POSE

ANIMAL CARTOONS CAN WALK LIKE ANIMALS OR HAVE HUMAN POSTURE

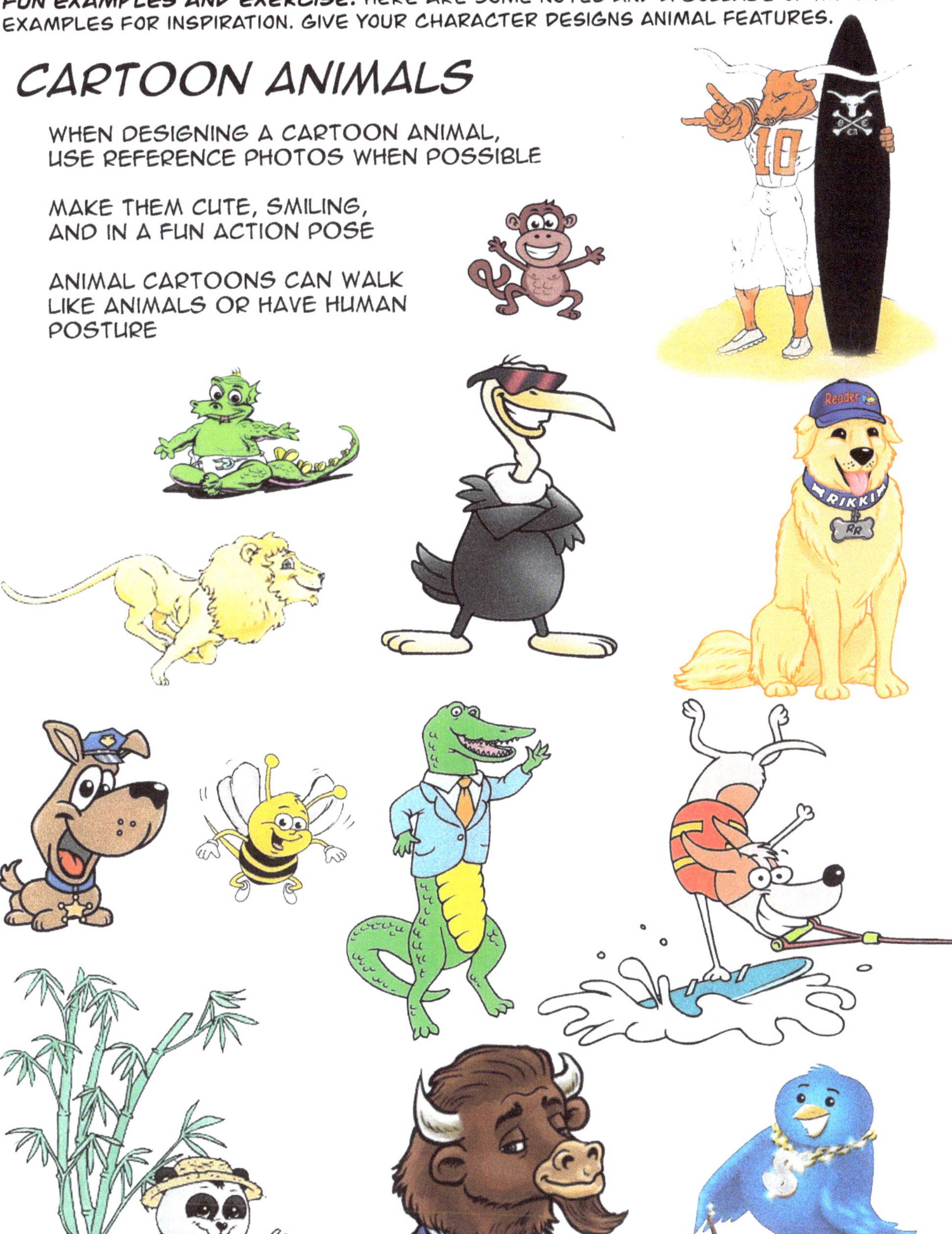

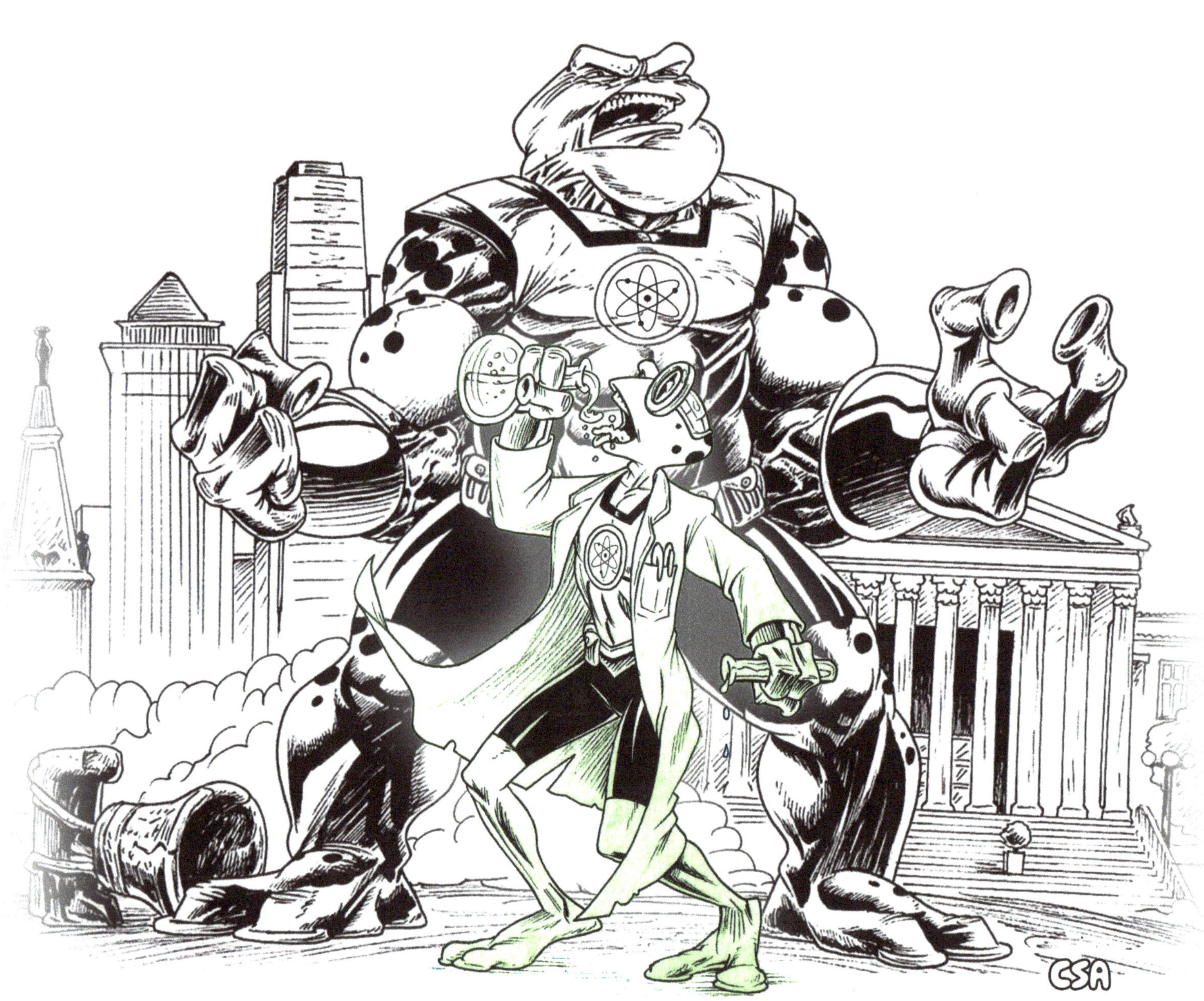

Expressions and Gestures

GREAT CARTOONISTS ARE ALSO GREAT ACTORS!

HOW CAN YOU KNOW HOW AN EXPRESSION SHOULD LOOK, UNLESS YOU'VE SEEN IT? ONCE YOU SEE, YOUR PENCIL WILL BELIEVE AND SO WILL YOUR READERS. THAT'S WHY YOU SHOULD HAVE A MIRROR NEXT TO YOUR DESK OR USE YOUR CAMERA TO RECORD YOURSELF AND FREEZE-FRAME TO GET THE DESIRED POSES.

THERE ARE NUMEROUS REAL-LIFE PROPS AND ONLINE TOOLS, LIKE DIGITAL MANNEQUIN APPLICATIONS. SOME OF THEM ARE USEFUL AND MUCH EASIER IN SOME WAYS BECAUSE YOU CAN LIGHT THE MODEL. HOWEVER, FEELING THE EXPRESSION IN YOUR BODY IS THE MOST NATURAL LEARNING METHOD.

IT'S INTERESTING TO DISCOVER HOW ONE TYPE OF CHARACTER WILL STAND OR MOVE DIFFERENTLY THAN ANOTHER. GET INTO THE ROLE AND BE TRUE TO YOUR CHARACTER. IN THE END, YOUR GESTURAL AND FACIAL EXPRESSIONS WILL BE MORE GENUINE THAN WHAT YOU COULD DERIVE FROM A SOULLESS WOODEN MANNEQUIN OR FROM WITHIN A 3D ENVIRONMENT.

IT'S AMAZING TOO HOW MUCH WE CAN CONTORT, EMOTE, COMPRESS, AND EXPAND OUR BODIES AND FACES. TAKE WHAT WE'RE ABLE TO DO AND EXAGGERATE THESE EXPRESSIONS FURTHER IN YOUR CARTOONS. AND GO BEYOND THE SIMPLE BASICS OF HAPPY, SAD, ANGRY, ETC. CRACK OPEN A THESAURUS AND GO DEEP AND COMPLEX WITH YOUR CHARACTER'S EXPRESSIONS, BUT ALL THE WHILE KEEP IT CLEAR FOR THE READER.

Expressions !!!

CHARACTER'S FEELINGS MUST BE UNDERSTOOD THROUGH THE POSITIONING OF THE BODY. THEIR FACIAL EXPRESSIONS SHOULD BE SECONDARY. EACH EXPRESSION HAS TO BE READABLE AS A STICK PERSON OR SILHOUETTE.

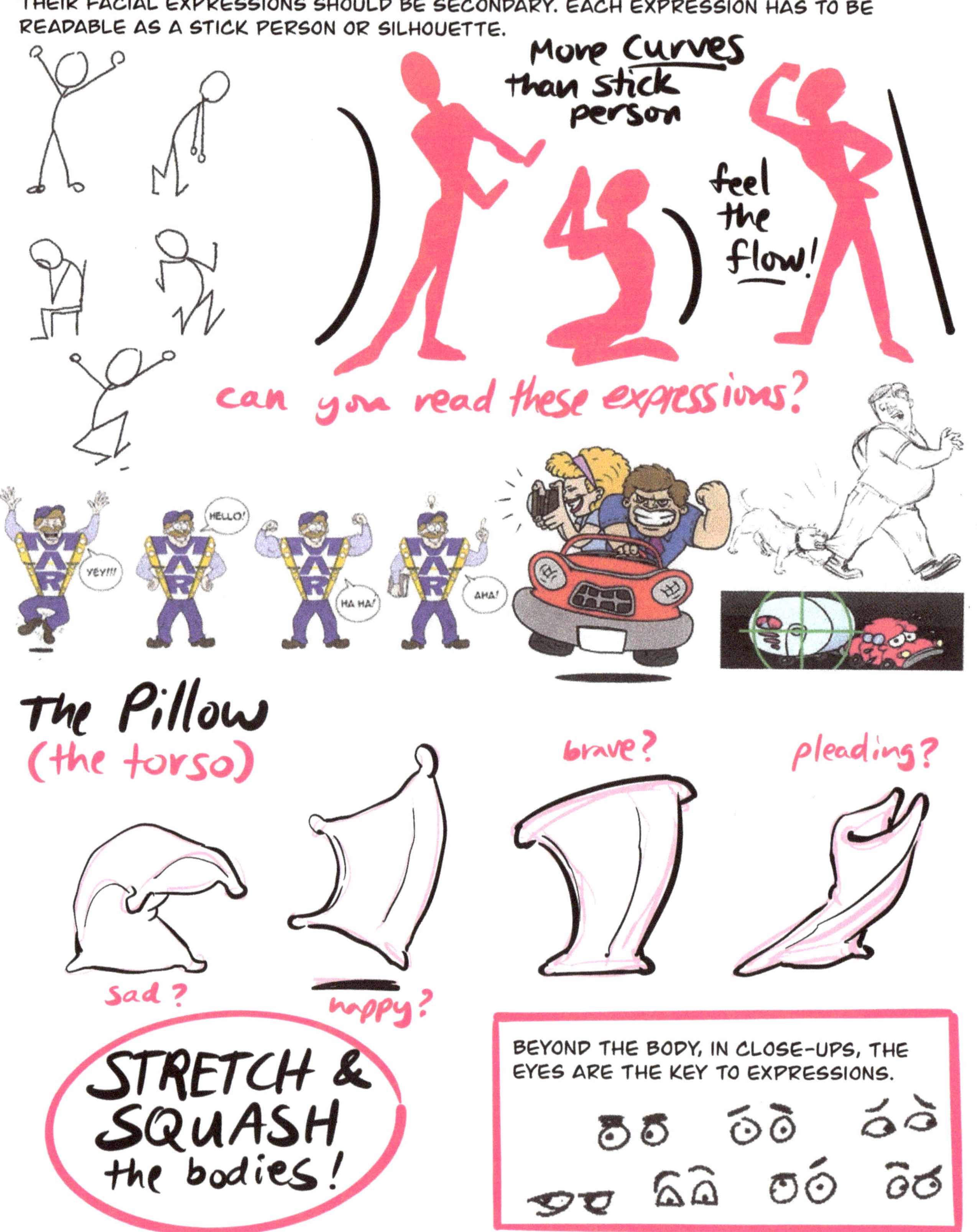

www.MasterpieceArtSchool.com

Stretch and Squash

STRETCH AND SQUASH IS AN ANIMATION PRINCIPLE WHICH IS VERY HELPFUL TO KNOW WHEN YOU'RE DRAWING CARTOONS. IMAGINE A BOUNCING BALL FILLED WITH AIR. WHEN IT LANDS ON THE GROUND, THE IMPACT MAKES IT CHANGE SHAPE. THE VOLUME STAYS THE SAME. ONLY THE EXTERIOR SHAPE COMPRESSES AND STRETCHES. FACES DO THE SAME THING WHEN EXPRESSIVE AND WHEN THEY ARE IN MOTION.

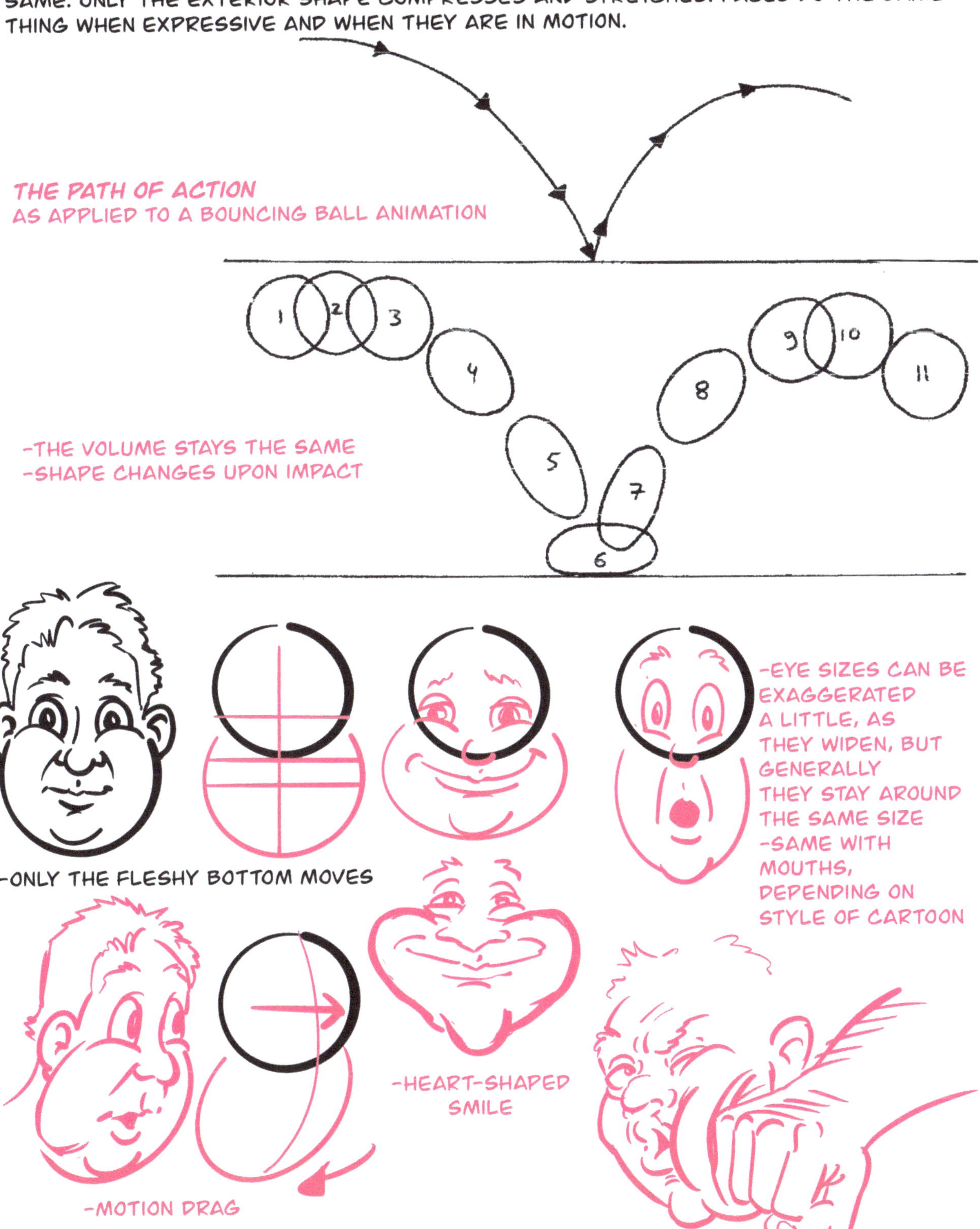

www.MasterpieceArtSchool.com

Gestural Exercise

TAKE ONE (OR MORE THAN ONE) OF YOUR CHARACTER DESIGNS FROM EARLIER AND CREATE AT LEAST *THREE DETAILED POSES* FOR THEM. THIS HELPS YOU AS A CARTOONIST TO LEARN ABOUT YOUR CHARACTER'S PERSONALITY. THROUGH YOUR DRAWINGS OF THEIR *PHYSICAL GESTURES,* YOU WILL GAIN A BETTER UNDERSTANDING OF HOW THEY WILL REACT IN VARIOUS SITUATIONS. EXPLORE THEIR EMOTIONAL RANGE. IF DRAWING A SUPERHERO, EXAGERATE AND STRETCH AND SQUASH THEIR BODY AS YOU WOULD A MORE CARTOONY CHARACTER. ADDITIONALLY, REMEMBER THAT A SUPER-HERO PUNCHING DOES NOT COUNT AS AN EXPRESSION.

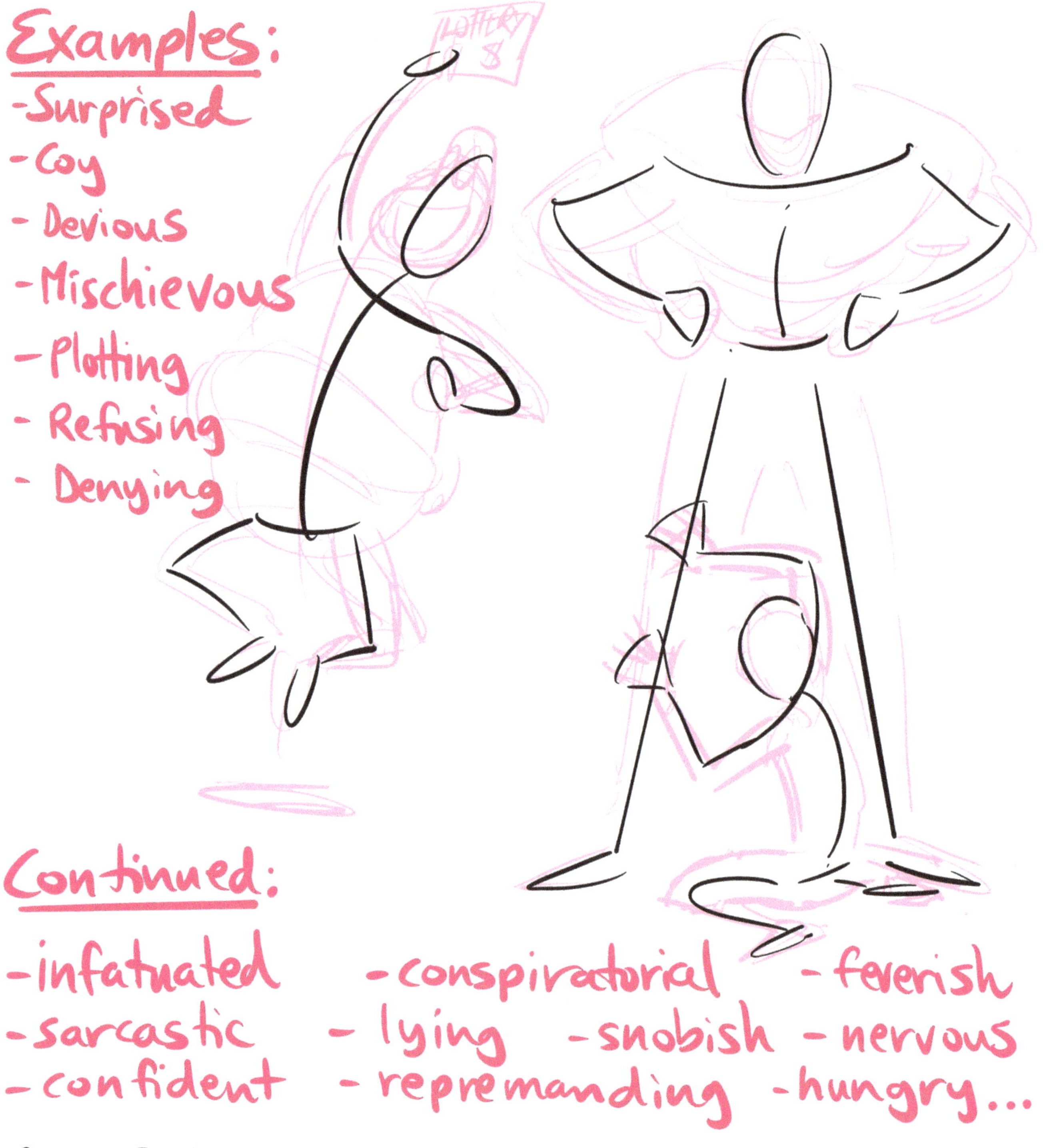

Examples:
- Surprised
- Coy
- Devious
- Mischievous
- Plotting
- Refusing
- Denying

Continued:
- infatuated
- sarcastic
- confident
- conspiratorial
- lying
- repremanding
- feverish
- snobish
- nervous
- hungry...

46

www.MasterpieceArtSchool.com

Drawing Techniques

ONCE YOU HAVE SOME NICE-LOOKING CHARACTERS, YOU MAY WANT TO PUT SOME FINISHING TOUCHES ON THE DRAWINGS. TO DO THAT, YOU NEED TO KNOW SOME BASIC DRAWING CONCEPTS AND TECHNIQUES.

FOR NOW, FOCUS ON ADDING BELIEVABLE CLOTHES AND PROPS TO YOUR CHARACTERS. THE BEST ADVICE IS TO DO YOUR RESEARCH. IF A CHARACTER IS A BALLERINA, LOOK CLOSELY AT THE PATTERNS OF THE TUTU RUFFLES AND THE STRAPS ON THEIR ANKLES. IF A CHARACTER IS A SOLDIER, RESEARCH THE TYPE OF SOLDIER THEY ARE AND FROM WHAT PERIOD IN HISTORY OR WHAT COUNTRY. THERE ARE SUBTLE DIFFERENCES TO THEIR OUTFITS AND UTILITIES.

SHADING TECHNIQUES HELP ADD REALISM AND TEXTURE TO CLOTHES AND PROPS.

LIGHTING IS VERY IMPORTANT TOO, AS IT CONTROLS MOOD AND MEANING. IMAGINE SOMEONE TELLING A SPOOKY STORY WITH A FLASHLIGHT UNDER THEIR CHIN OR A SOLITARY FIGURE UNDERNEATH A LAMP POST. KEEP LIGHTING MINIMAL ON CHARACTERS WITHOUT BACKGROUNDS BUT LATER ON WHEN THESE CHARACTERS ARE ADDED TO SCENES, THEN THE MAGIC HAPPENS.

THESE DRAWING TECHNIQUES ARE ALSO USED TO GIVE A THREE DIMENSIONAL FEEL TO YOUR TWO DIMENSIONAL DRAWINGS.

Sketching, Drawing, & Inking

-SKETCHING   -DRAWING   -INKING

"x" means fill in black

THERE IS A NOTABLE DIFFERENCE BETWEEN SKETCHING, DRAWING, AND INKING. SKETCHING CAN BE VERY ROUGH, FOR THUMBNAILS OR BREAKDOWNS OF A CHARACTER OR COMIC PAGE. A DRAWING IS THE NEXT STAGE WHERE YOUR IDEAS COME TO LIFE. INKING IS WHERE "THE MAGIC HAPPENS" AND THE DETAIL AND SHADING IS ADDED.

DRAWINGS, AS OPPOSED TO SKETCHES, ARE MORE POLISHED ARTWORKS WITH VERY CLEAR LINES. INKING IS THE CLEANEST FORM OF BLACK AND WHITE ILLUSTRATION. WHEN INKING, YOU'RE ESSENTIALLY TRACING OVER A TIGHT DRAWING. EACH STAGE LEAVES A LITTLE ROOM FOR EMBELLISHMENT. GENERALLY, ONE LEADS TO ANOTHER, FROM LOOSE PENCIL LINES IN THE SKETCHING STAGE, TO TIGHTER LINES IN THE DRAWING STAGE, AND FINALLY VERY CRISP LINES IN THE INKING STAGE.

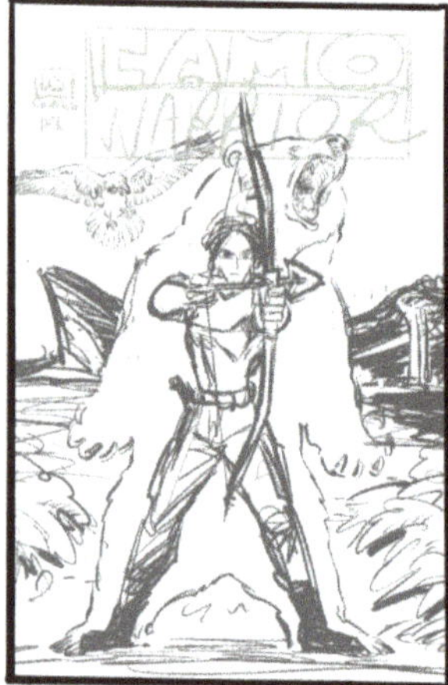

– PRELIMINARY SKETCH / THUMBNAIL / BREAKDOWN

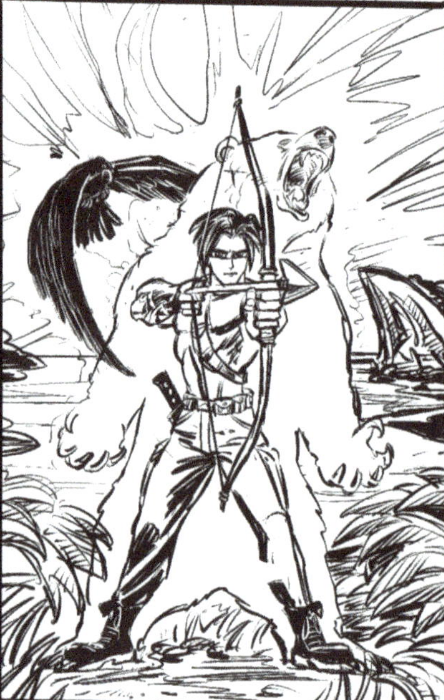

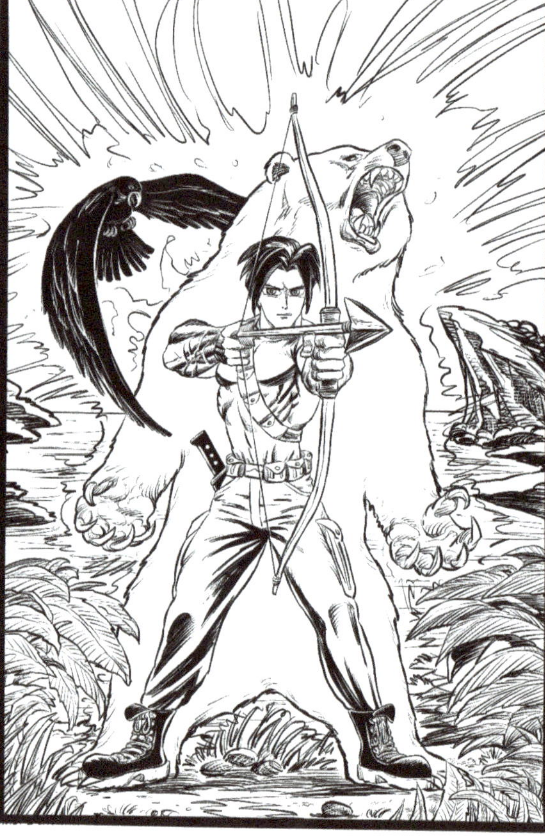

– DRAWING ABOVE

– INKING ON RIGHT

–FINAL COVER, LEFT

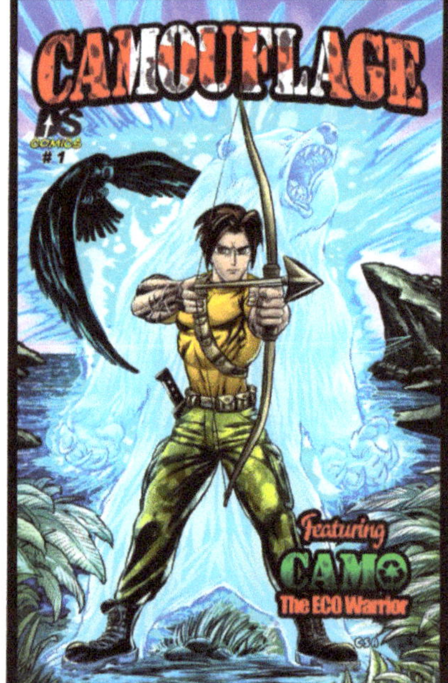

AS YOU CAN SEE, THE SKETCH IS DIFFERENT THAN THE FINAL IN SLIGHT WAYS. THE CROW IS SKETCHED DIFFERENTLY AND THERE'S A ROUGH PLACEMENT OF WHERE THE COVER LOGO WILL BE. OFTEN, ARTISTS SKETCH MULTIPLE IDEAS BECAUSE SKETCHING IS DONE QUICKLY. THIS EARLY PHASE IS GREAT FOR EXPERIMENTATION.

IN THE DRAWING PHASE, YOU CAN DEVELOP YOUR IDEAS FURTHER AND REDRAW SOME ELEMENTS THAT DIDN'T WORK AS WELL IN THE FIRST STAGE. IF YOU STILL NEED TO MAKE CHANGES IN THE DRAWING PHASE, JUST ERASE.

A LOT OF PROFESSIONAL COMIC OR MANGA ARTISTS THAT PLAN TO PENCIL AND INK THEIR OWN ARTWORK DO LOOSER DRAWINGS THAN IF IT WOULD BE IF IT WOULD BE INKED BY SOMEONE ELSE. IT'S WISE, EVEN WHEN INKING YOURSELF, TO WORK AS CLEAN AS POSSIBLE SO THAT ALL YOU'RE EMBELLISHING ON ARE THE EXCESSIVE DETAILS AND NOT THE ACTUAL COMPOSITION, ANATOMY, OR PERSPECTIVE.

COLOR CAN LOOK NICE BUT A GREAT DRAWING SHOULD COMMUNICATE CLEARLY IN BLACK AND WHITE.

EASY AND FUN CARTOONING TECHNIQUES FOR DRAWING COMICS AND MANGA

Shading Techniques

WITH SHADING, NEATNESS COUNTS. FOR HATCHING AND CROSSHATCHING, DRAW YOUR LINES THE SAME THICKNESS AND ALL GOING IN THE SAME DIRECTION, AT THE SAME ANGLE. DO NO RUSH YOUR SHADING.

THE LIGHT SOURCE IN THESE EXAMPLES IS ON THE UPPER RIGHT. FOR BLENDING, REMEMBER THAT LIGHT TRAVELS AROUND SPHERICAL OBJECTS SO THERE IS A LIGHT BAND ON THE FAR EDGE OF THE SHADOW SIDE.

HATCHING –ILLUSTRATED WITH A BRUSH PEN STYLE

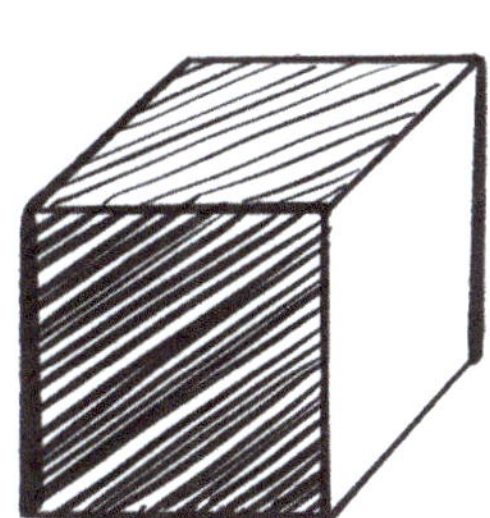
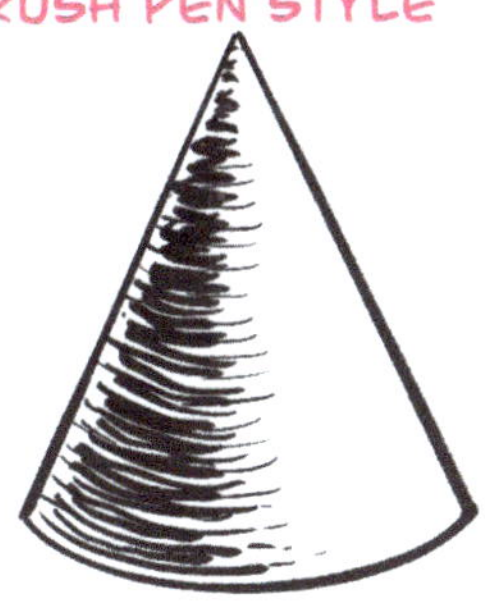
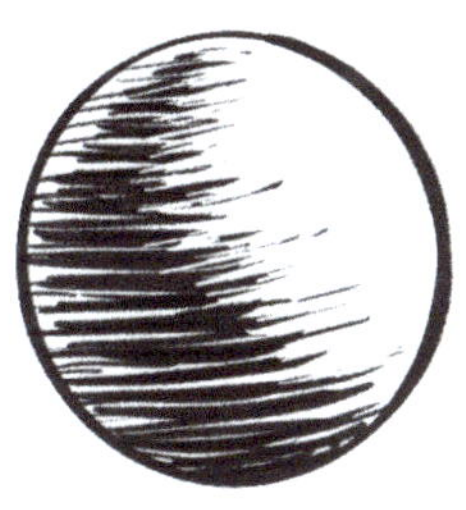

CROSSHATCHING –ANGLE YOUR LINES FOR STYLISH RESULTS

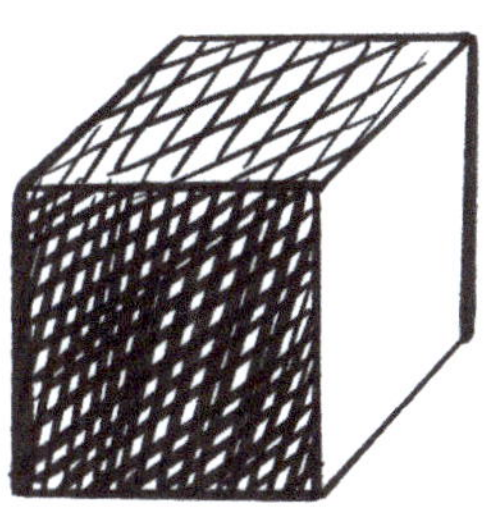
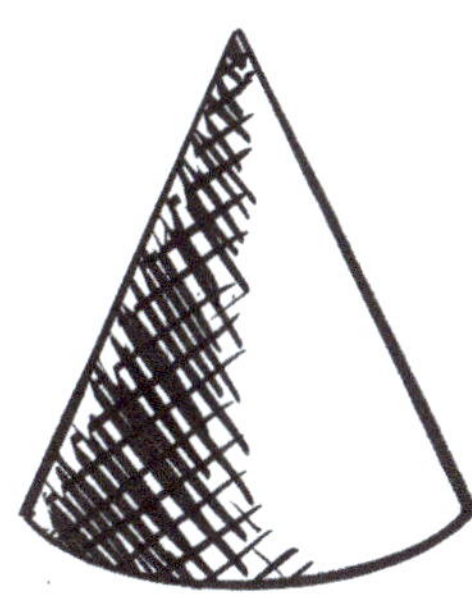
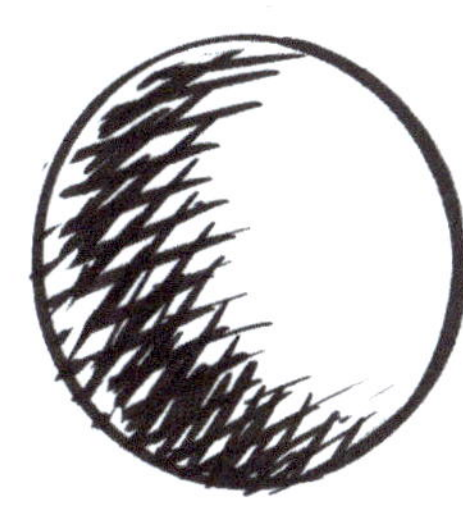

BLENDING –BEST ACHIEVED WITH THE SIDE OF YOUR PENCIL

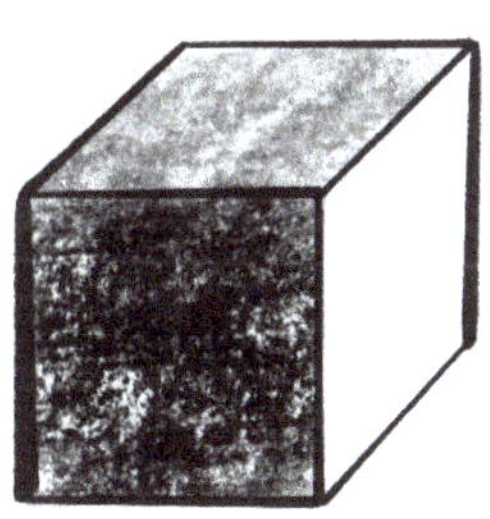
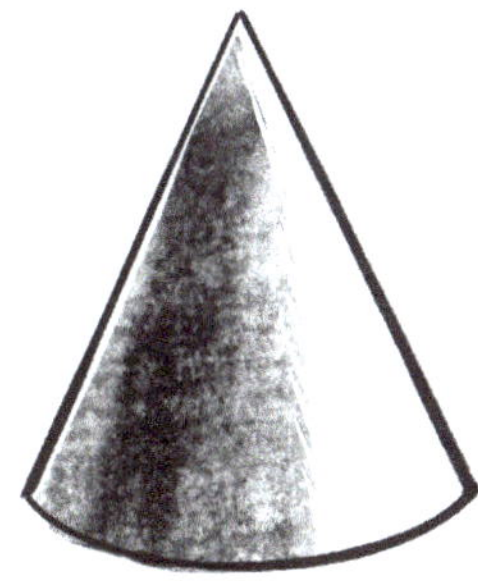
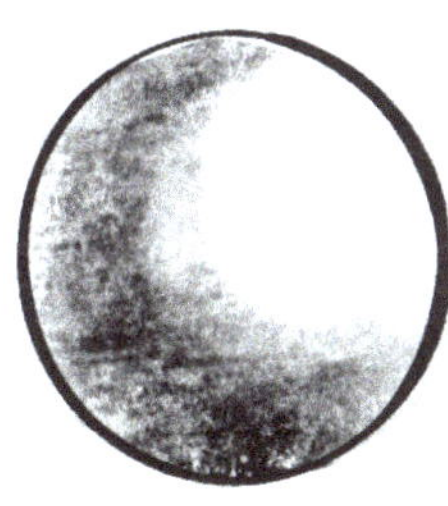

STIPPLING –ARGUABLY THE MOST BEAUTIFUL BUT ALSO REQUIRES THE MOST PATIENCE

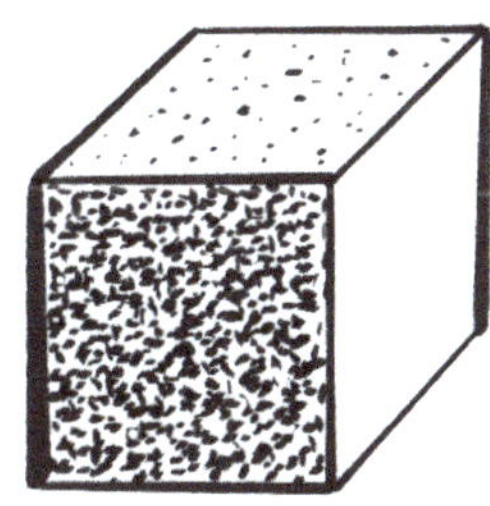
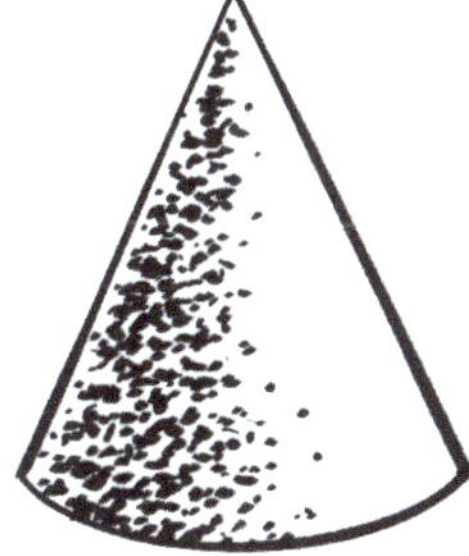
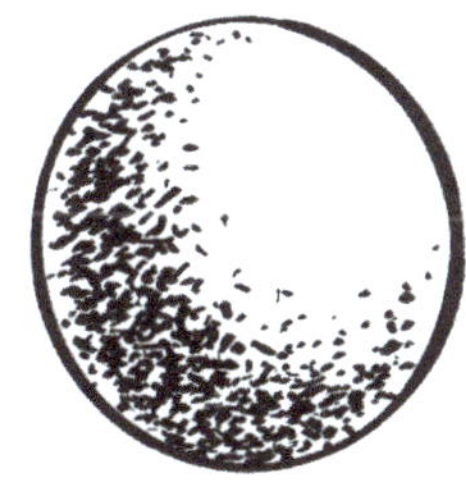

Styles & Lines

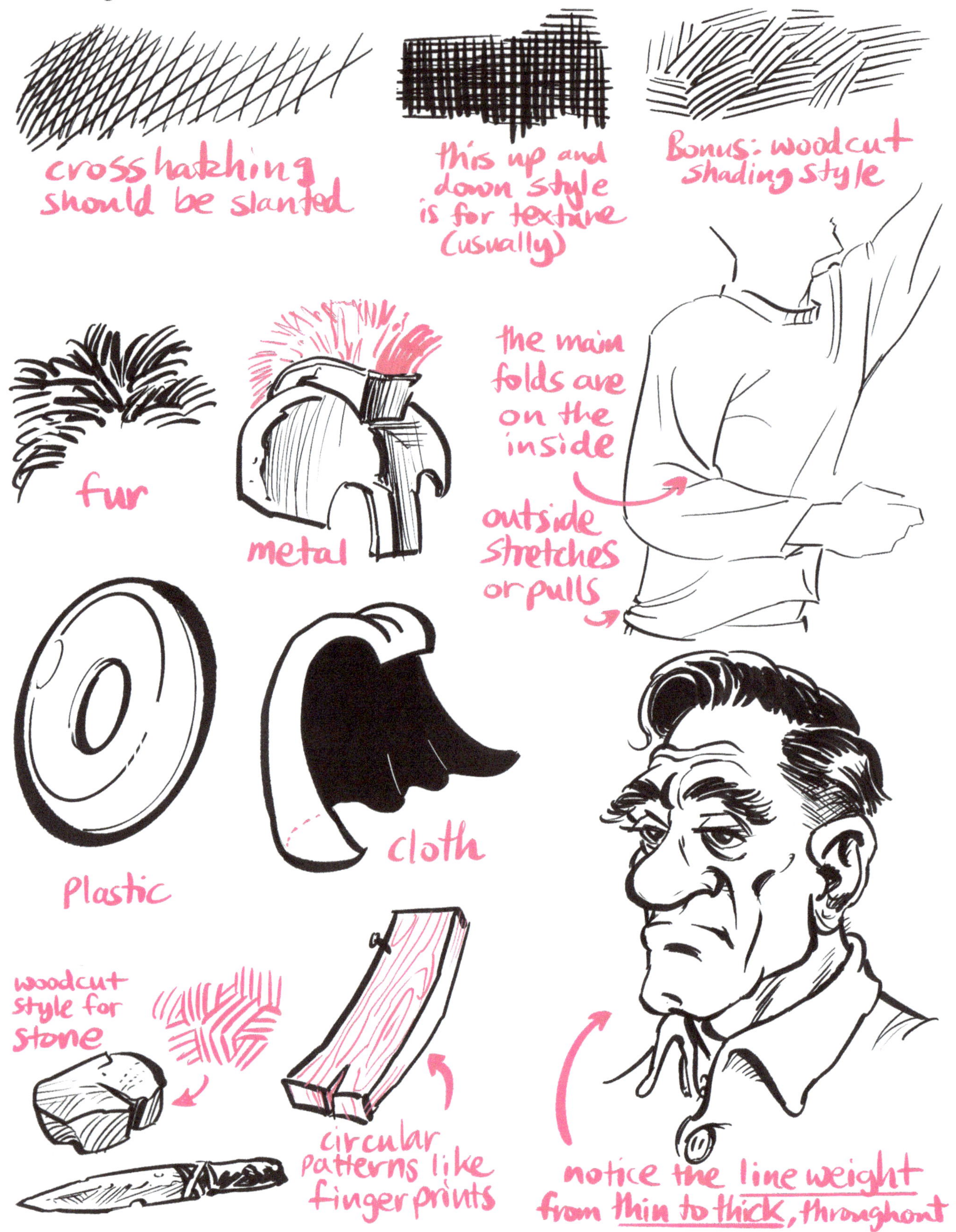

Light & Shadows

IT'S MOST SIMPLE TO THINK OF LIGHT AS COMING FROM ONE SINGLE SOURCE, LIKE THE SUN. WITH ARTIFICIAL LIGHT, THERE CAN BE MULTIPLE SOURCES WITH MULTIPLE COLOURS. THE POSITION OF THE LIGHT SOURCES AFFECT THE ANGLES OF THE SHADOWS ON A CHARACTER'S FACE OR BODY OR A ROOM OR BUILDING. NATURAL LIGHT CAN BE DRAWN WITH SOFTER SHADING WHILE ARTIFICIAL LIGHT CAN HAVE MORE CONTRAST AND DRAWN WITH BOLDER SHADOWS. DRAWING A CHARACTER ALL IN SHADOW, LIKE A SILHOUETTE, CAN HAVE A STRONG EFFECT AND CAN OPEN UP THE READER'S IMAGINATION.

IN EVENLY-LIGHT SITUATIONS, A CHARACTER'S OR BACKGROUND'S FEATURES CAN APPEAR CLEARER. ALTERNATELY, WHERE YOU POSITION AN ARTIFICIAL LIGHT SOURCE CAN AFFECT THE MOOD OF THE SCENE. LIKE A LOW LIGHT SOURCE CAN GIVE A SPOOKY EFFECT ON THE FACE AND TALL SHADOWS, SUCH-AS A CAMPFIRE GHOST STORY. IF THE LIGHT SOURCE IS ABOVE, THE CHARACTER MAY APPEAR OVERPOWERED. SIDE LIGHTING CAN BE A GOOD INDICATOR OF THE LOCATION OR USED AS A DIRECTIONAL DEVICE FOR PROGRESSING THE STORY IF THE CHARACTER THEN HAS TO TURN TOWARD THE LIGHT IN A PANELED-SEQUENCE.

IT'S ADVISED TO HAVE A THREE DIMENSIONAL MODEL AND A LIGHT BULB TO LIGHT IT AND THEN APPLY THE LIGHTING YOU OBSERVE TO YOUR IMAGINARY CHARACTER OR SCENE.

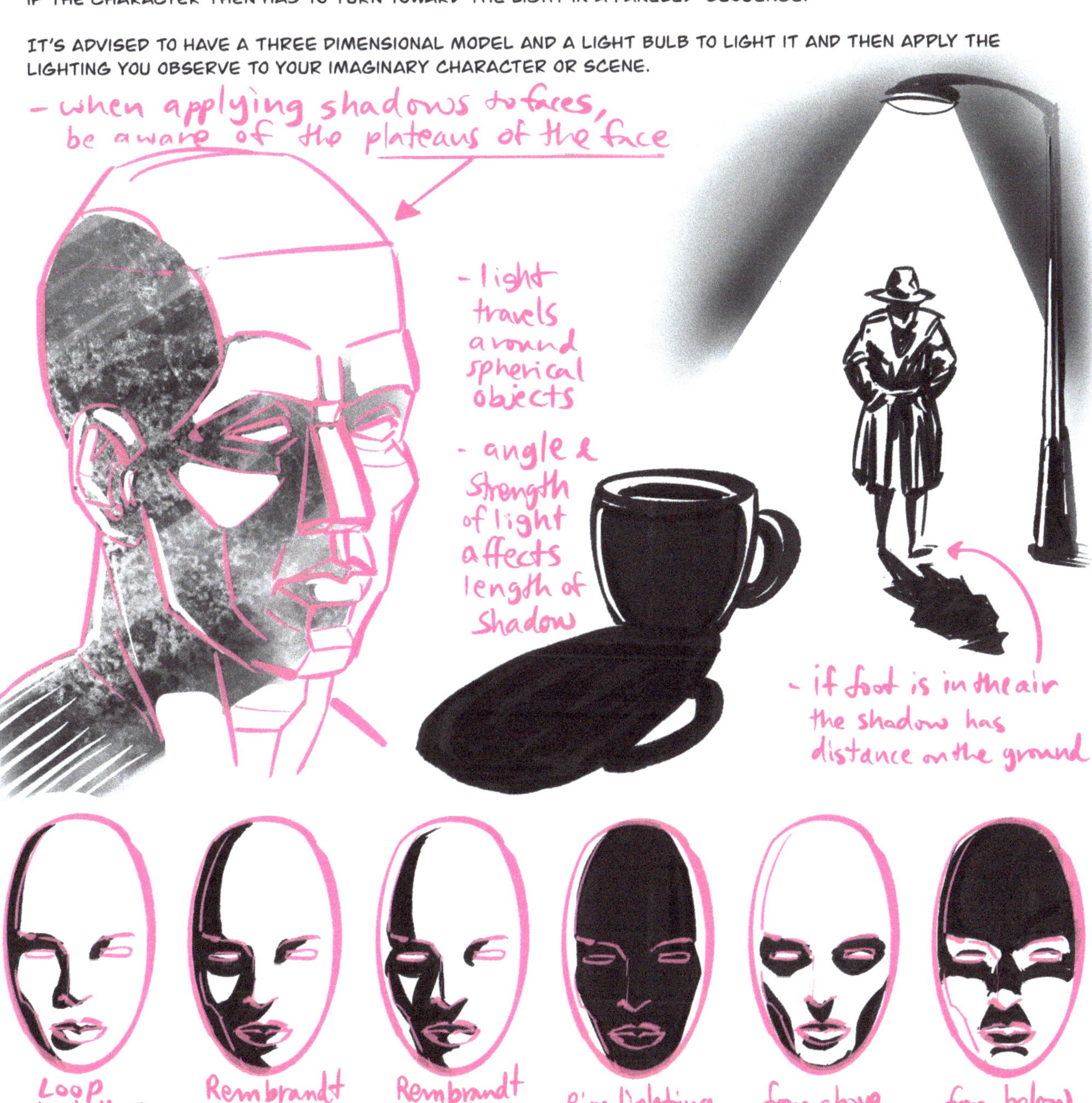

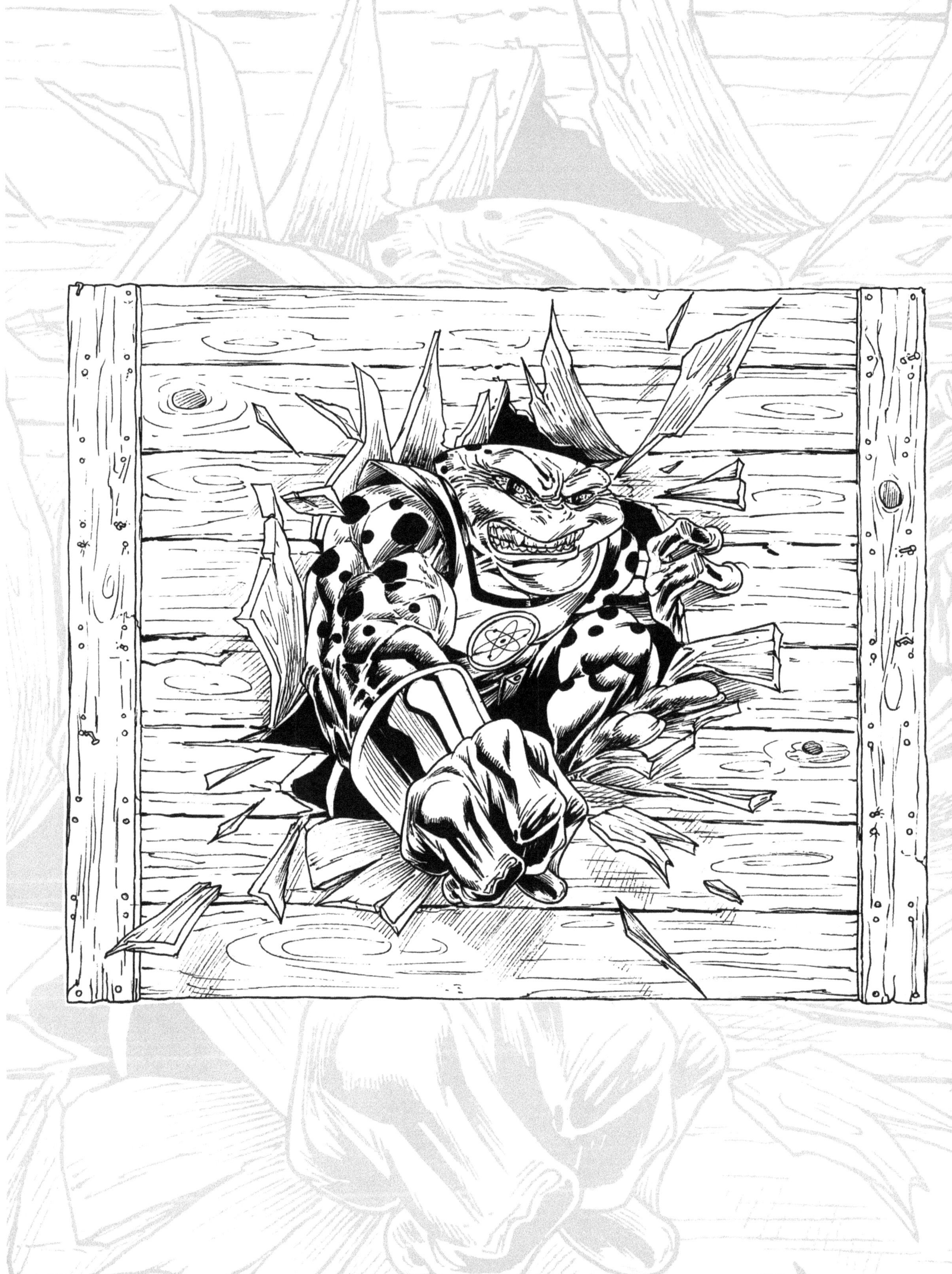

Perspective

WHEN DESIGNING CHARACTERS, YOU GET THE IMPRESSION THAT THERE'S STILL ROOM FOR SUBJECTIVITY IN THEIR INTERPRETATION. WITH BACKGROUNDS, LESS SO.

BUILDINGS, ROADS, AND OBJECTS ALL HAVE TO LOOK LIKE THEY ARE SET EVENLY ON THE GROUND AND PART OF THE REAL WORLD. THE BEST WAY TO REPRESENT OUR SURROUNDINGS REALISTICALLY IS THROUGH THE THREE DIFFERENT TYPES OF PERSPECTIVE.

THIS IS THE PART WHERE YOU BRING OUT YOUR RULER. BUT DON'T BE DISCOURAGED. PERSPECTIVE IS VERY FUN BECAUSE YOU GET TO CREATE ENVIRONMENTS FOR YOUR IMAGINED CHARACTERS.

IT'S POSSIBLE FOR PERSPECTIVE TO GET COMPLEX WHEN YOU'RE TRYING TO INVENT SOME ARCHITECTURAL WONDER FROM SCRATCH AND TRYING TO DRAW IT FROM SOME ODD ANGLE. HOWEVER, EVEN THOUGH WHAT WE'RE REVIEWING IN THESE LESSONS ARE THE THEORETICAL BASICS OF PERSPECTIVE, IT'S NOTABLE THAT YOU CAN TAKE THESE FUNDAMENTAL TECHNIQUES EXTREMELY FAR WITH YOUR IMAGINATION.

PERSPECTIVE IS THE FOUNDATION OF THE STORIES THAT YOU TELL WITHIN EACH PICTURE OF YOUR PANELED COMICS.

One Point Perspective

THIS IS THE PART WHERE YOU MIGHT NEED TO USE A RULER. PERSPECTIVE IS A SERIES OF ANGLES THAT MAKE OBJECTS IN NATURE LOOK REALISTIC. PERSPECTIVE IS APPLIED TO SCENERY AND EXTERIOR AND INTERIOR OF BUILDINGS BUT PERSPECTIVE IS ACTUALLY USED IN CHARACTER DRAWINGS TOO. WHEN YOU TILT A CHARACTER'S HEAD, YOU'RE USING PERSPECTIVE.

THERE ARE THREE MAIN TYPES OF PERSPECTIVE, ONE POINT, TWO POINT, AND THREE POINT. PERSPECTIVE LINES ARE DRAWN LIGHTLY. THEY ARE A GUIDE THAT WE BUILD OUR CLEAN-LINED ENVIRONMENT ONTO. IN EACH TYPE OF PERSPECTIVE, ONE CONSTANT IS THE HORIZON LINE. WHAT CHANGES IS THE NUMBER OF VANISHING POINTS, RESPECTIVELY.

THE HORIZON LINE IS AN INDICATOR THAT SEPARATES THE GROUND FROM THE SKY. THE VIEWER'S EYE LEVEL CAN BE ABOVE OR BELOW THE HORIZON LINE. OBJECTS THAT ARE ABOVE THE HORIZON LINE TOWER ABOVE US, WHILE OBJECTS THAT ARE BELOW THE HORIZON LINE WE LOOK DOWN UPON (OBJECTIVELY NOT FIGURATIVELY).

AS OBJECTS FADE FROM OUR VIEW INTO THE DISTANCE, THEY APPEAR SMALLER TO OUR EYES. THE VANISHING POINT IS OUR FOCAL POINT. IT'S THE POINT THAT ALL OBJECTS DISAPPEAR INTO. THE VANISHING POINT CAN BE A LONG STREET WE'RE FOLLOWING OR A GUIDE FOR US TO UNDERSTAND THE ANGLES OF OUR FURNITURE WITHIN OUR SPACE. THE LINES ABOVE THE HORIZON LINE ARE ANGLED UPWARD AND THE LINES BELOW THE HORIZON LINE ARE ANGLED DOWNWARD. ALL OTHER LINES OF OBJECTS ARE DRAWN EITHER PARALLEL WITH THE HORIZON LINE OR STRAIGHT UP AND DOWN AT A 90 DEGREE ANGLE.

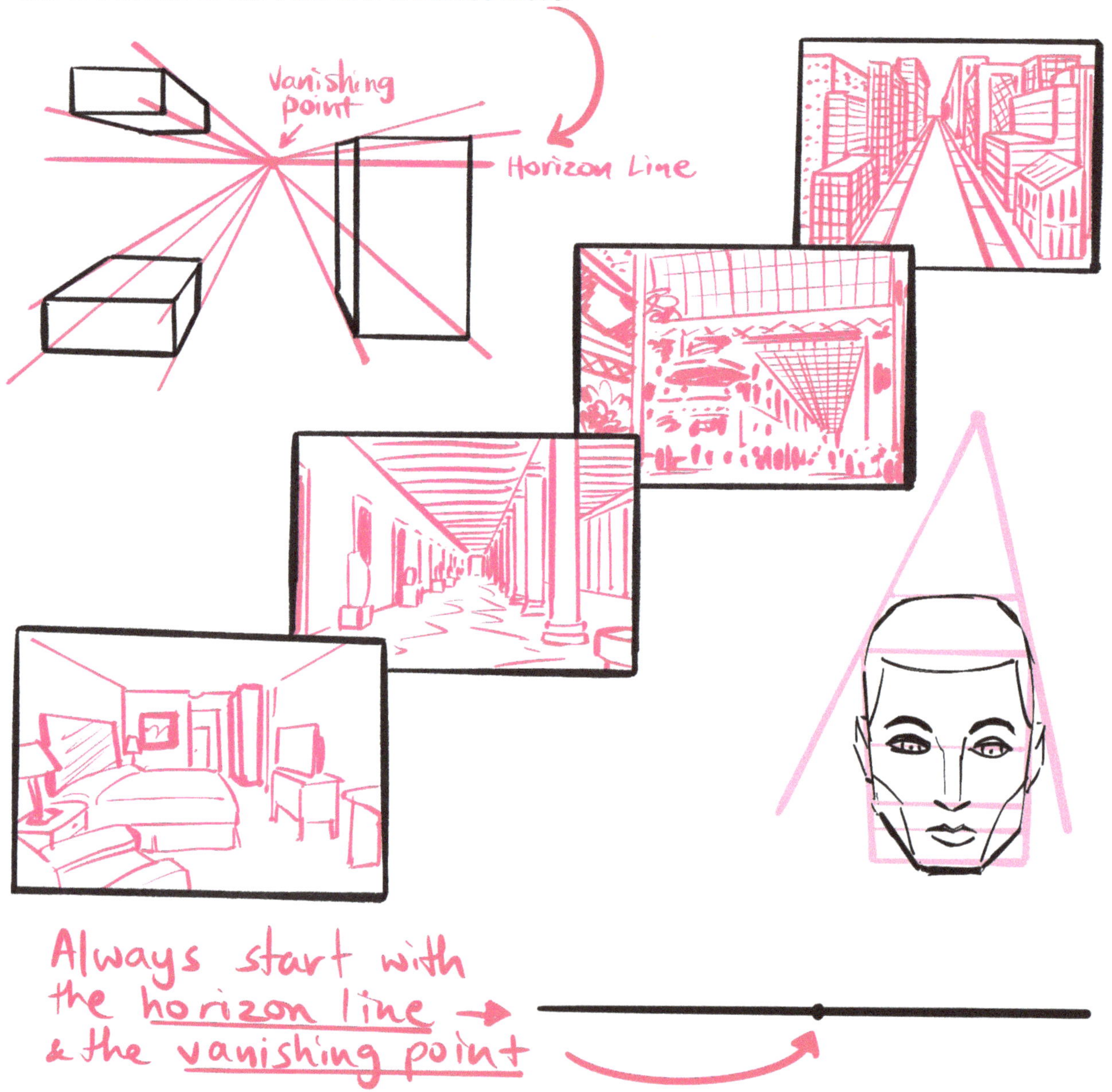

One Point Examples

SEE IF YOU CAN FIND THE HORIZON LINE AND THE VANISHING POINT IN THE EXAMPLES BELOW. THEN TRY CREATING YOUR OWN SCENES. REMEMBER THAT PEOPLE ARE DRAWN IN PERSPECTIVE TOO!

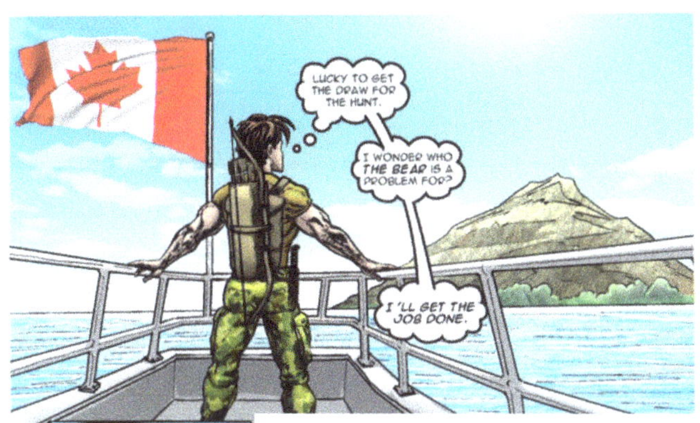

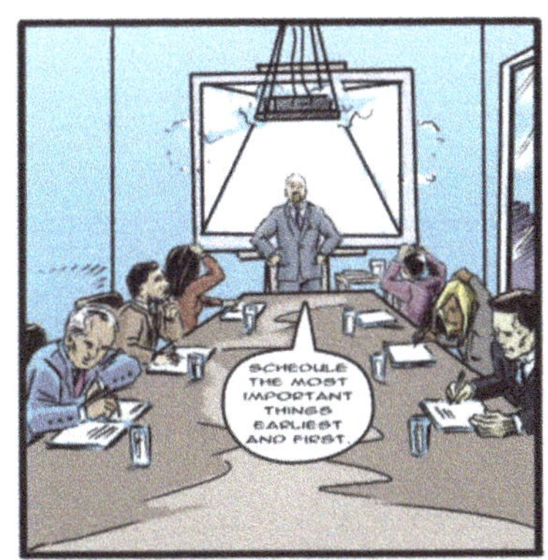

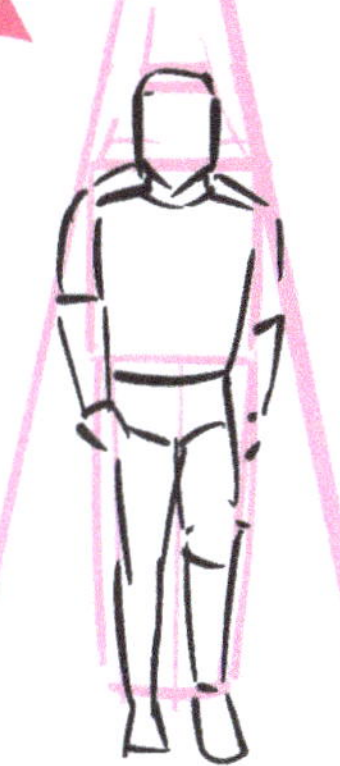

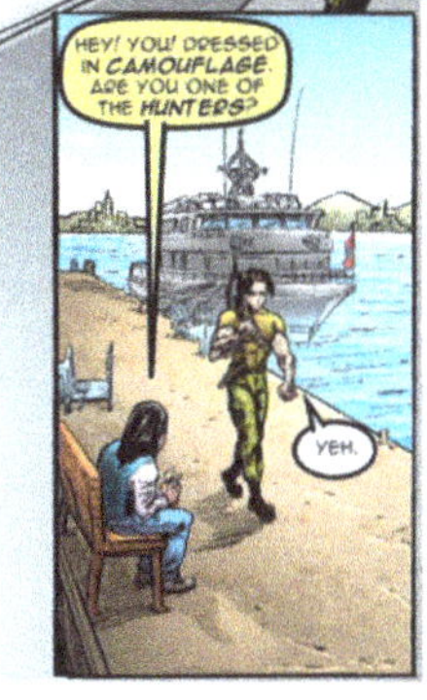

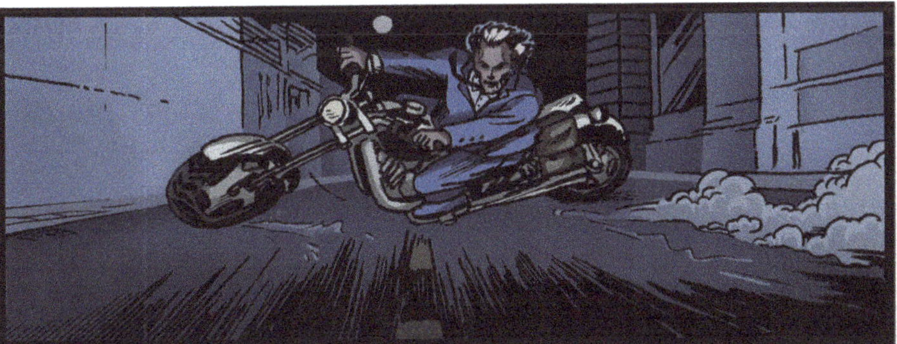

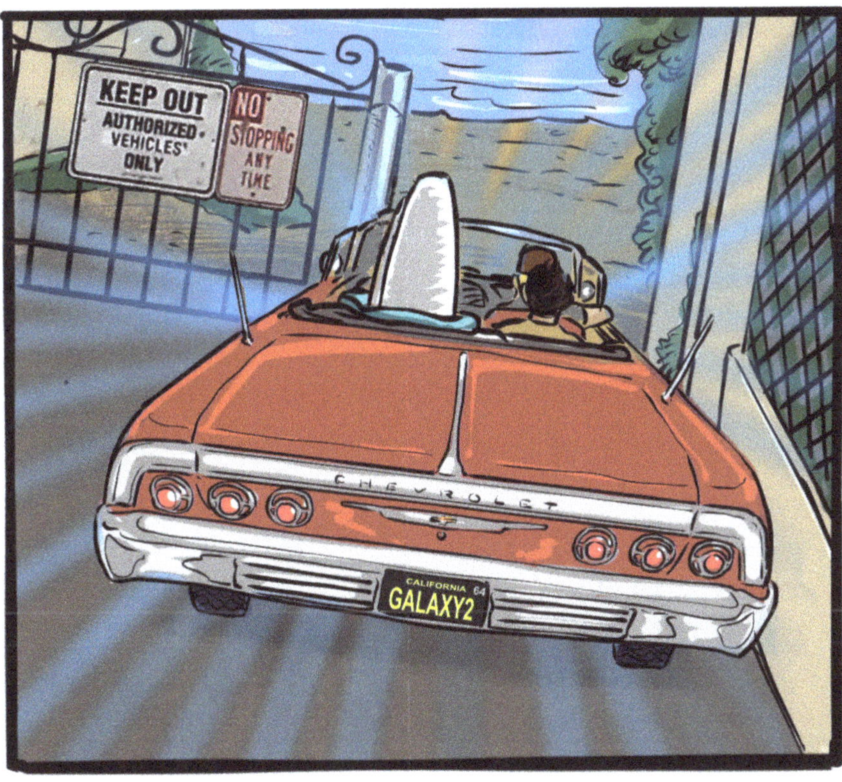

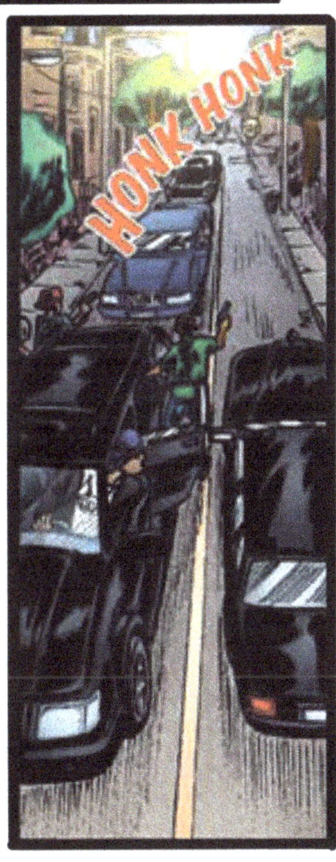

Two Point Perspective

IMAGINE YOU'RE AT AN INTERSECTION AND YOU CAN SEE DOWN BOTH ROADS. THAT'S WHEN YOU NEED TO USE THE TWO POINT PERSPECTIVE WITH TWO VANISHING POINTS. ALSO, TWO POINT PERSPECTIVE CAN BE BE USED TO DRAW OBJECTS LIKE BOXES, CHAIRS, CARS, OR EVEN THREE-DIMENSIONAL LETTERING.

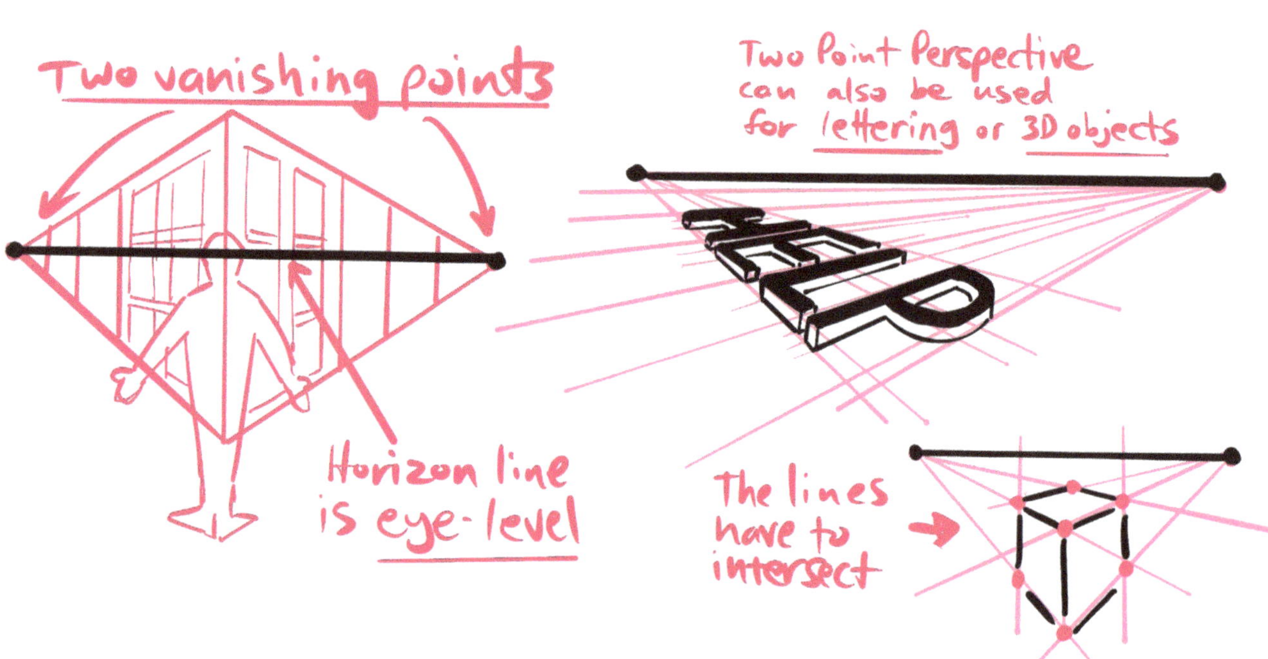

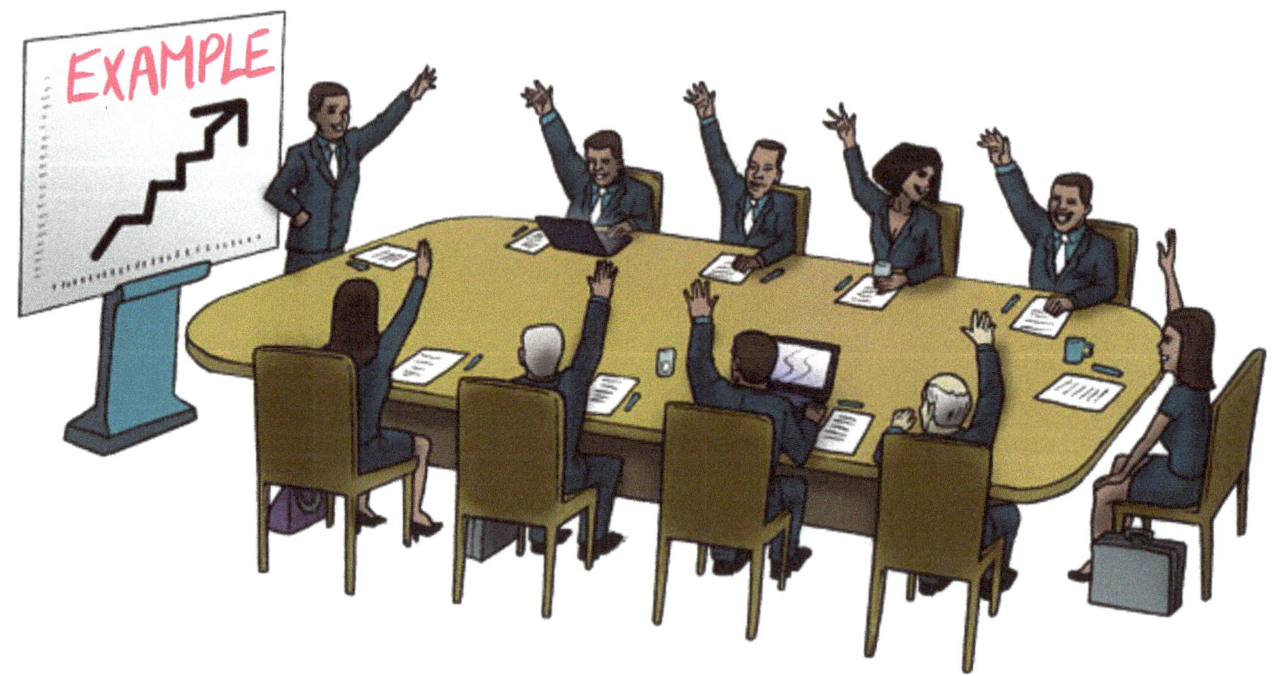

Three Point Perspective

IN ONE POINT PERSPECTIVE, THE LINES OF YOUR OBJECT HAD TO BE PARALLEL TO YOUR HORIZON LINE OR AT A 90 DEGREE VERTICAL ANGLE. WITH TWO POINT PERSPECTIVE, ONLY THE VERTICAL LINES HAD TO BE AT A 90 DEGREE ANGLE, THE REST OF THE LINES COULD BE HOWEVER, AS LONG AS THEY INTERSECTED. THAT RESTRICTED OUR VIEW. ESSENTIALLY, WE WERE ALWAYS VIEWING OBJECTS FROM A STAGNANT AND STANDING POSITION. NOW, WITH THREE POINT PERSPECTIVE, BY ADDING A THIRD POINT, WE CAN HAVE A MORE DYNAMIC VIEW OF OBJECTS. IF THE OBJECT IS BELOW US, IT'S AS IF WE HAVE AN AERIAL VIEW (WE'RE FLOATING OR IN A PLANE ABOVE BUILDINGS). IF THE OBJECT IS ABOVE US, IT'S AS IF IT'S LEVITATING (LIKE A U.F.O. OR AN AIRBORNE OBJECT). THE OBJECT ITSELF DETERMINES OUR PERSPECTIVE, MORE THAN THE GROUND IT SITS ON.

WHEN DRAWING IN THREE POINT PERSPECTIVE, IT'S RECOMMENDED THAT THE THREE VANISHING POINTS ARE PLACED OUTSIDE THE ILLUSTRATED PANEL. THE FARTHER APART THE TWO VANISHING POINTS WHICH ARE ON THE HORIZON LINE ARE, THE CLOSER FOREGROUND OBJECTS CAN APPEAR. OTHERWISE THEY MIGHT SEEM NARROW AND SMALL IN THE CENTER OF YOUR DRAWING WITH EMPTY SPACE AROUND. WITH THREE POINT PERSPECTIVE, SOMETIMES THE EDGE OF YOUR ILLUSTRATED PANEL CAN SHOW THE OBJECTS SKEWED. (SEE CITYSCAPE PANEL BELOW.) HOWEVER SKEWED BUILDINGS MAY APPEAR, EVERYTHING IS CORRECT IF YOU FOLLOW YOUR PERSPECTIVE GRID. BELIEVE IN THE RULES OF PERSPECTIVE AND FOLLOW THE TECHNIQUES. UPON THOSE GRIDS AND STRUCTURES, YOU CAN BE CREATIVE WITH DECOR AND SHADING.

Examples:

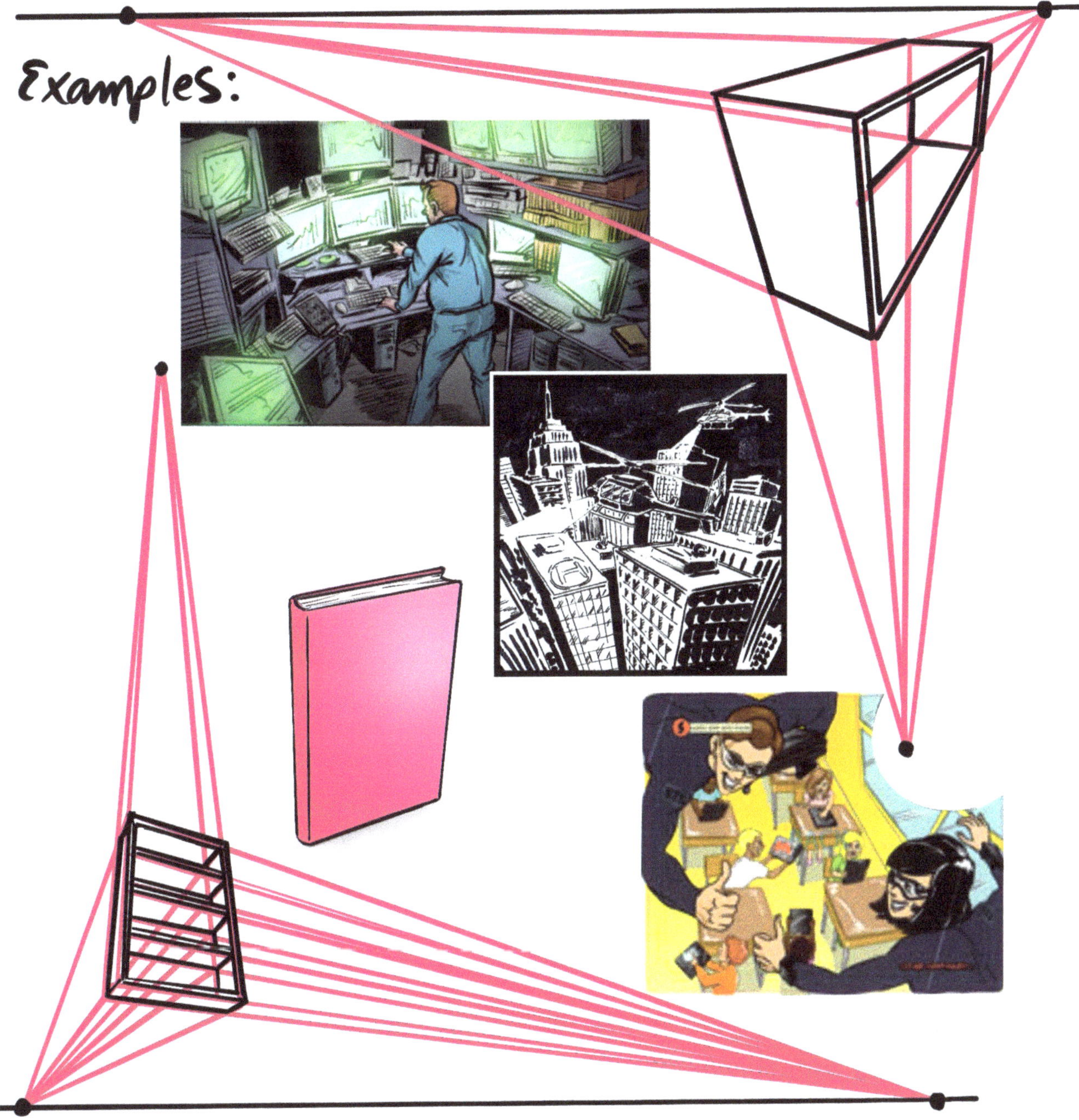

Further Perspectives

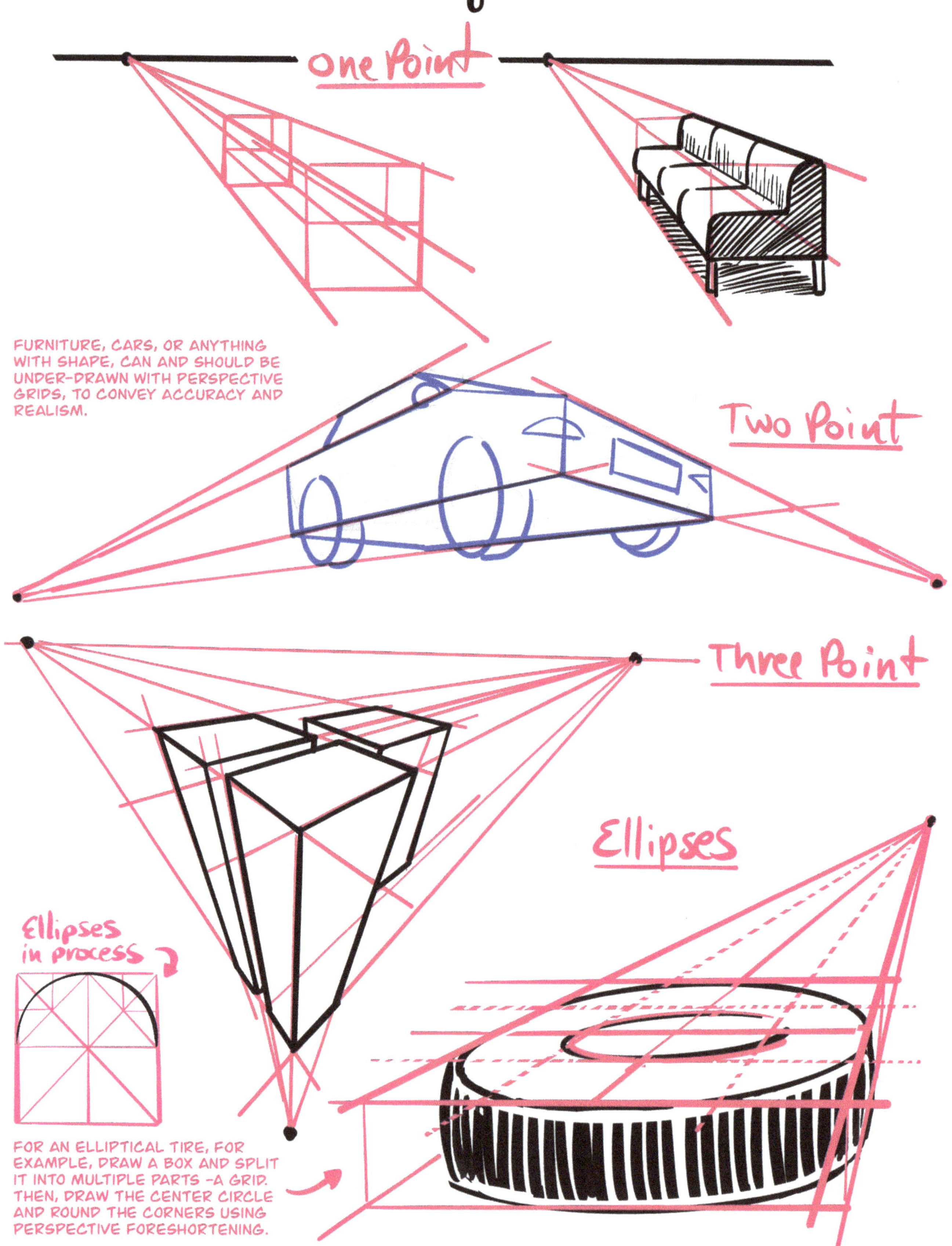

Four & Five Points

PERSPECTIVE CAN KEEP GETTING MORE COMPLEX, WITH FOUR AND FIVE POINT PERSPECTIVES. IN FOUR POINT PERSPECTIVE, THE VERTICAL LINES BETWEEN THE NORTH AND SOUTH POINTS ARE CURVED. HOWEVER, THE POINTS FROM THE EAST AND WEST POINTS EXTEND IN STRAIGHT LINES.

4 Point Perspective:

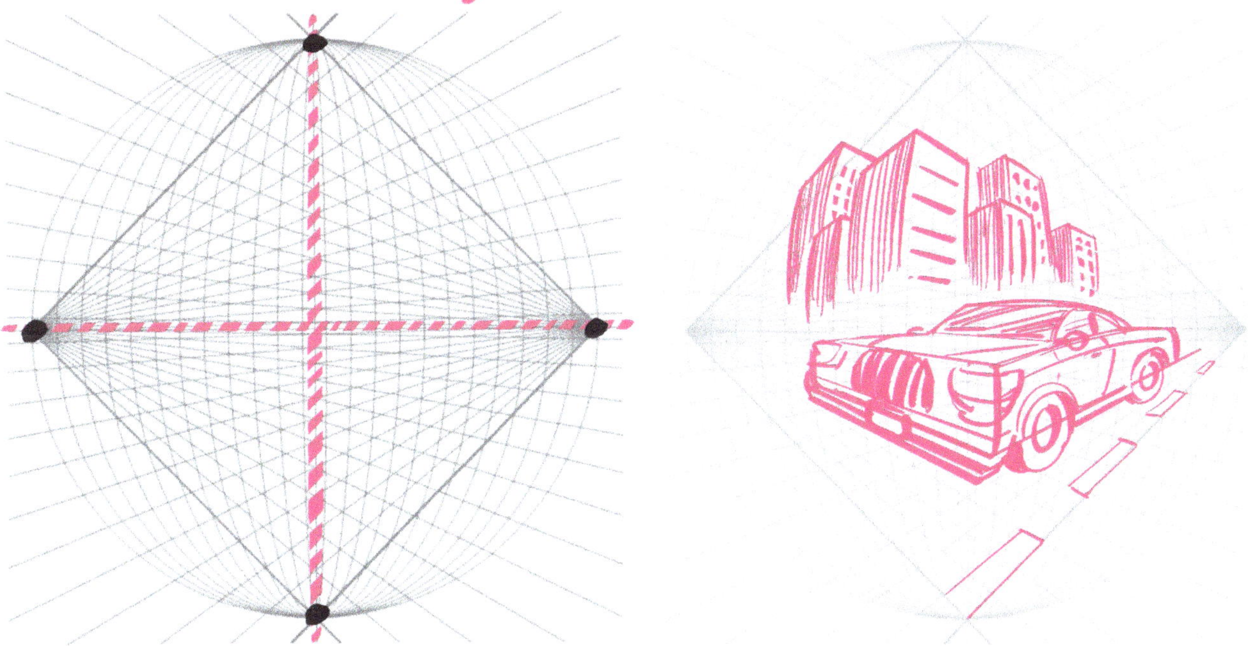

WITH FIVE POINT PERSPECTIVE, THE LINES FROM ALL THE HEMISPHERES ARE CURVED, BUT THE FIFTH POINT FROM THE CENTER (WHERE THE HORIZON LINES CONVERGE) COMES STRAIGHT OUT TOWARD THE VIEWER, CREATING A FISHEYE OR PEEPHOLE EFFECT.

5 Point Perspective / Fisheye Effect:

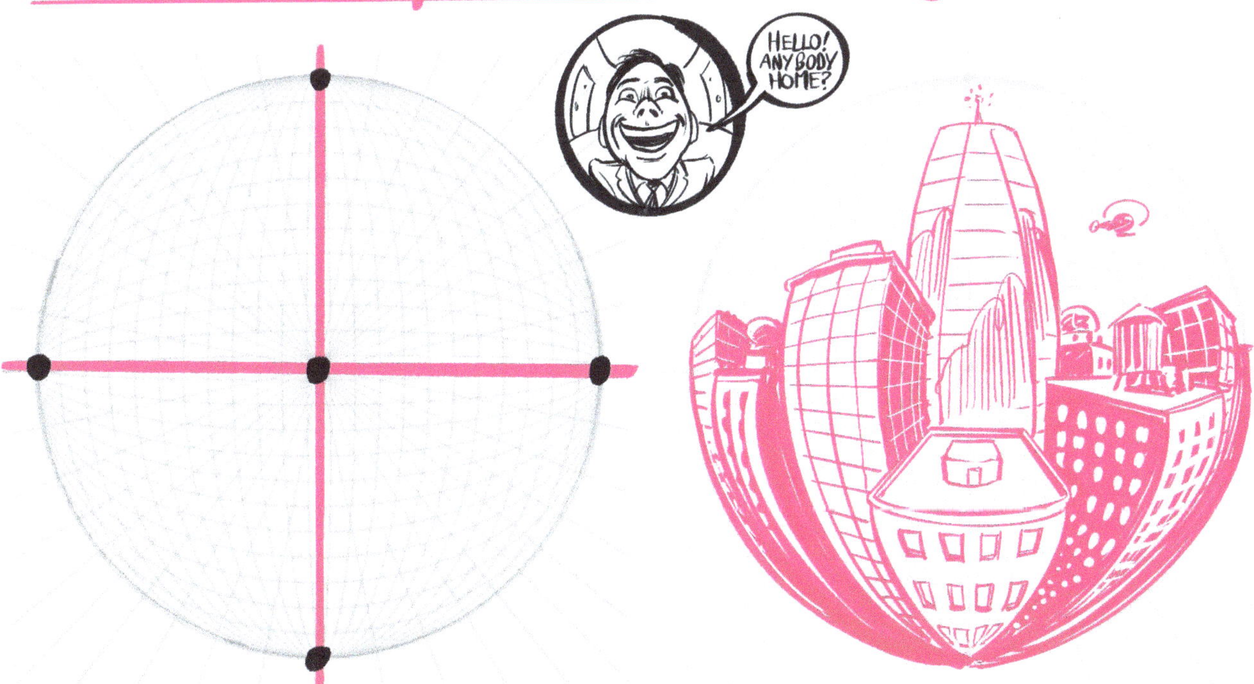

Characters in Perspective

Perspective Tips

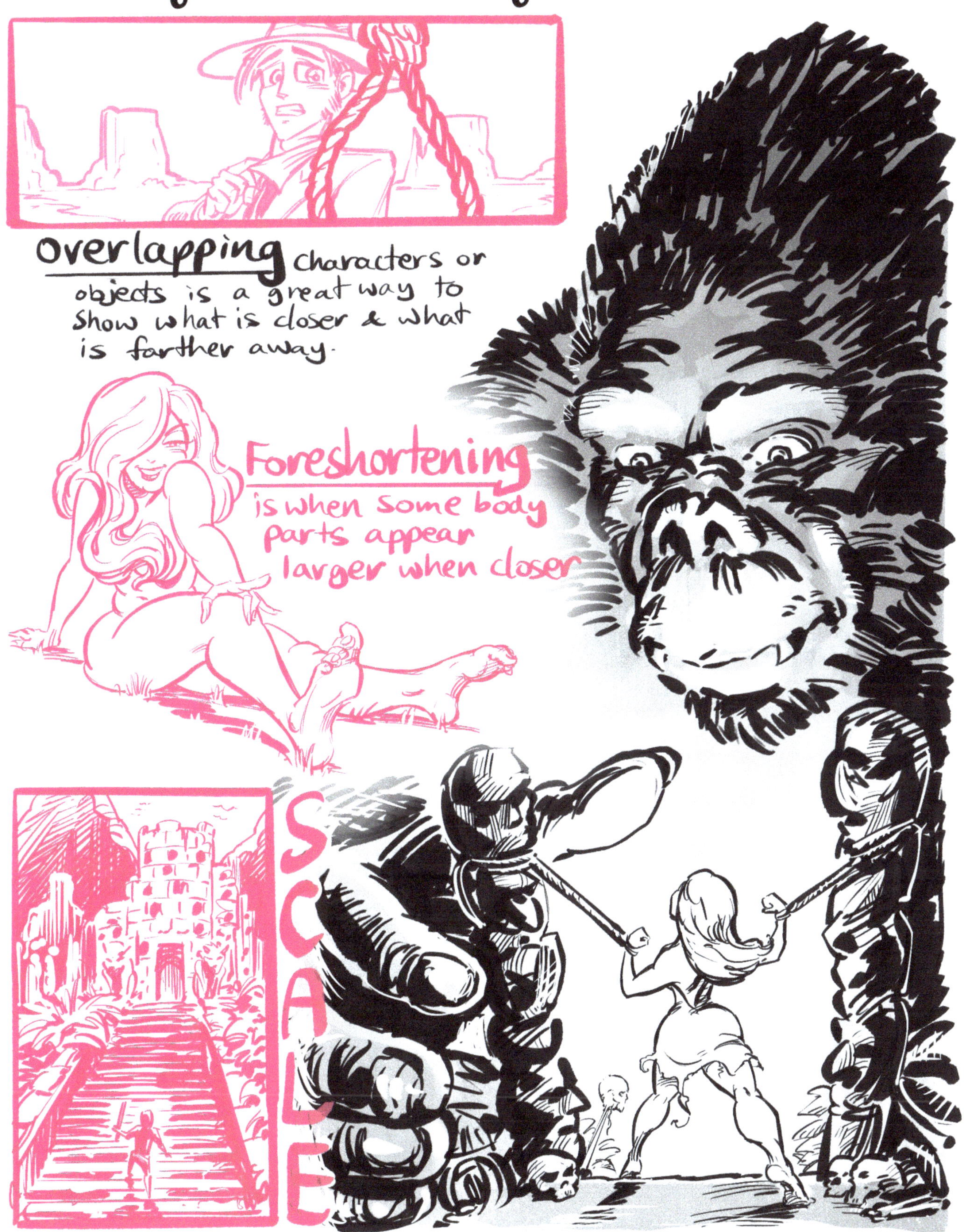

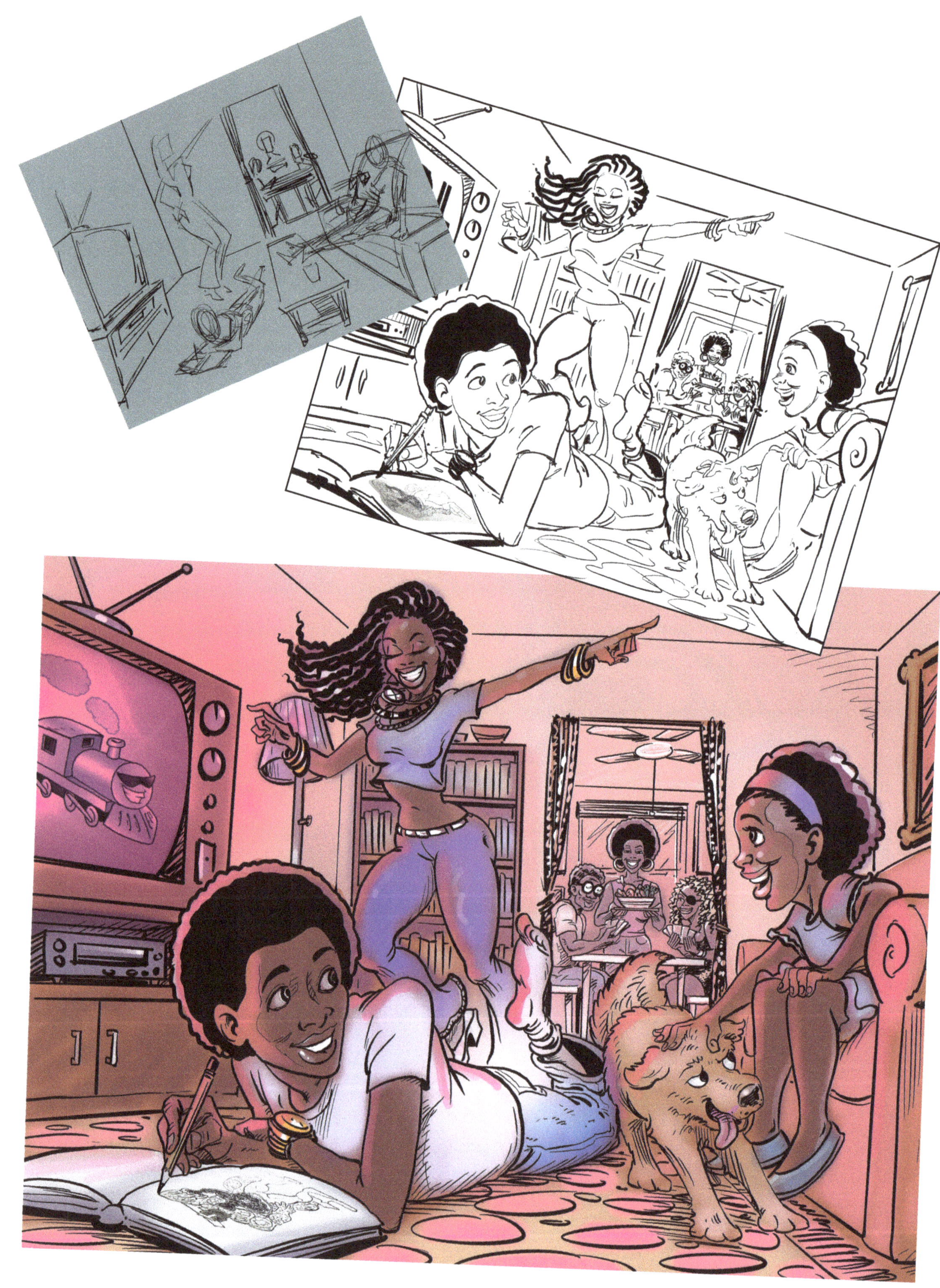

Comics/Manga Storytelling

WHEN I WAS A YOUNG BOY, I'D SIT IN FROM OF THE TELEVISION WITH ONE FOOT ON THE COFFEE-TABLE AND MY LINED NOTEBOOK IN MY LAP. SATURDAY MORNINGS, COLOURFUL ANIMATED SHOWS WOULD FLASH ON THE SCREEN. ON WEEKDAY EVENINGS, TELEVISED WRESTLING. I'D SKETCH ALL THE WHILE.

FOR ANY CHARACTER I'D SEE, WHETHER ANIMATED OR IN THE MUSCULAR FLESH, I'D INVENT MY OWN VERSION OF THEM. DOZENS OF NOTEBOOKS WERE FILLED WITH MY CHARACTERS, IN DIFFERENT OUTFITS AND EPOCHS. THE FLINT OF MY IMAGINATION SPARKED WITH POSSIBILITIES.

IT WAS ONLY A MATTER OF TIME UNTIL THOSE CHARACTERS HAD TO BE PUT INTO SEQUENCE. THAT'S WHERE COMICS CAME IN. IT'S A NATURAL EVOLUTION TO GO FROM CHARACTER DESIGN TO COMICS. MANY MORE DOZENS OF SKETCHBOOKS STACKED IN MY ROOM.

ONE YEAR AWAY FROM FINISHING HIGH SCHOOL, I REMEMBER THINKING OF MY GOALS. ALL I DREAMED OF DOING WAS MAKING COMICS. THEN, I NEVER DREAMED MUCH MORE.

AS A PROFESSIONAL FREELANCE ARTIST FOR TWENTY YEARS, DRAWING NORTH AMERICAN MANGA WAS MY FAVOURITE TYPE OF JOB. A COUPLE OF THOUSAND PAGES LATER, I'VE DEVELOPED A HANDFUL OF QUICK AND TRUE TECHNIQUES THAT CAN HELP YOU MAKE THE BEST SEQUENTIAL ART.

STARTING WITH SINGLE-PANEL CARTOONS, WE'LL GO INTO THE PRINCIPLES OF STORY-TELLING AND COVER EVERYTHING FROM COMPOSITION, PAGE LAYOUT, AND COVERS. LETTERING AND SPECIAL EFFECTS AND A BUNCH OF OTHER FUN STUFF TOO!

One Panel Cartoon

TAKE OUR CHARACTERS AND CREATE A ONE PANEL CARTOON THAT DEPICTS THAT CHARACTER, AND OTHERS, IN A SCENARIO THAT IS CUTE, FUNNY, AND IS EASY TO UNDERSTAND. DRAW SIMPLE BACKGROUNDS FOR NOW. FOCUS ON RELAYING YOUR IDEA. DON'T WORRY ABOUT WORD BUBBLES EITHER. YOU CAN INCORPORATE THE TEXT WITHIN THE IMAGE OR OUTSIDE. EVEN BETTER, MAKE IT SILENT. YOUR CONCEPT SHOULD BE COMPREHENSIVE WITHOUT ANY WORDS WHATSOEVER. BE CREATIVE AND HAVE FUN WITH IT!

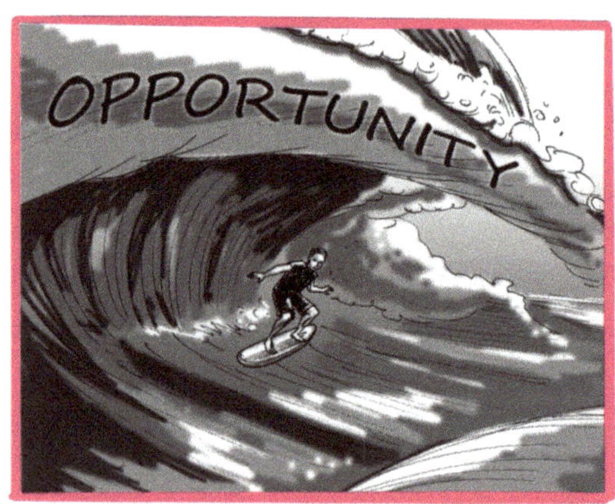

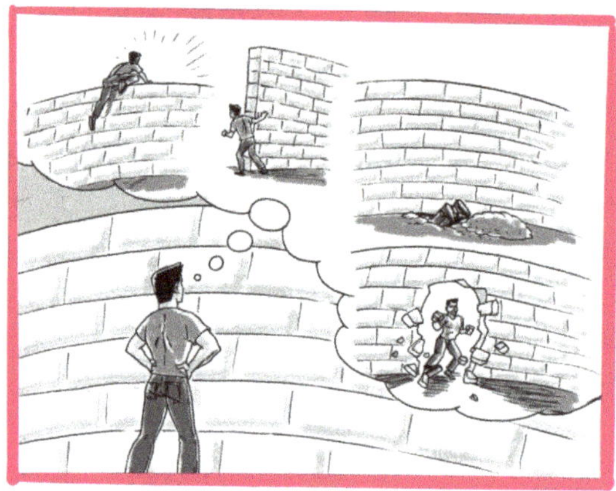

Where there's a will, there's a way.

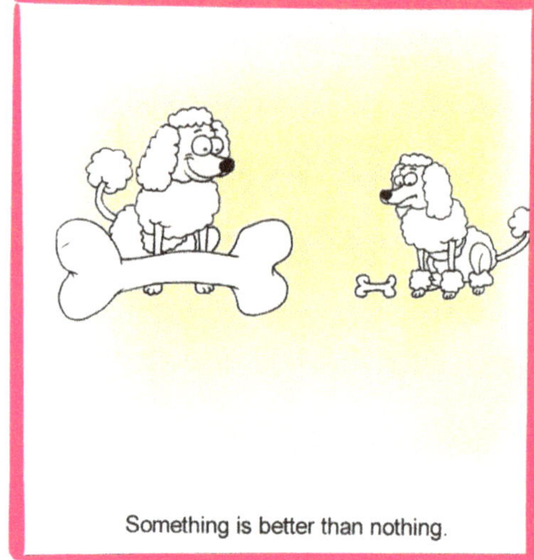

Something is better than nothing.

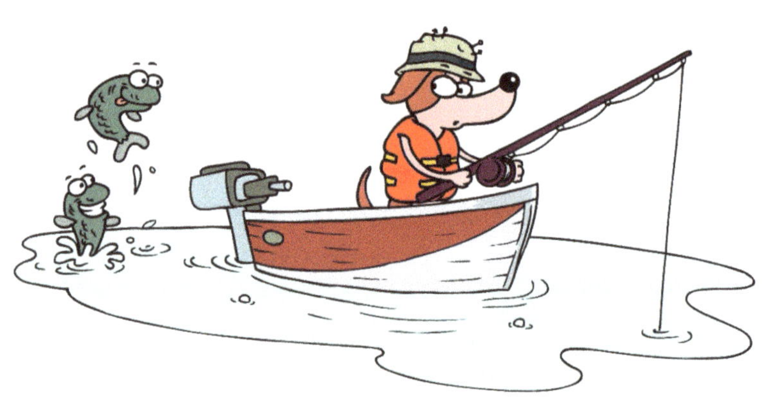

BEFORE STARTING:

-NOTE YOUR IDEA

-WRITE YOUR SPEECH OR DESCRIPTION

-SKETCH YOUR CHARACTER(S) AND BACKGROUND

-DRAW YOUR CARTOON IN PENCIL ON A FULL PAGE

-INK YOUR CARTOON NEATLY WITH PEN

DRAW A ONE PANEL CARTOON!

WITH ONE PICTURE:

-TELL A STORY
-EXPRESS AN IDEA
-MAKE PEOPLE UNDERSTAND
-MAKE IT HUMOROUS

ONCE YOU'VE DRAWN 5-6 SINGLE PANEL CARTOONS, TRY A TWO PANEL CARTOON. A TWO PANEL CARTOON IS BASICALLY A SETUP AND A PUNCHLINE. IN THE FIRST PANEL SETUP THE PREMISE AND THEN THE JOKE. ACTION AND REACTION!

Three Panel Storytelling

EVERY STORY HAS THREE PARTS: AN INCITING INCIDENT, THE REACTION, AND THE RESOLUTION. IN THE BEGINNING, THE PLACE, THE CHARACTERS, AND THE PLOT POINTS HAVE TO BE ILLUSTRATED. EVERYTHING IN THE BULK OF THE STORY ARC BUILDS TOWARD A MAIN CONFLICT OR A CLIMAX. AND IN THE CONCLUSION, ALL CONFLICTS ARE RESOLVED AND THE STORY WRAPS UP NEATLY (OR SOMETIMES IS LEFT WITH A CLIFFHANGER).

EVEN A TWO PANEL CARTOON SHOULD HAVE A SETUP AND A PUNCHLINE.

INTRODUCTION

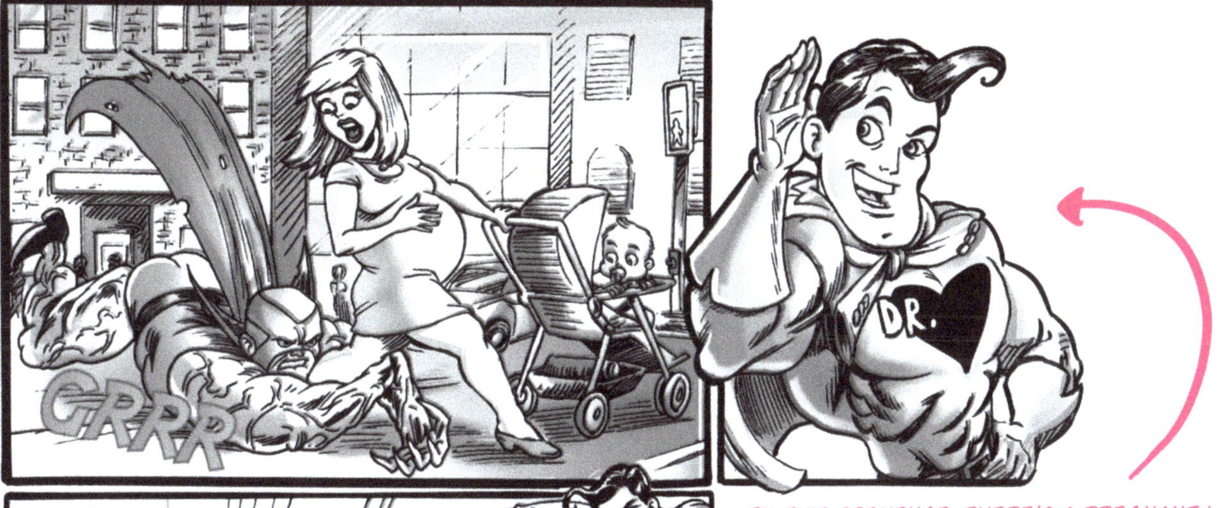

IN THIS SEQUENCE, THERE'S A PREGNANT LADY BEING ATTACKED BY A VILLAIN. BY THE END OF THE INTRODUCTION, OUR HERO HEARS THE CALL TO ACTION. THEN, IN THE CLIMAX, OUR HERO DEFEATS THE VILLAIN AND RESCUES THE MOTHER AND CHILD. IN THE END, EVERYONE IS SAFE AND HAPPY!

CLIMAX

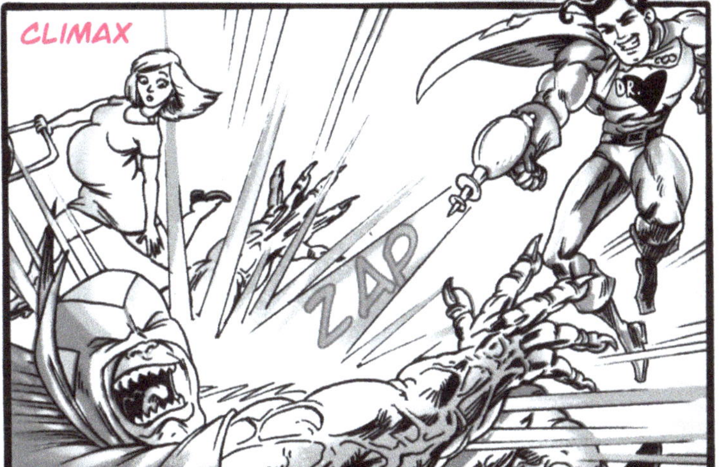

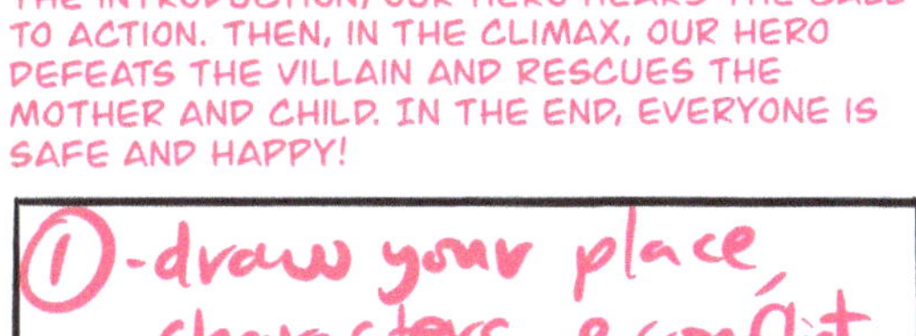

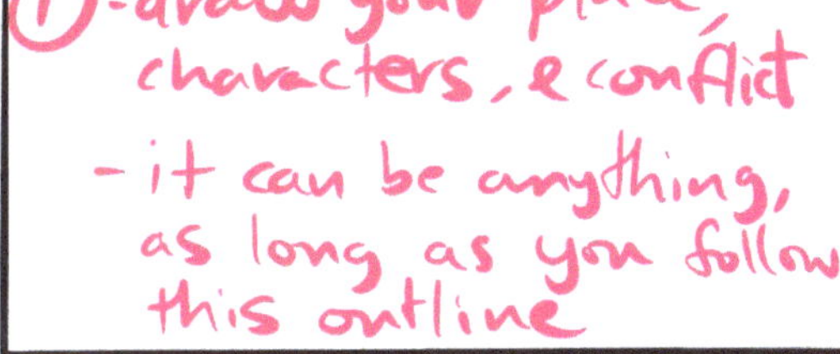

CONCLUSION

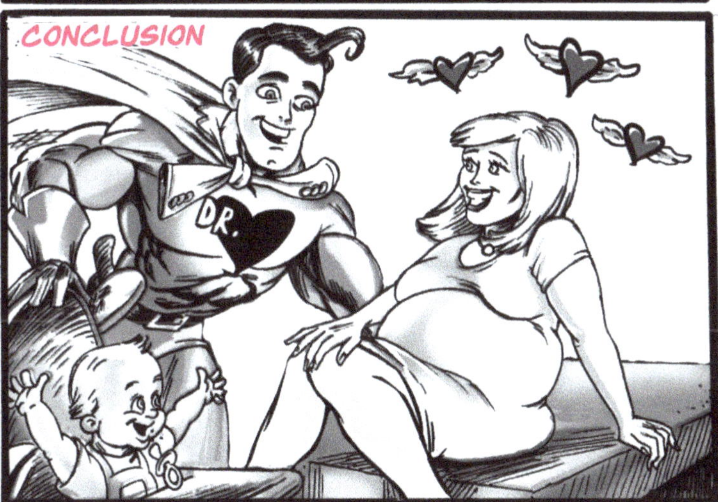

③ - how does your story resolve?
- your characters should have learned something or evolved

Scripting

THERE ARE A FEW POPULAR WAYS TO WRITE A COMIC OR A MANGA. THE FIRST TWO ARE FOR WRITERS THAT ARE PARTNERED WITH ILLUSTRATORS. THE "MARVEL METHOD" IS WHEN A WRITER GIVES AN ARTIST A PLOT, NAMELY A COUPLE OF PARAGRAPHS OF STORY OR A VERBAL DESCRIPTION, AND THE ARTIST GOES OFF AND CREATES ALL THE SEQUENTIAL DRAWINGS. THE ARTIST IN THIS METHOD IS IN CHARGE OF THE PACING AND THE VISUAL DIRECTION BUT AT THE END THE WRITER COMES BACK AND SCRIPTS THE NARRATION AND DIALOGUE FOR EACH PANEL. THIS METHOD CAN SPEED UP THE PRODUCTION. THE WRITER IS THE IDEA PERSON, WHILE THE ARTIST HAS FREEDOM OF INTERPRETATION.

THE SECOND METHOD IN WHICH THE WRITER AND ARTIST ARE TWO DIFFERENT PEOPLE IS FOR THE WRITER TO PROVIDE AS DETAILED A SCRIPT AS THEY CAN AND FOR THE ARTIST TO FOLLOW IT TO A TEE. SOME WRITERS EVEN PROVIDE THUMBNAIL SKETCHES FOR PANEL DIRECTION. SINCE EVERYTHING IS SPELLED OUT FOR THEM AND THEY CAN FOCUS ON THE DETAILS, THIS HAS SOME APPEAL TO ARTISTS. COMMUNICATION WHILE EMPLOYING ANY METHOD IS IMPORTANT, SO BOTH WRITERS AND ARTISTS CATER TO EACH OTHERS' STRENGTHS. FOR EXAMPLE, A WRITER MAY CHANGE ELEMENTS OF THEIR STORY TO SUIT WHAT THE ARTIST IS STRONGEST AT DRAWING.

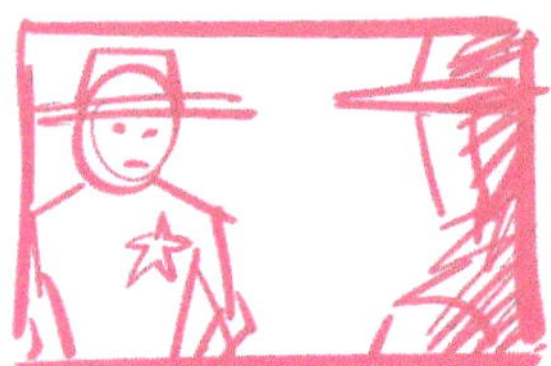
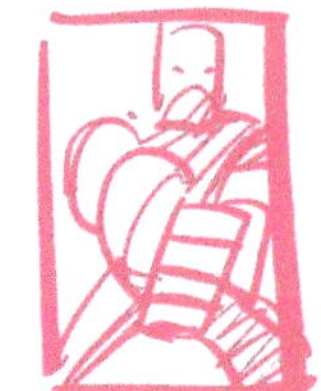
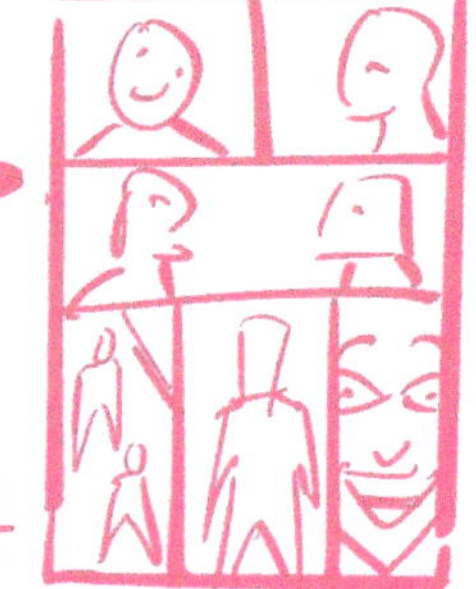

THUMBNAILS

- can specify direction beyond the script

- Artists also use these small ("thumb-sized") drawings to work out their ideas, often before writing a script

WHEN AN ARTIST CAN ALSO WRITE FOR HIS OR HER SELF, THAT'S WHEN THERE ARE MORE WAYS TO GET RESULTS. THEY CAN START WITH SKETCHING MAJOR SCENES THEY HAVE IN MIND AND THEN REARRANGE THEM BASED ON HOW THEY WANT TO PACE THE STORY. OR THEY COULD WRITE AN OUTLINE, PAGE BY PAGE OR PANEL BY PANEL, AND THEN START DRAWING ANYWHERE WITHIN THAT FRAMEWORK. REGARDLESS ON THEIR CREATIVE APPROACH, AN ARTIST MUST BE JUST AS GOOD A WRITER (AND VISE VERSA), WHEN THEY ARE HANDLING BOTH DUTIES. IF DONE WELL, BEING A TWO-IN-ONE CREATOR GIVES A PERSON THE MOST CONTROL AND FREEDOM AND POTENTIALLY THE MOST ADMIRATION, PRAISE, AND SELF-SATISFACTION.

Template

TITLE OF BOOK - ISSUE #1

25/10/2022 by Your Name - yourname@email.com

PAGE ONE

Panel 1: This is where the ACTION is described. Compositional notes can be given.

LOCATION CAPTION: Columbus Circle, New York City. Two friends meet in front of Central Park.

CHARACTER 1:   Hey, how are you?

CHARACTER 2:   Great! How about…

PANEL 2: Both characters turn toward the sound with surprise on their faces.

SFX: CRASH!

- Location Caption can be a Narrative Caption, etc.
- Formating should include the elements above, at least

Composition

HOW YOU COMPOSE PANELS FOR COMICS OR OTHER MEDIUMS LIKE FINE ART OR FILM DEPENDS ON THE EMOTIONS YOU'RE TRYING TO CREATE IN THE READER OR VIEWER. THE SEQUENCE MATTERS TOO, TO BUILD UP THE STORY TO ITS CLIMAX. THE PASSAGE OF TIME CAN BE CONVEYED QUICKLY WITH SMALL CONSECUTIVE PANELS OR SLOWLY WITH A BIG PANEL THAT TAKES THE READER MORE TIME TO ADMIRE. PANEL SHAPES CAN ALSO INFLUENCE THE ACTION IN MANGA AND COMICS. WARPED PANELS CAN INDICATE A DREAM SEQUENCE OR JAGGED PANELS CAN BE USED TO DRAW ATTENTION TO AN IMPACTFUL ACTION. PANEL COMPOSITIONS HAVE AN OVERALL GREAT EFFECT ON PAGE FLOW AND THE EASE WITH WHICH WE READ STATIC OR SEQUENTIAL IMAGES.

ALTHOUGH THERE ARE DOZENS OF HIGHLY EFFECTIVE PANEL COMPOSITION IDEAS, HERE ARE A FEW OF MY MOST NOTABLE COMPOSITIONS (IN A WIDESCREEN FORMAT).

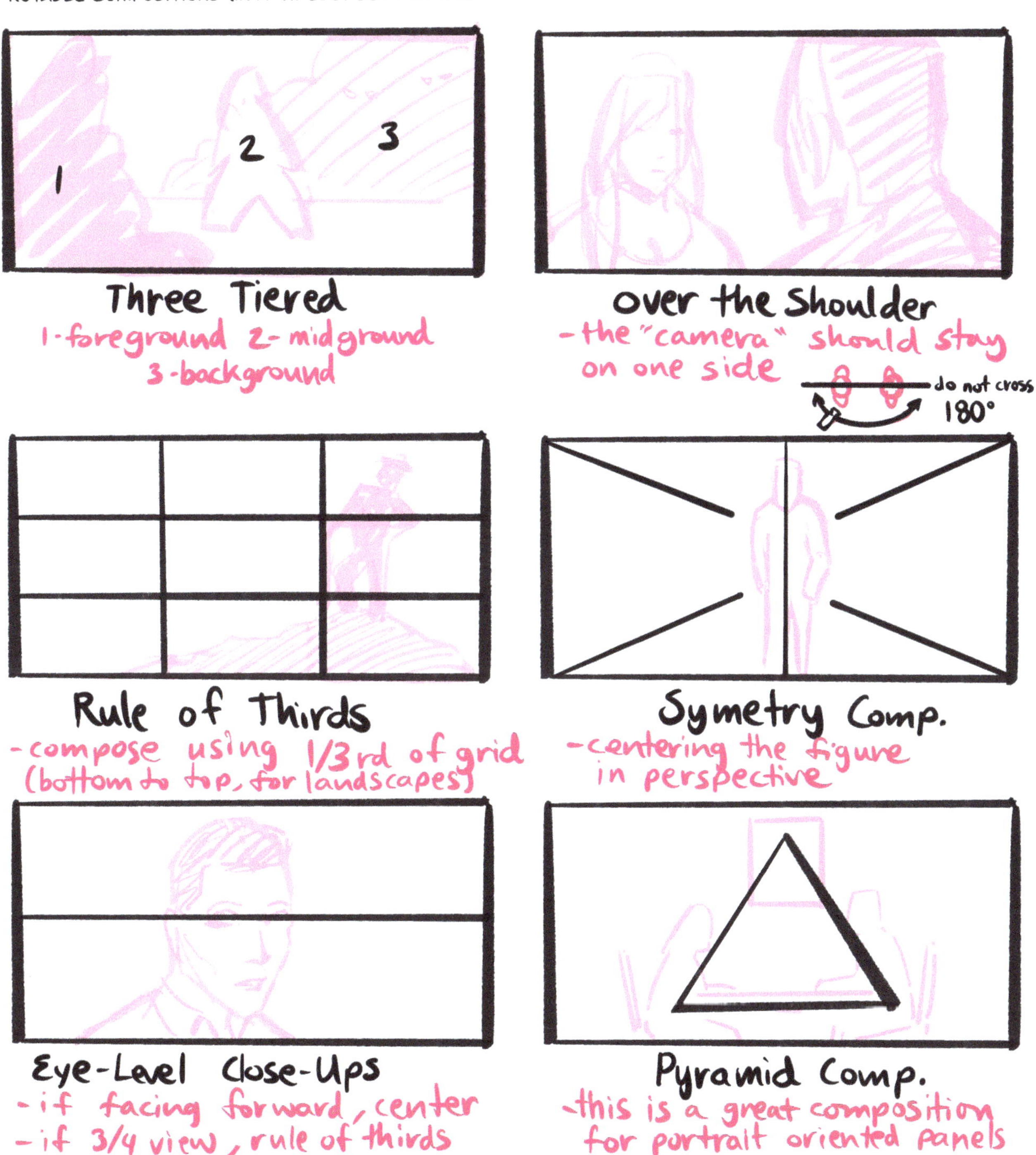

Three Tiered
1-foreground 2-midground
3-background

over the Shoulder
- the "camera" should stay on one side

Rule of Thirds
- compose using 1/3rd of grid
(bottom to top, for landscapes)

Symetry Comp.
- centering the figure in perspective

Eye-Level Close-Ups
- if facing forward, center
- if 3/4 view, rule of thirds

Pyramid Comp.
- this is a great composition for portrait oriented panels

Panels & Pacing

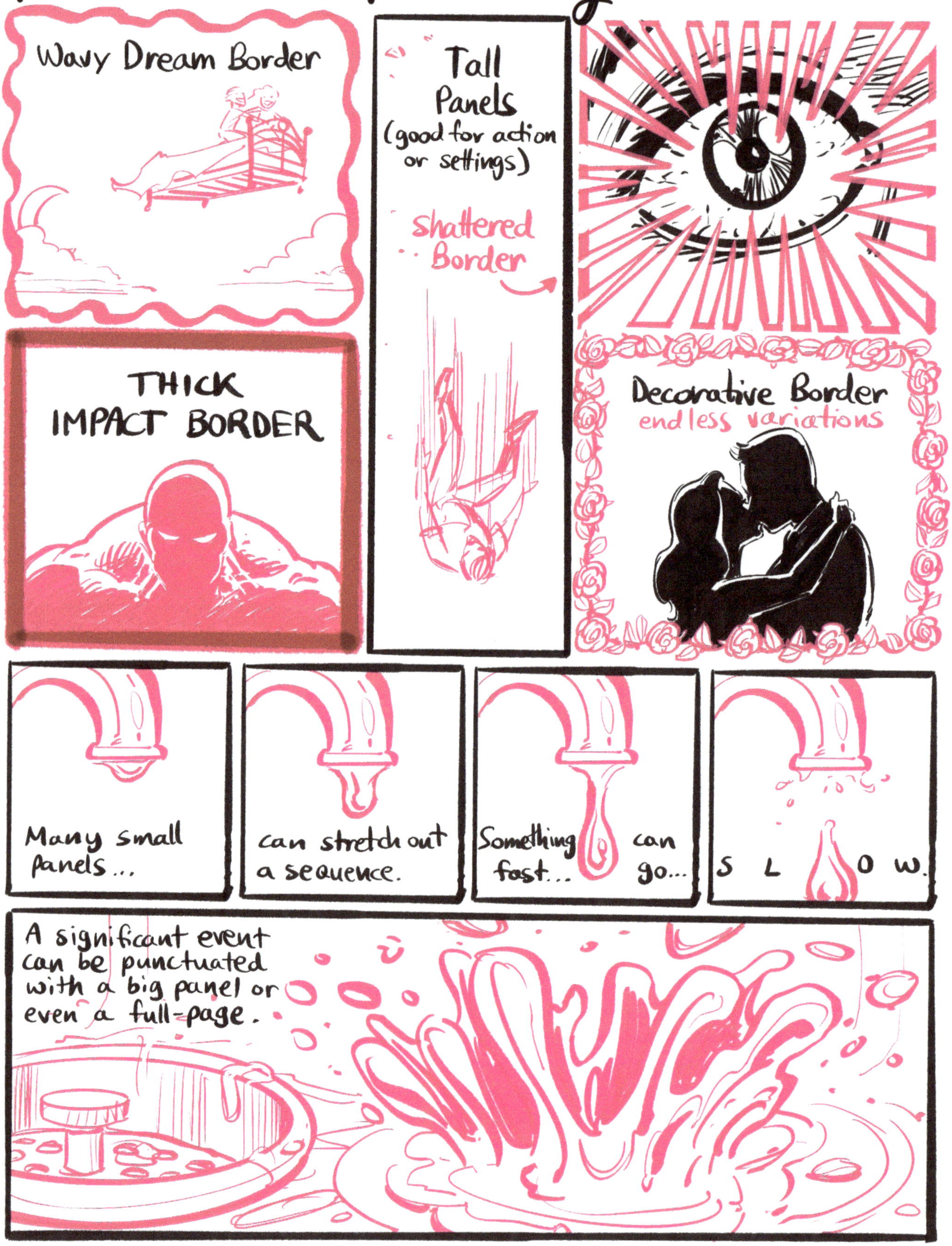

Wavy Dream Border

Tall Panels
(good for action or settings)

Shattered Border

THICK IMPACT BORDER

Decorative Border
endless variations

Many small panels...

can stretch out a sequence.

Something fast... can go...

S L O W.

A significant event can be punctuated with a big panel or even a full-page.

Page Layout

IN MANGA AND COMICS, PAGE FLOW IS JUST AS IMPORTANT AS STORYTELLING. IN FACT, PAGE LAYOUT IS THE ART OF THE STORY. THE FLOW OF THE ACTION, PANEL TO PANEL, IS WHAT MAKES A STORY EITHER PLEASANT TO READ OR TEDIOUS. ONE PANEL SHOULD EASILY LEAD TO THE NEXT. WE READ FROM TOP LEFT TO BOTTOM RIGHT. YOUR JOB AS AN ARTIST IS TO MAKE THAT A VERY SMOOTH TRANSITION, LEADING THE READER TO FLIP THE PAGE. EACH PAGE SHOULD HAVE A COMPLETE ACTION AND YOU SHOULD BE ABLE TO UNDERSTAND WHAT IS HAPPENING WITHOUT ANY WORDS. YOU ARE ALSO OPEN TO EXPERIMENT WITH DESIGN ELEMENTS THAT ADVANCE THE STORY AND MAKE IT WORTHWHILE FOR READERS TO LINGER ON YOUR ARTWORK.

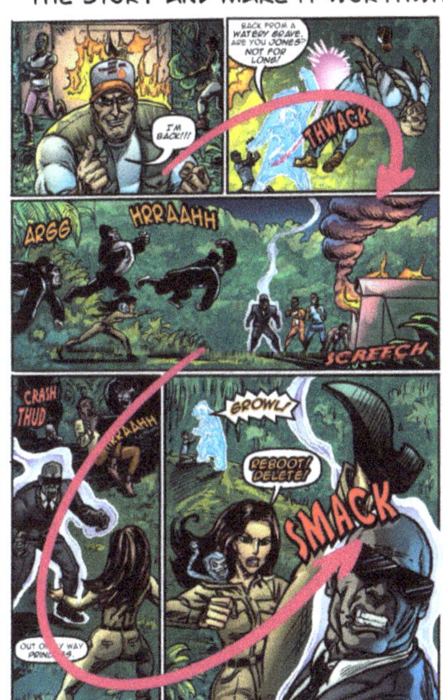

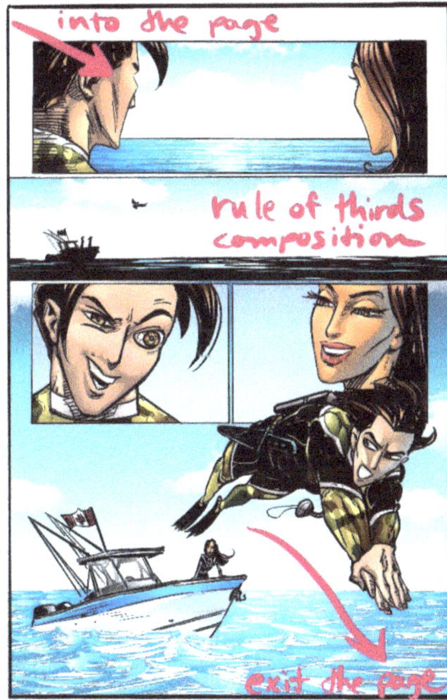

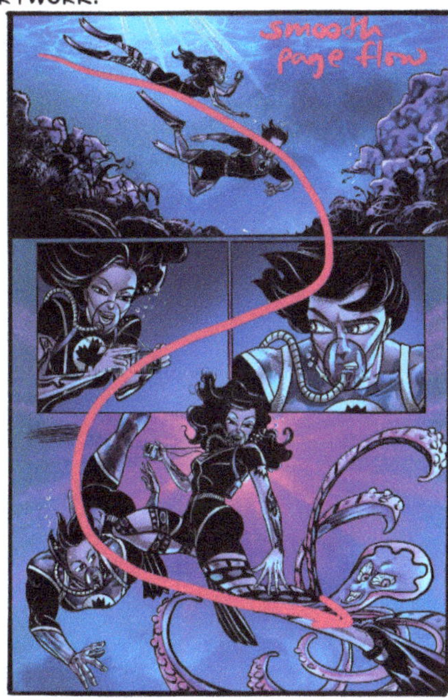

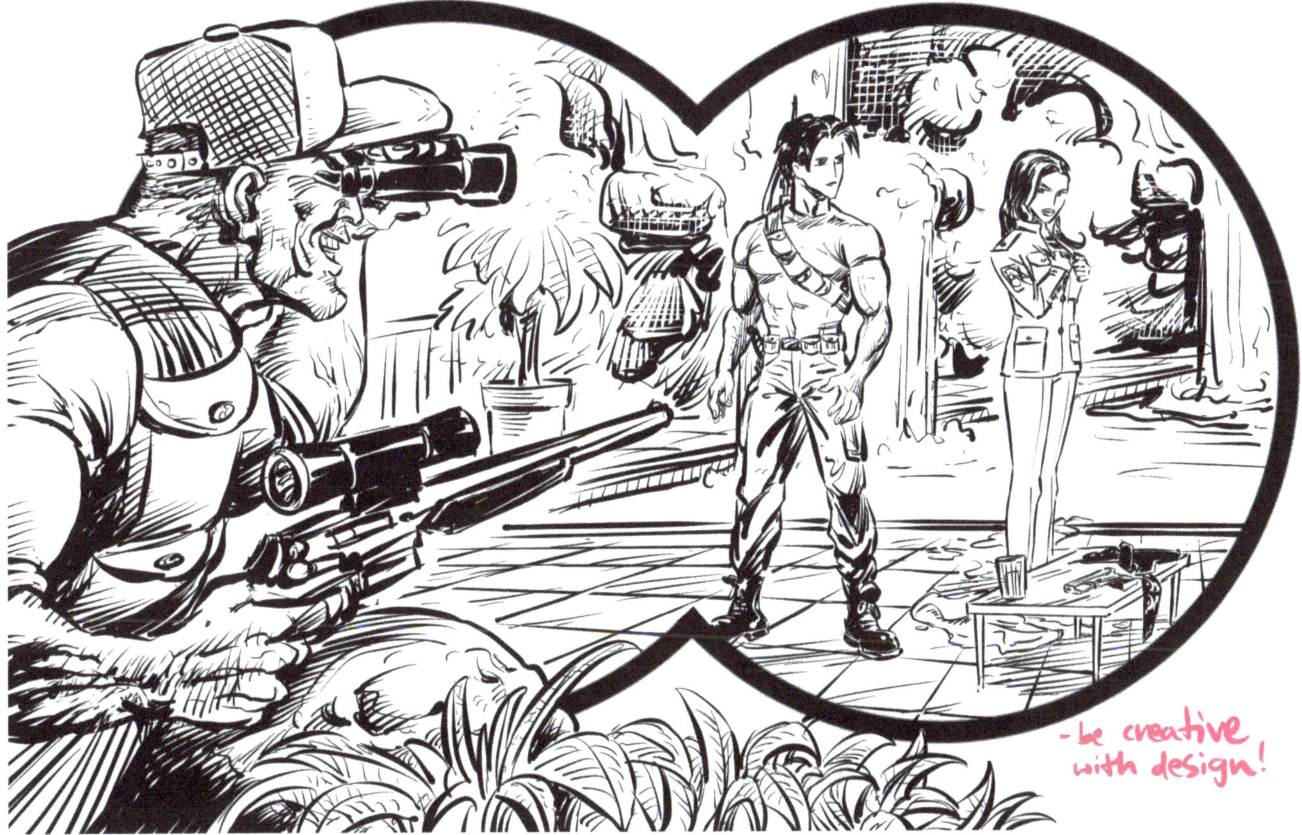

Web Manga

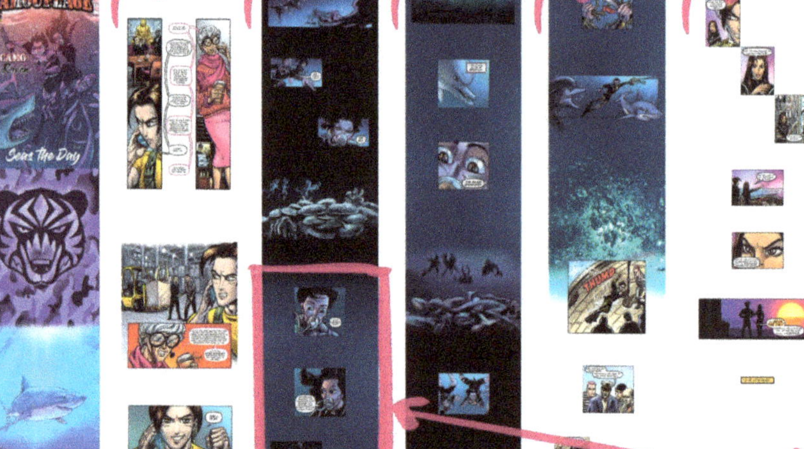

THE READING EXPERIENCE IS DIFFERENT FOR WEB COMICS. READERS SCROLL UP AND DOWN, AS OPPOSED TO FROM TOP-LEFT TO BOTTOM-RIGHT IN A TRADITIONAL COMIC. THERE ARE SOME BENEFITS THOUGH, WITH WEB MANGA. NAMELY, *SUSPENSE*!

IN TRADITIONAL COMICS, YOU HAVE THE PRINTED PRODUCT IN YOUR HANDS AND CAN TELL WHAT'S COMING UP BUT WITH WEB MANGA, YOU SCROLL THROUGH THE STORY ONE PANEL AND ONE WORD BUBBLE AT A TIME. WHAT READERS SEE IS ONLY WHAT IS VISIBLE ON THEIR PHONE OR COMPUTER MONITOR AND THE STORIES ARE PUBLISHED AS LONG SCROLLS.

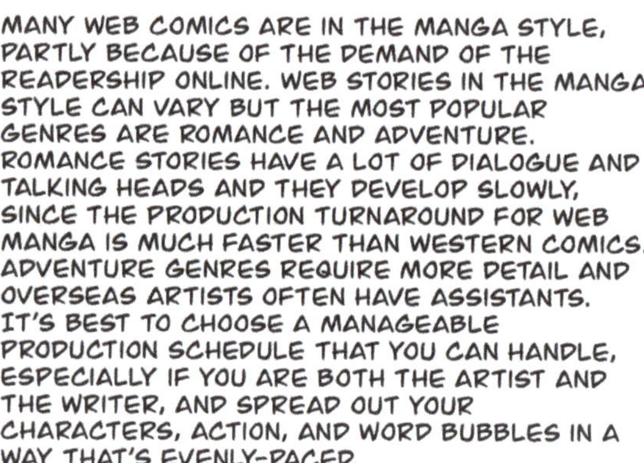

Approximate phone format

Typical PC view

MANY WEB COMICS ARE IN THE MANGA STYLE, PARTLY BECAUSE OF THE DEMAND OF THE READERSHIP ONLINE. WEB STORIES IN THE MANGA STYLE CAN VARY BUT THE MOST POPULAR GENRES ARE ROMANCE AND ADVENTURE. ROMANCE STORIES HAVE A LOT OF DIALOGUE AND TALKING HEADS AND THEY DEVELOP SLOWLY, SINCE THE PRODUCTION TURNAROUND FOR WEB MANGA IS MUCH FASTER THAN WESTERN COMICS. ADVENTURE GENRES REQUIRE MORE DETAIL AND OVERSEAS ARTISTS OFTEN HAVE ASSISTANTS. IT'S BEST TO CHOOSE A MANAGEABLE PRODUCTION SCHEDULE THAT YOU CAN HANDLE, ESPECIALLY IF YOU ARE BOTH THE ARTIST AND THE WRITER, AND SPREAD OUT YOUR CHARACTERS, ACTION, AND WORD BUBBLES IN A WAY THAT'S EVENLY-PACED.

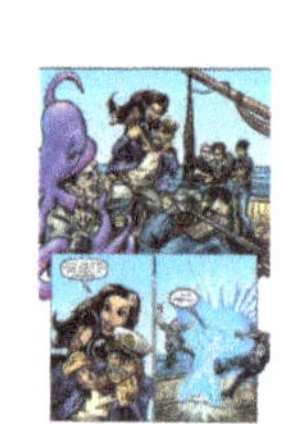
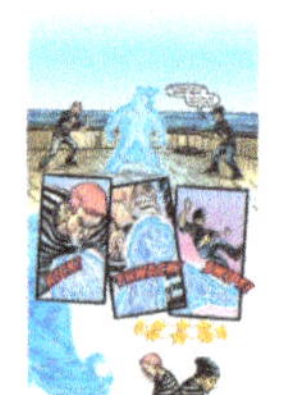
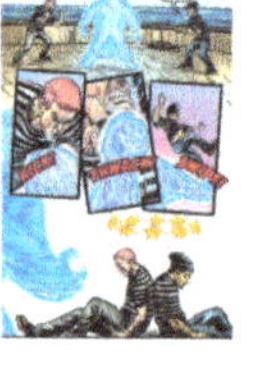
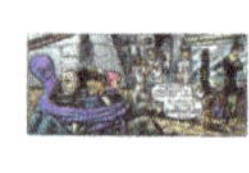

With some editing, you can re-format a traditional 6.9" x 10.4" comic into the specs of popular online platforms or your own website or app (distribution options are endless, for gaining new readers)

Cover Art

THE MAGIC OF GREAT COVER ART IS A COMBINATION OF HAVING A STRONG COMPOSITION AND USING DIRECTIONAL DEVICES TO LEAD THE EYE. THE PYRAMID COMPOSITION IS ONE OF THE MOST POPULAR BECAUSE IT CAN BE SO EFFECTIVE. IT'S PARAMOUNT THAT WHEN USING THE PYRAMID, THERE IS SPACE AROUND THE SIDES AND ON TOP. DON'T DRAW THINGS TOO CLOSE TO THE EDGE AND MAKE SURE THAT THE CHARACTERS ARE CENTERED AND THE ELEMENTS ARE WELL-BALANCED ON THE PAGE. THE TOP ALWAYS HAS MORE SPACE BECAUSE THAT'S WHERE THE TITLE GOES.

THE FOCUS SHOULD ALWAYS BE THE CENTER OF YOUR COMPOSITION. ALL CHARACTERS AND OBJECTS SHOULD POINT TOWARD OR FRAME WHATEVER IS IN THE CENTER.

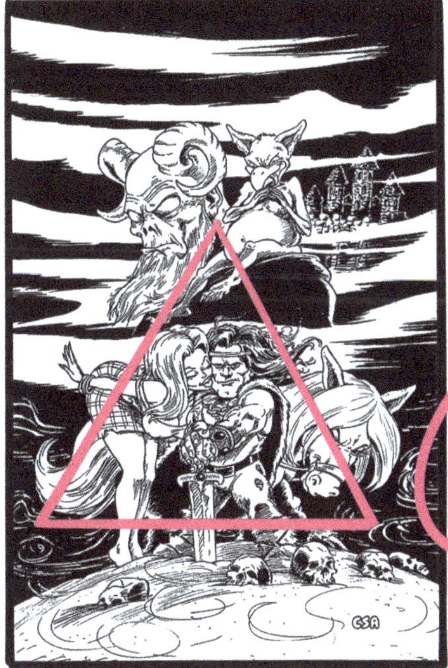

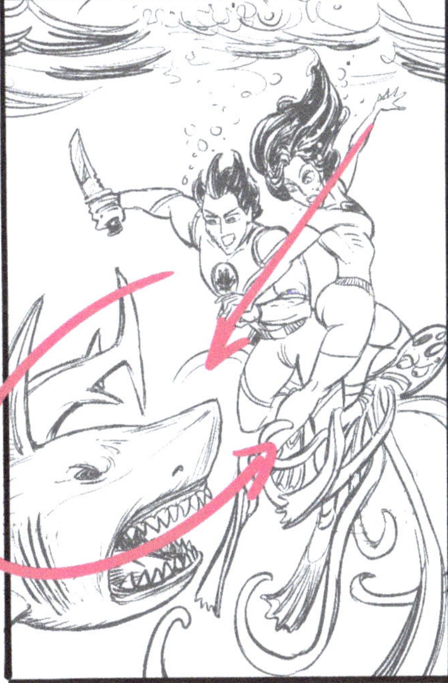

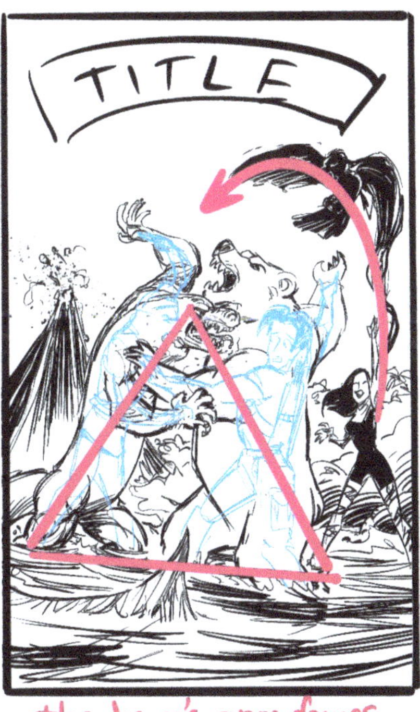

notice how the main character's face is in the center of the page

the shark frames the page & points toward the octopus

the bear's arm frames the girl & the raven brings the eye back in

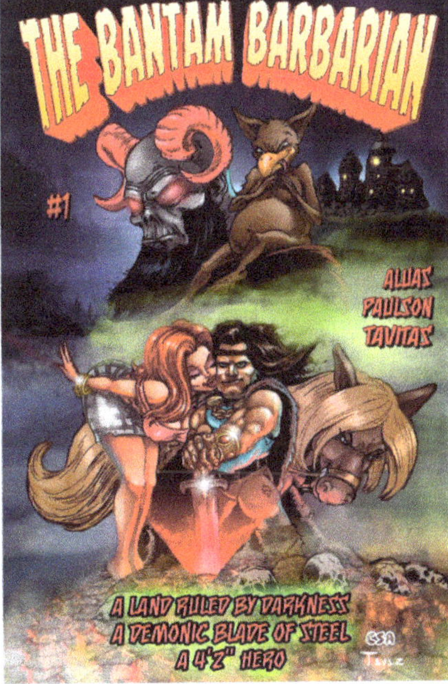

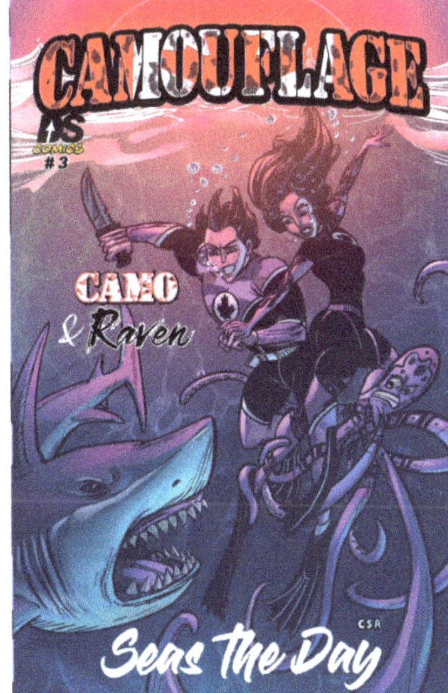

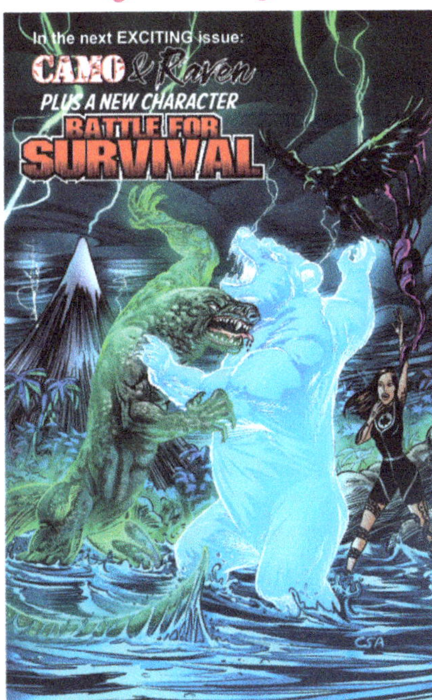

Word Bubbles

WORD BUBBLES COME IN MANY DIFFERENT FORMS AND YOU CAN CERTAINLY BE MORE INNOVATIVE THAN THESE EXAMPLES BELOW, BUT DEFINITELY START WITH THESE BECAUSE THESE ARE UNIVERSAL. A SPEECH BUBBLE IS TYPICALLY OVAL. YOU CAN EMPHASIZE LOUDNESS OR TONE BY MAKING THE OVAL JAGGED. THOUGHT BUBBLES ARE LIKE CLOUDS. YOU CAN DIFFERENTIATE BUBBLES BASED ON THE CHARACTER THAT IT'S ASSOCIATED WITH. FOR EXAMPLE, AN EVIL CHARACTER MIGHT HAVE A SHADED BUBBLE OR A THICK BORDER AROUND IT. IF THE SOUND IS COMING FROM AN ELECTRONIC SPEAKER, THE BUBBLE SHOULD LOOK DIFFERENT. WORD BUBBLES ARE PART OF THE ART. BE THOUGHTFUL AND EXPRESSIVE WITH THEM. ADDITIONALLY, YOU CAN USE EFFECTS TO ILLUSTRATE SOUNDS OR CHARACTER REACTIONS.

IN THIS AGE, THERE ARE MANY FONTS THAT YOU CAN USE TO MAKE IT EASY ON YOURSELF TO LETTER WORD BALLOONS. BUT IF YOU'RE LETTERING BY HAND, USE A CONSISTENT GRID.

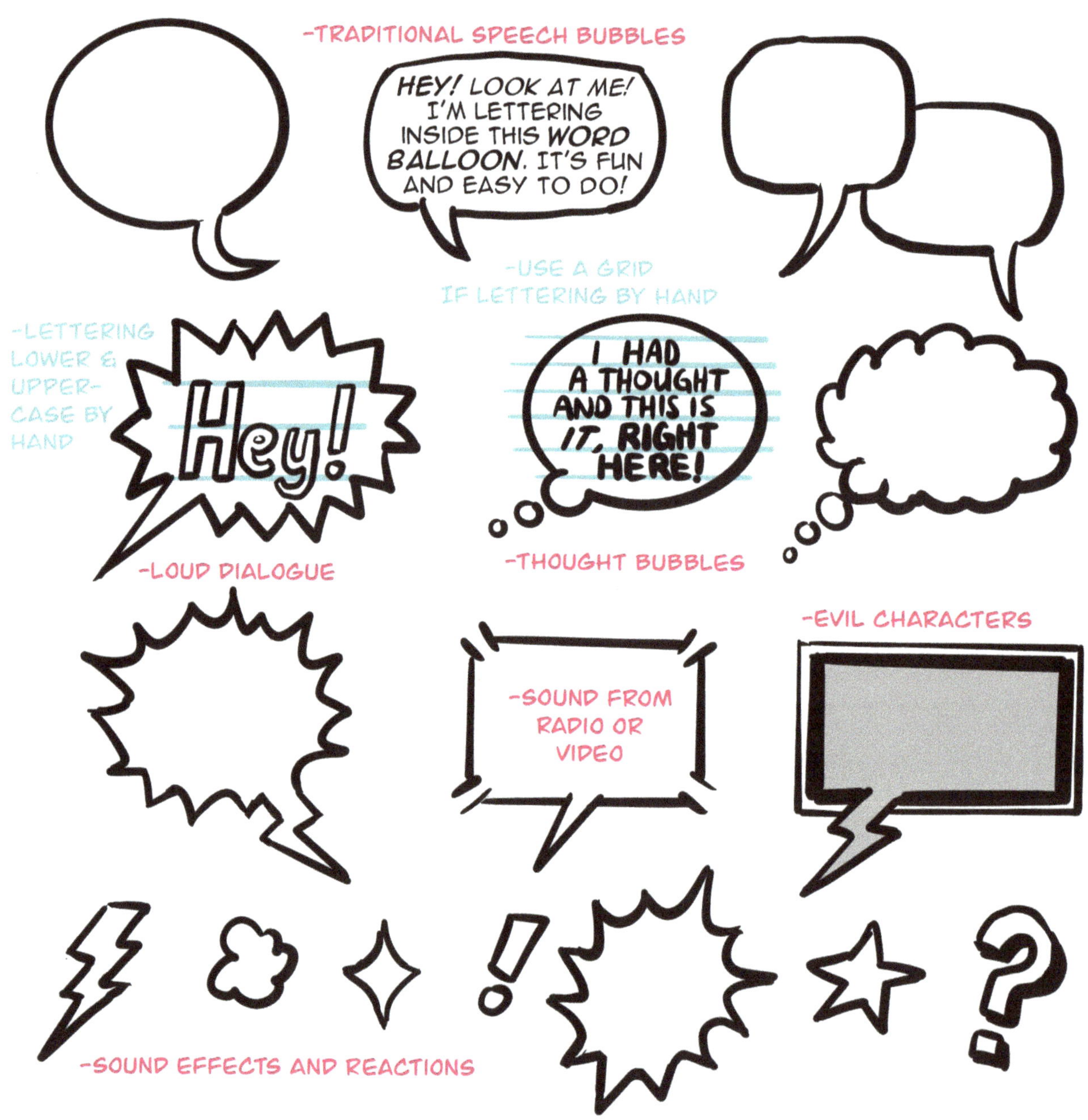

Lettering Titles & Logos

WHETHER IT'S A COMIC BOOK LOGO OR A DESIGN FOR A PRODUCT OR BUSINESS, AN ARTIST HAS TO CONSIDER THE THEME. ANY GRAPHICS THAT ARE INTEGRATED INTO THE LOGO SHOULD REFLECT THE WORDS OR TITLE. HERE ARE A BUNCH OF EXAMPLES BELOW. YOU CAN CREATE YOUR LOGO DESIGN DIGITALLY OR BY HAND. THE MEDIUM ISN'T IMPORTANT, AS LONG AS THE END RESULT IS COLORFUL AND LOOKS PROFESSIONAL.

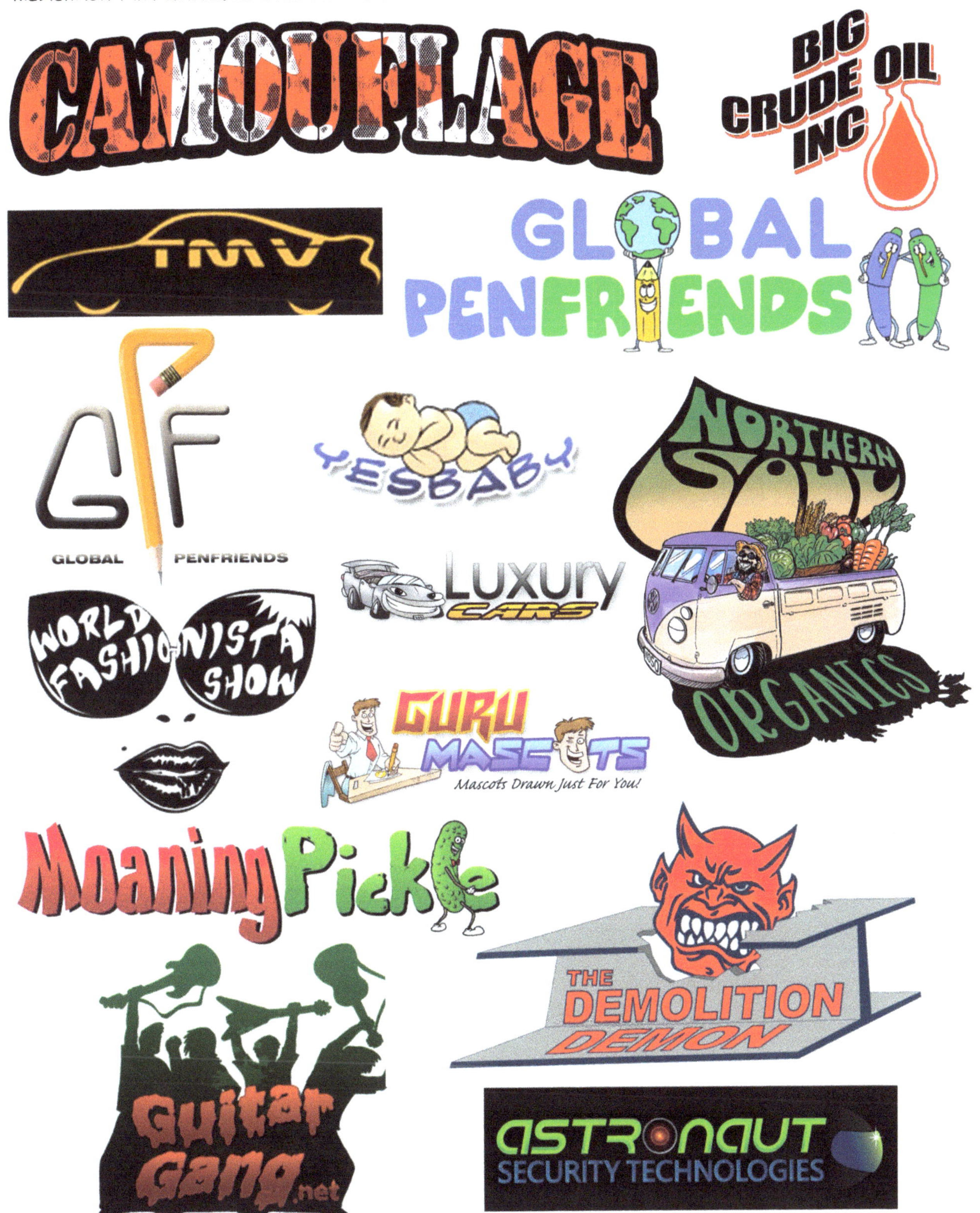

Manga & Comic Action

MOTION IN COMICS AND MANGA HAS TO BE DEPICTED WITH EXPRESSIVE LINES. LIKEWISE, SOUND IS EXPRESSED THROUGH PHONETIC EFFECTS. MOST OFTEN, IN SEQUENTIAL ART, WE FRAME OUR DRAWINGS. WITHIN A GIVEN PANEL, WE CAN EMPHASIZE THE ACTION WITH LINES THAT CONVEY MOVEMENT. ACTION LINES CAN SHOW SOMETHING POWERFUL HAPPENING TO A CHARACTER OR THEY CAN SHOW THE MOVEMENT OF THE CHARACTER.

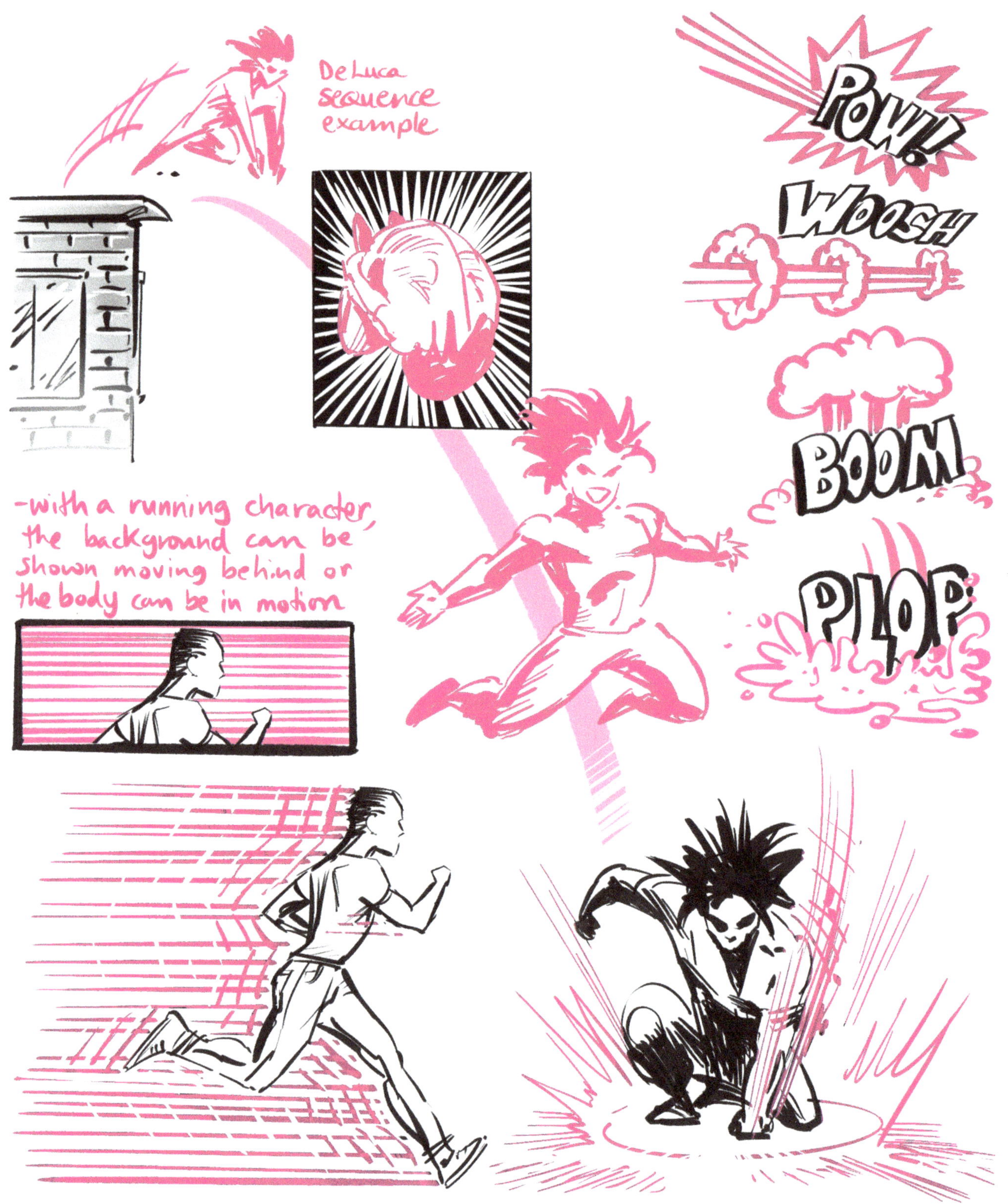

Special Effects

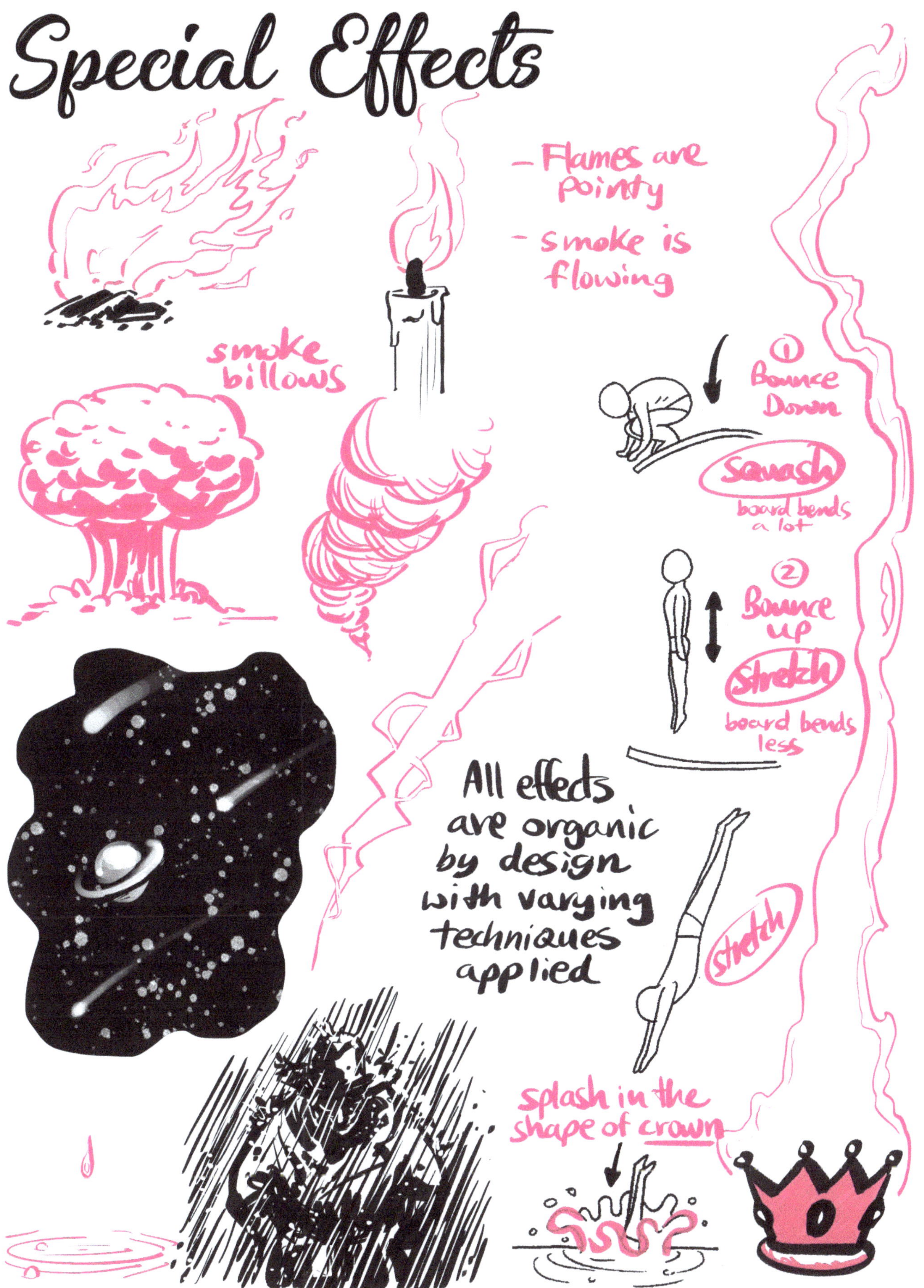

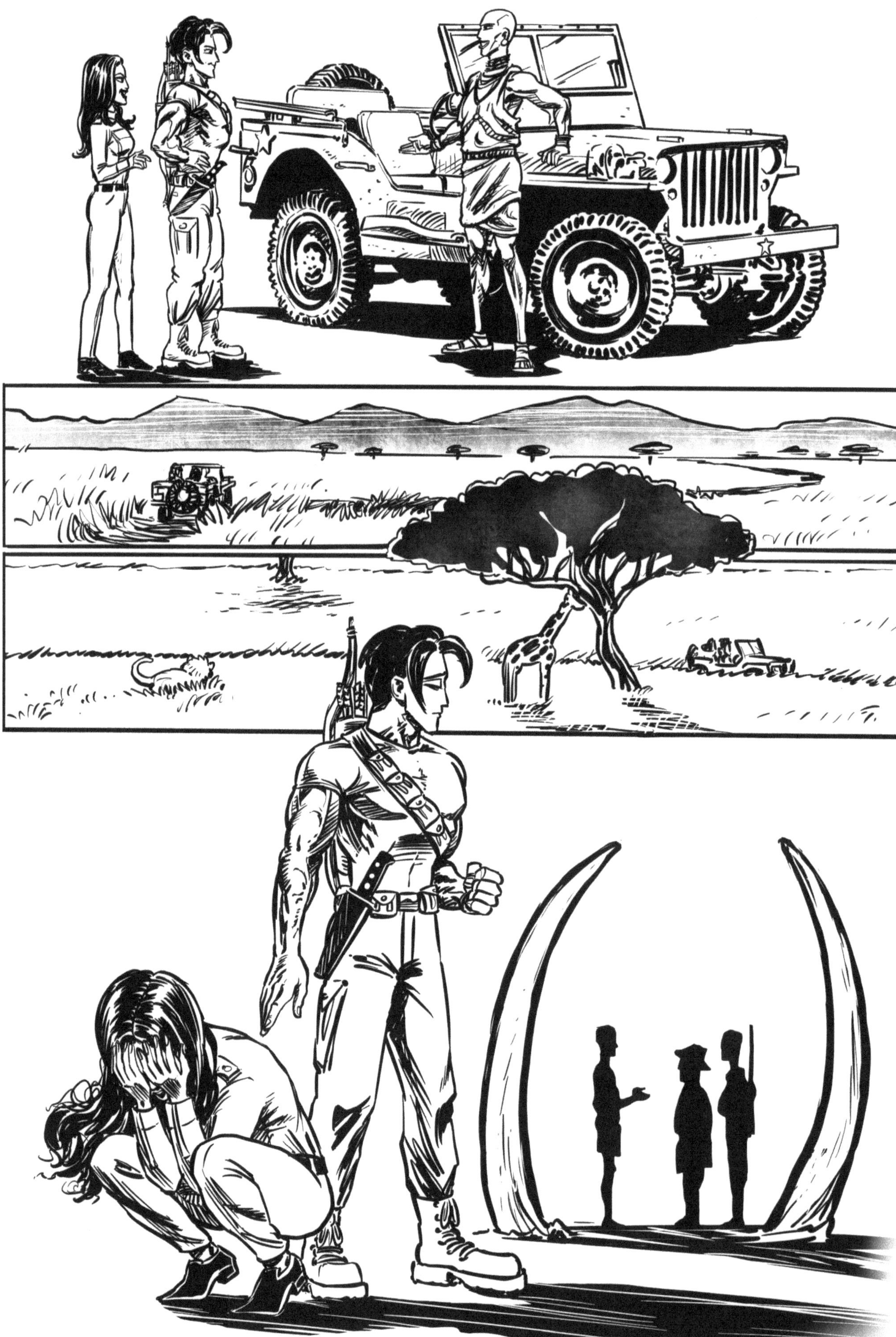

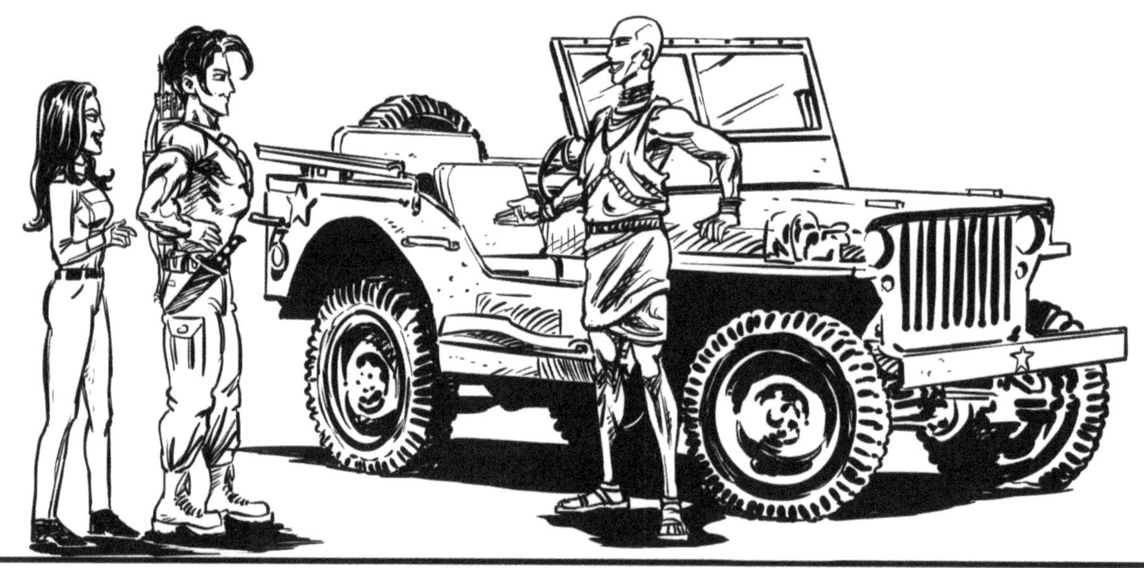

Continuing Comics/Manga

THIS IS A FUN EXERCISE WHERE YOU TAKE THE FIRST COUPLE OF PANELS OF A STRIP AND YOU INVENT THE REST. THE REQUEST IS TO KEEP THE SAME CHARACTERS. YOU CAN ADD NEW ONES BUT CONTINUE WITH THESE FOR A WHILE.

USE THE SKILLS YOU DEVELOPED TO FIGURE OUT THE SHAPES USED TO DESIGN THESE CHARACTERS AND MIMIC THEIR DESIGN, ADDING NEW EXPRESSIONS. IT SHOULD LOOK LIKE THE SAME ARTIST DID EACH SEQUENCE.

ADD LETTERING TOO AND WHATEVER DIALOGUE OR NARRATIVE YOU CAN CONCEIVE. KEEP THE STYLE CONSISTENT BUT UNLEASH YOUR IMAGINATION WITH STORY IDEAS AND SCENARIOS.

TRY AND MAKE EACH PAGE A COMPLETE SHORT STORY, FINDING INSPIRATION IN THE PANEL SIZES AND SHAPES. BY THE LAST PANEL, THERE SHOULD BE SOME RESOLUTION. IT CAN BE FUNNY, SERIOUS, SURREAL, IT'S UP TO YOU!

PANEL SHAPES ARE PROVIDED AT THE START, THEN YOU CAN MAKE UP YOUR OWN PANEL SIZES. LATER YOU CAN USE THE TEMPLATES TO INVENT YOUR OWN COMICS AND MANGA FROM SCRATCH!

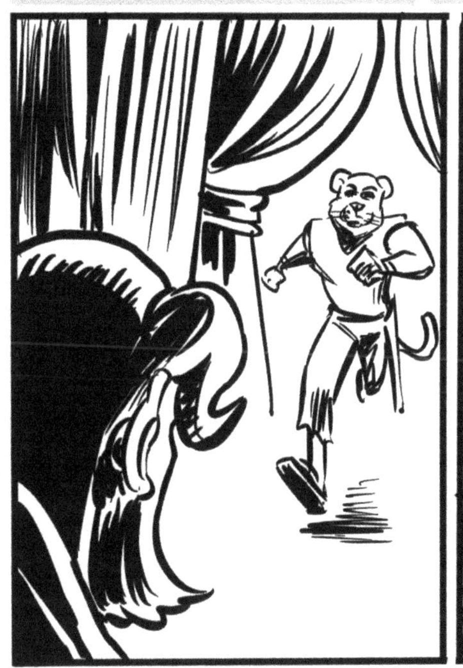

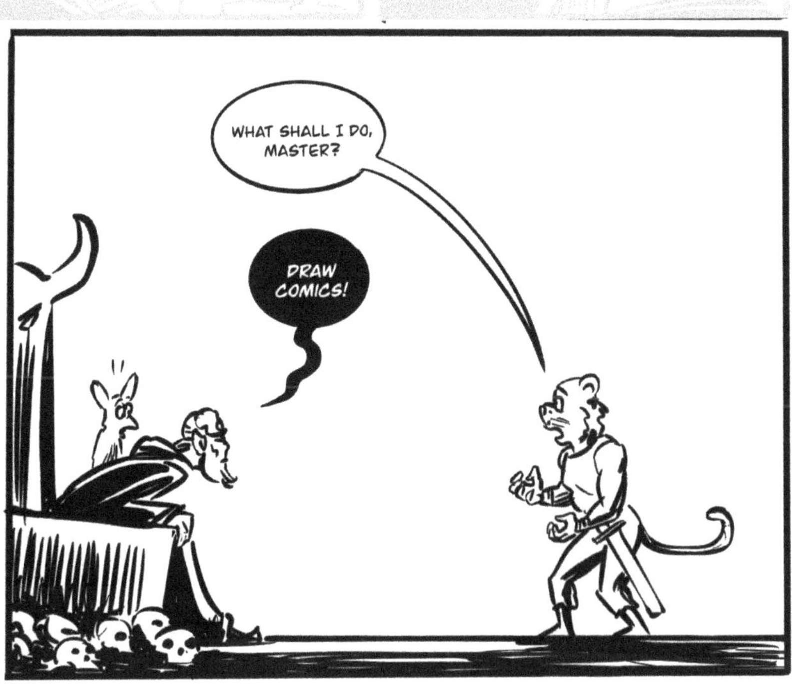

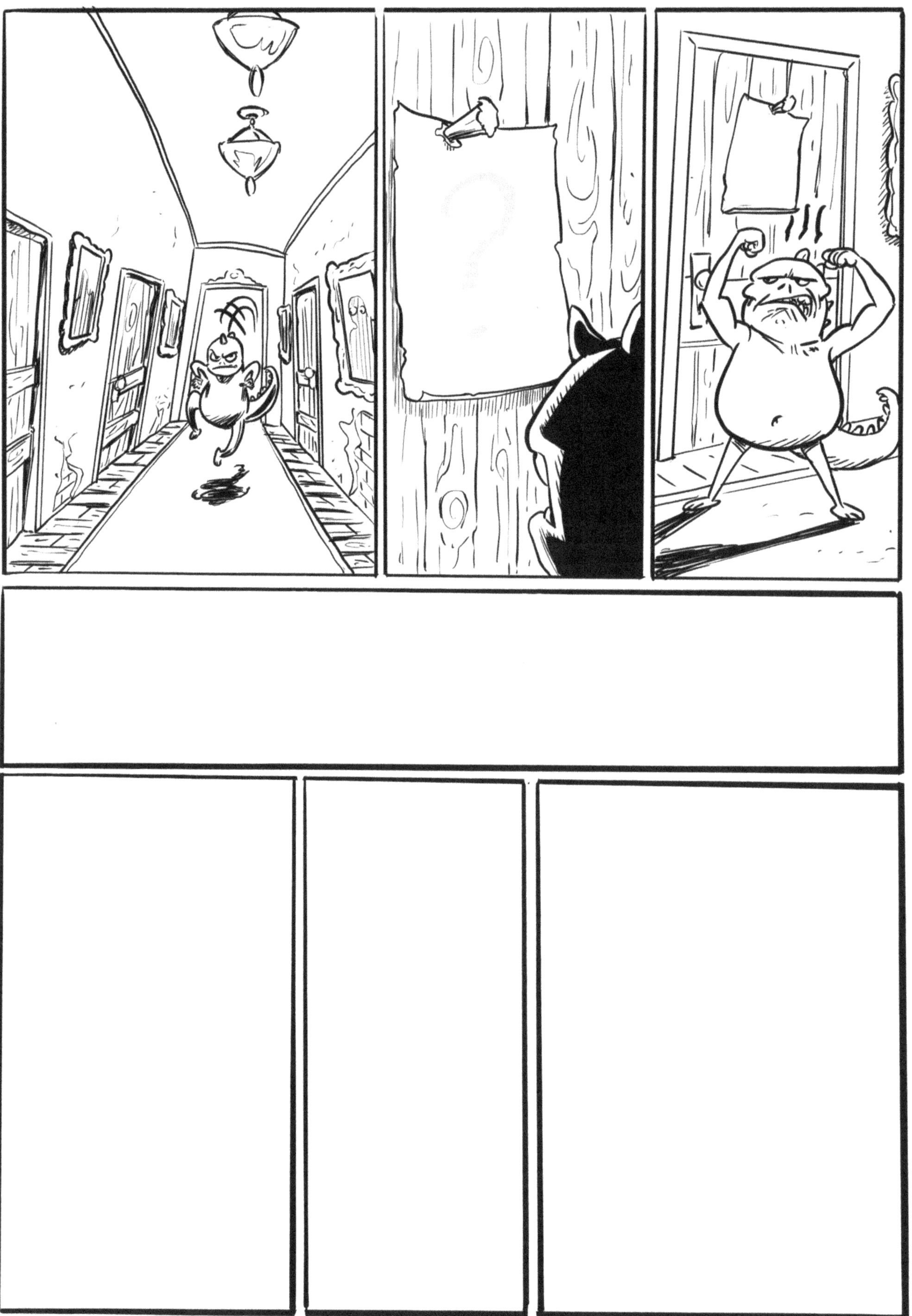

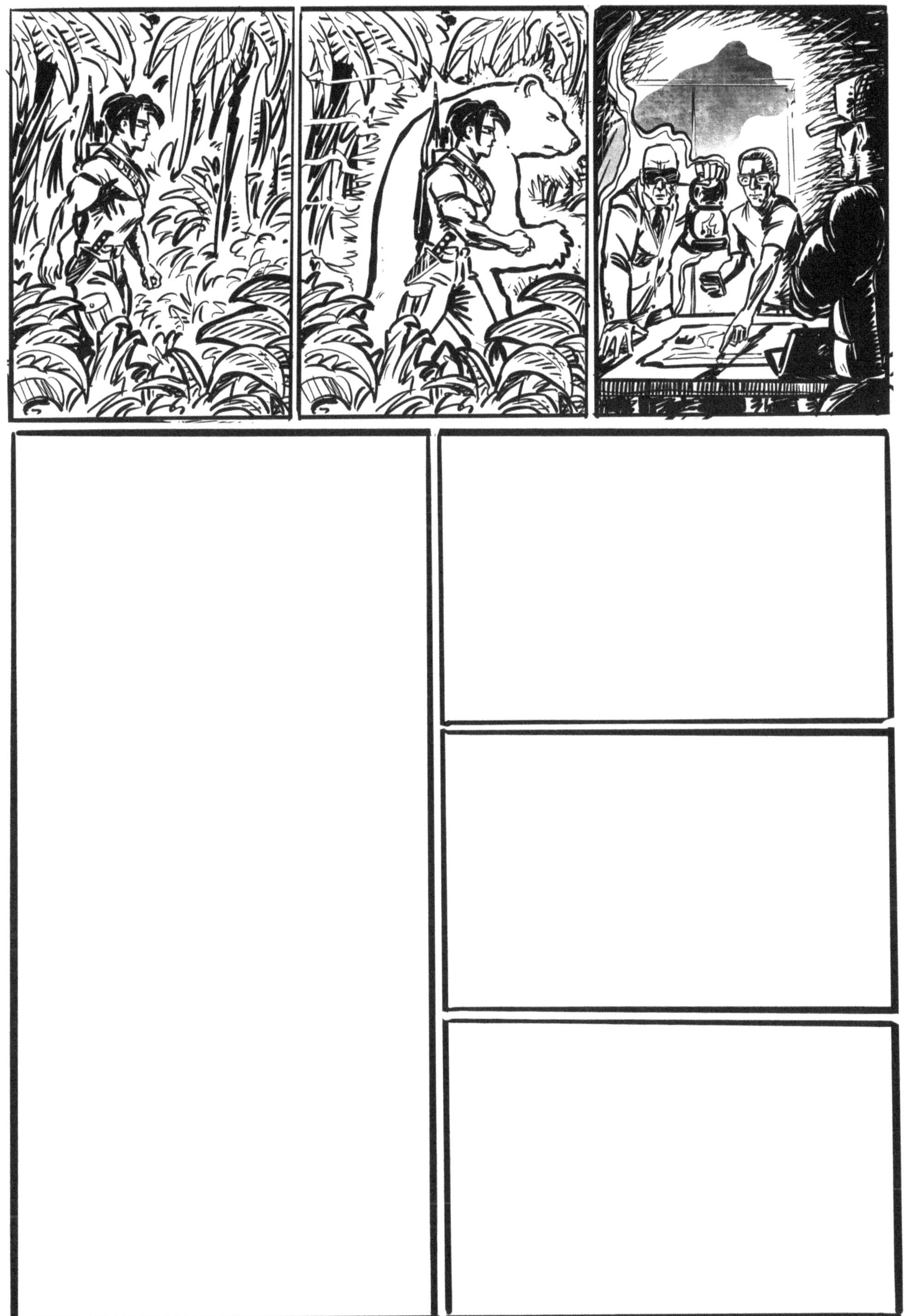

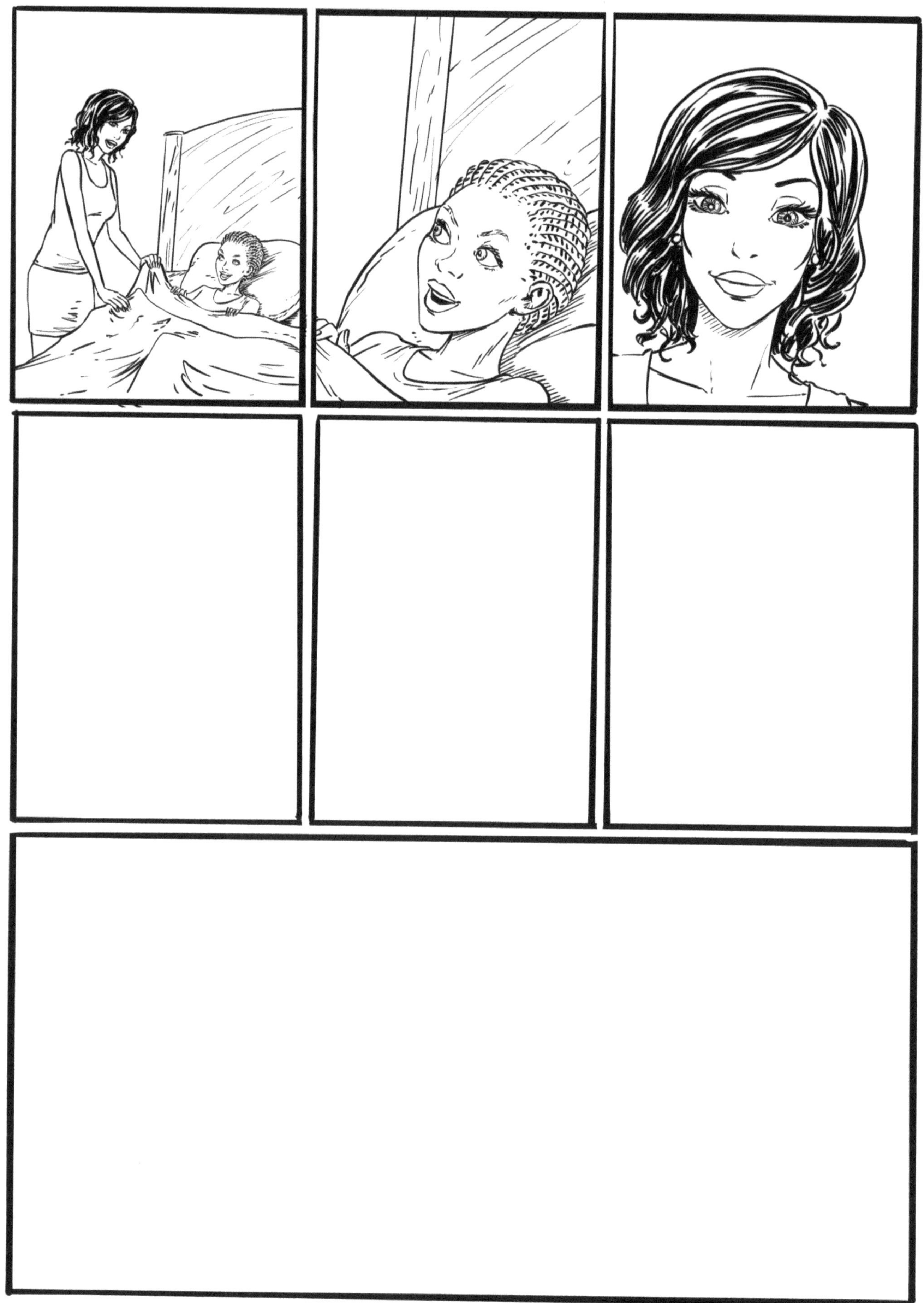

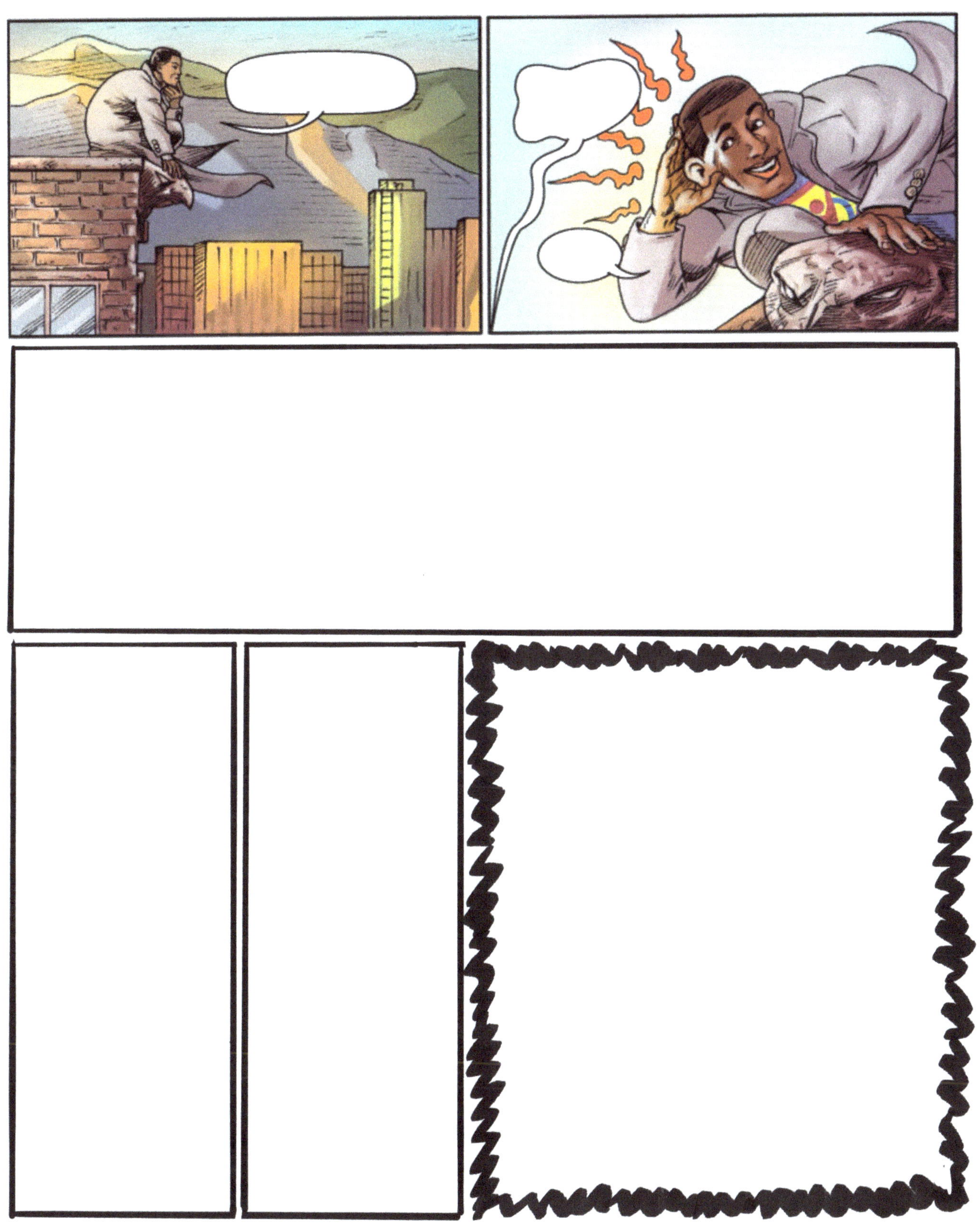

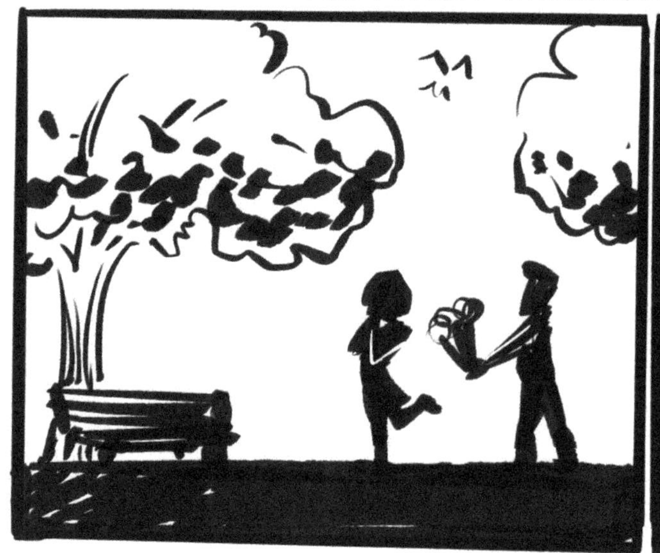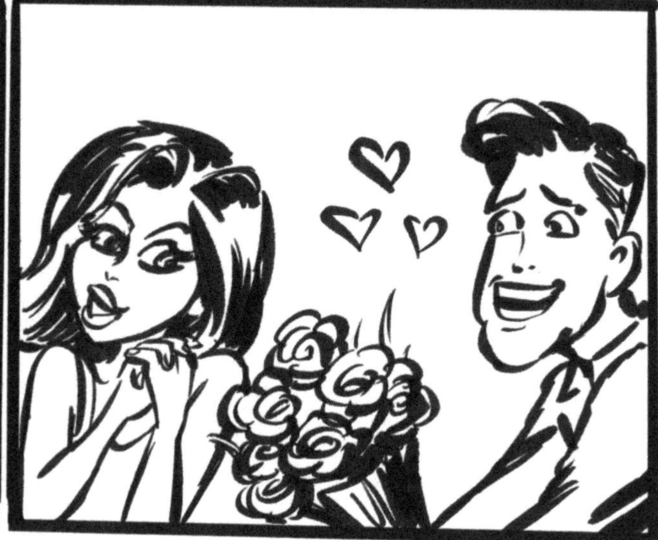

WHAT HAPPENS NEXT?

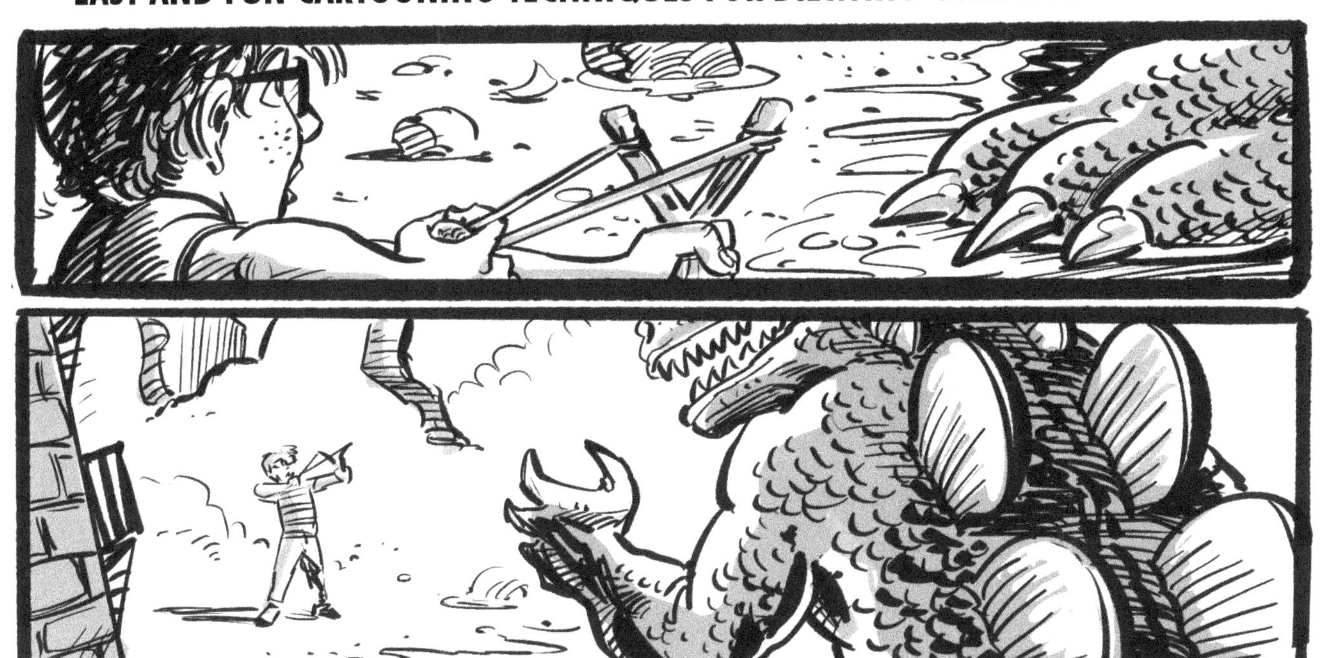

WHAT HAPPENS NEXT?

Trim line

Margin area

margin area

Be Creative!

Comic/Manga Template

Trim line

Trim line

margin area

margin area

Trim line

Bonus Material & Gallery

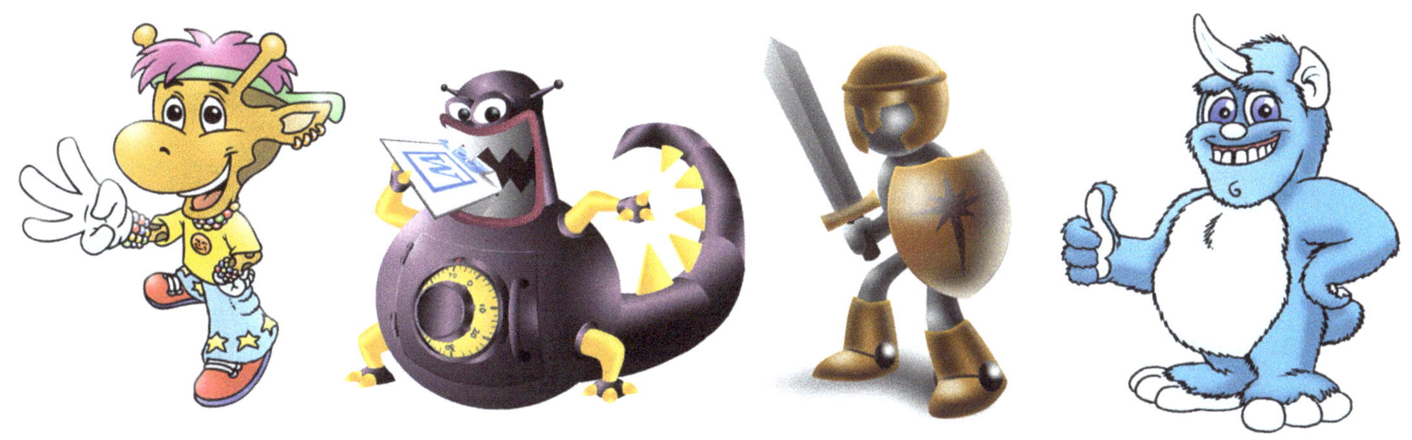

THANK YOU FOR COMING ALONG THIS REALLY FUN RIDE DRAWING COMICS AND MANGA!

ALTHOUGH IT IS DEFINITELY POSSIBLE TO GO MORE IN-DEPTH ON EACH OF THE PRECEDING POINTS, THIS BOOK IS A PERFECT STARTING PLACE FOR DEVELOPING OR IMPROVING YOUR DRAWING SKILLS. IT DEFINITELY DESERVES MULTIPLE READINGS. EACH PAGE IS RICH WITH INFO AND IT'S EASY TO MISS THINGS. TO PILE ON MORE INFORMATION, HERE ARE SOME BONUS PAGES. I MENTION COLOUR FOR EXAMPLE, WHICH IS EXTRA FROM THE DRAWING FOCUS OF THE BOOK, AND I'M INCLUDING SOME EXTRA TIPS AND FUN ARTWORKS TO INSPIRE YOU. FEEL FREE TO COPY ANYTHING YOU LIKE AND REMEMBER TO PRACTICE AND HAVE FUN!

THANKS AGAIN FOR YOUR GENUINE INTEREST AND YOUR HARD WORK!

GOOD LUCK WITH YOUR COMICS AND MANGA PROJECTS!

AND PLEASE SHARE YOUR THOUGHTS AND KEEP IN TOUCH!

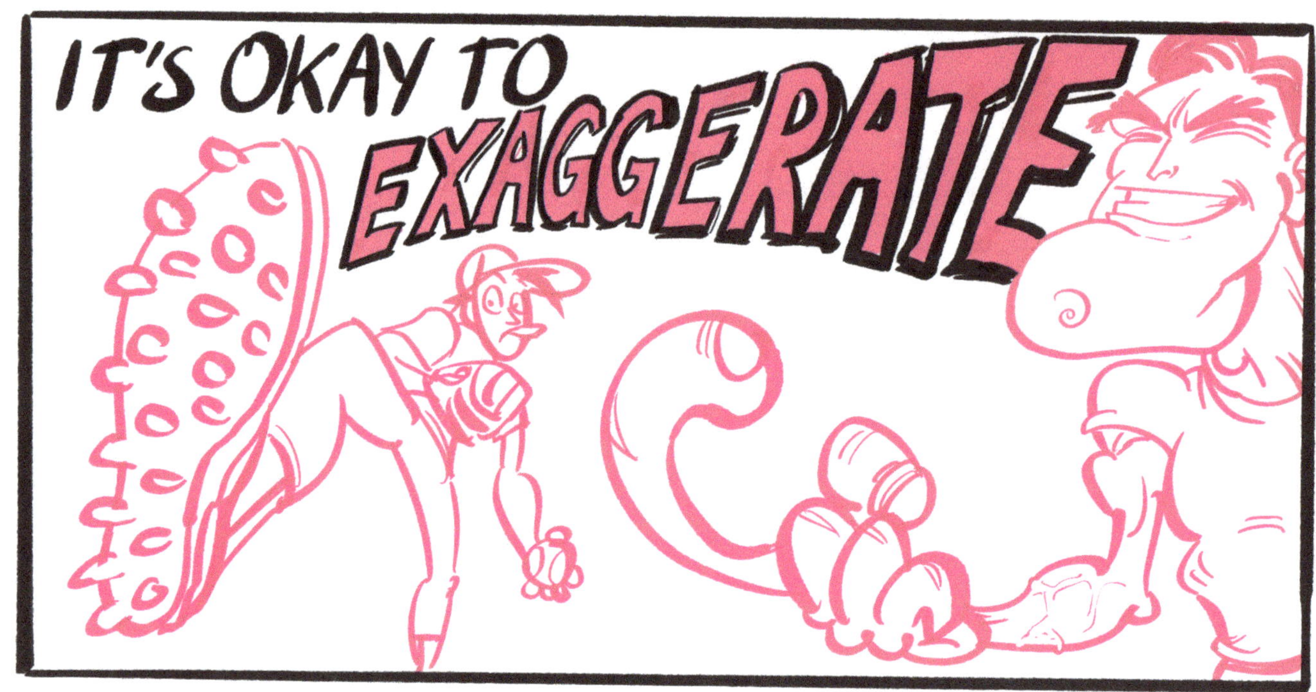

FACE EXPRESSIONS

FOCUS ON <u>EMOTIONS</u>
* <u>EYES</u> = MOST EXPRESSIVE
* CHEEKS & EYES <u>STRETCH</u> & <u>SQUASH</u>
* TOP OF HEAD & NOSE DO NOT CHANGE — BUT <u>HAIR</u> CAN <u>MOVE</u>

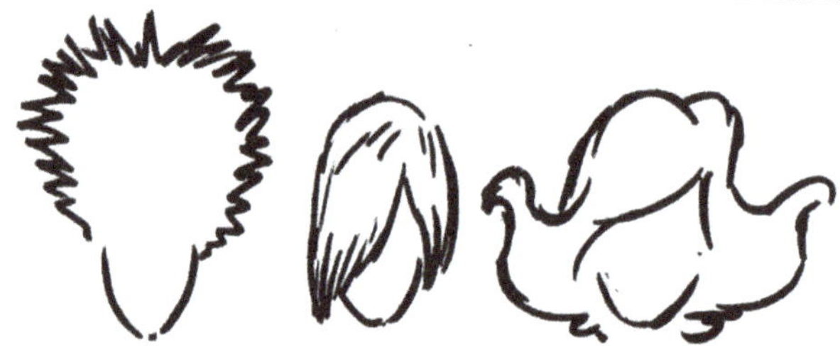

BODY EXPRESSIONS

FOCUS ON <u>EMOTIONS</u>
* SHOULD BE CLEAR AS STICK PERSON
* EXAGGERATE (& ACT IT OUT)

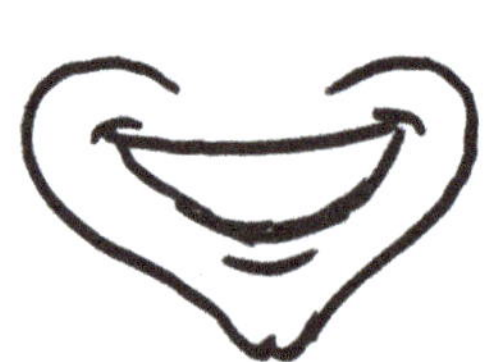
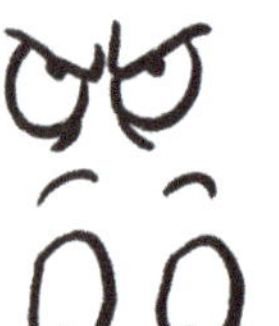
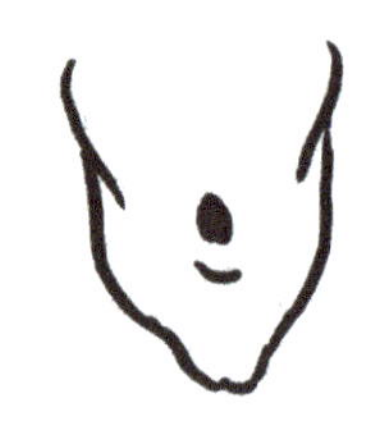
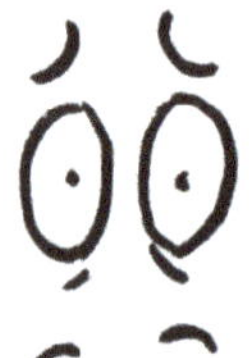
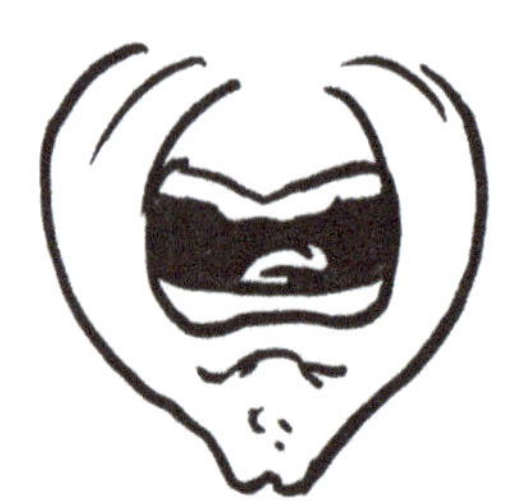
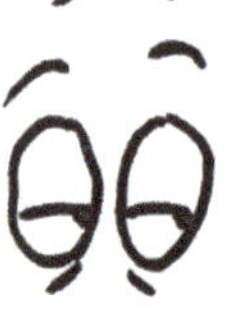

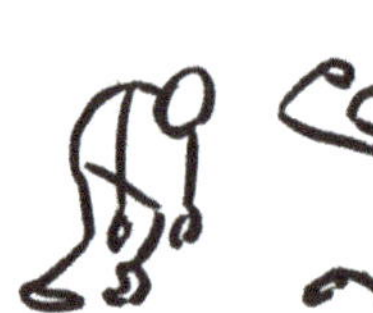
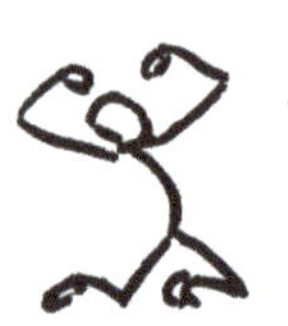
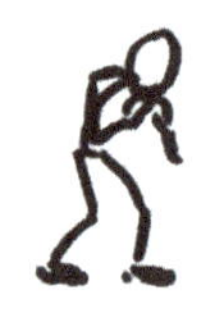
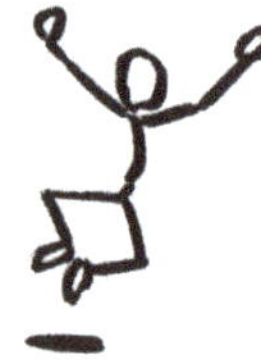
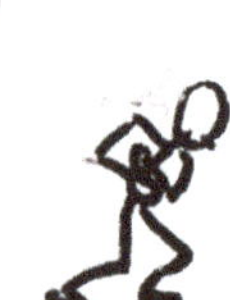

TORSO/PILLOW EXPRESSIONS
* <u>STRETCH</u> & <u>SQUASH</u> !!!

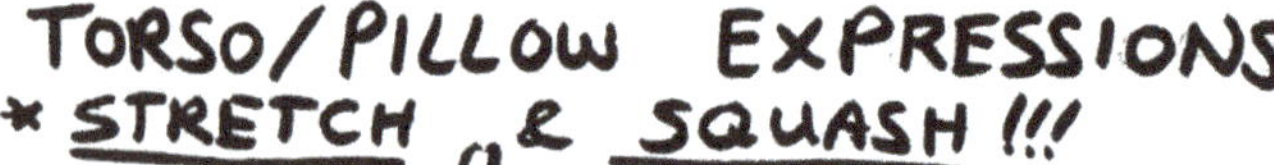
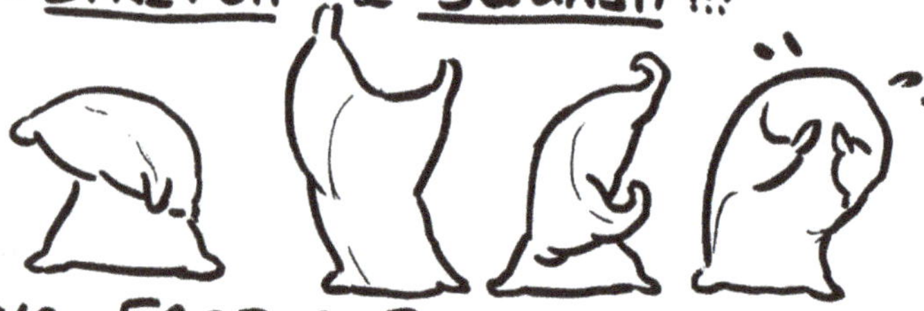

→ DRAW YOUR CHARACTER'S FACE & BODY...

Even the <u>Pros</u> use shapes!

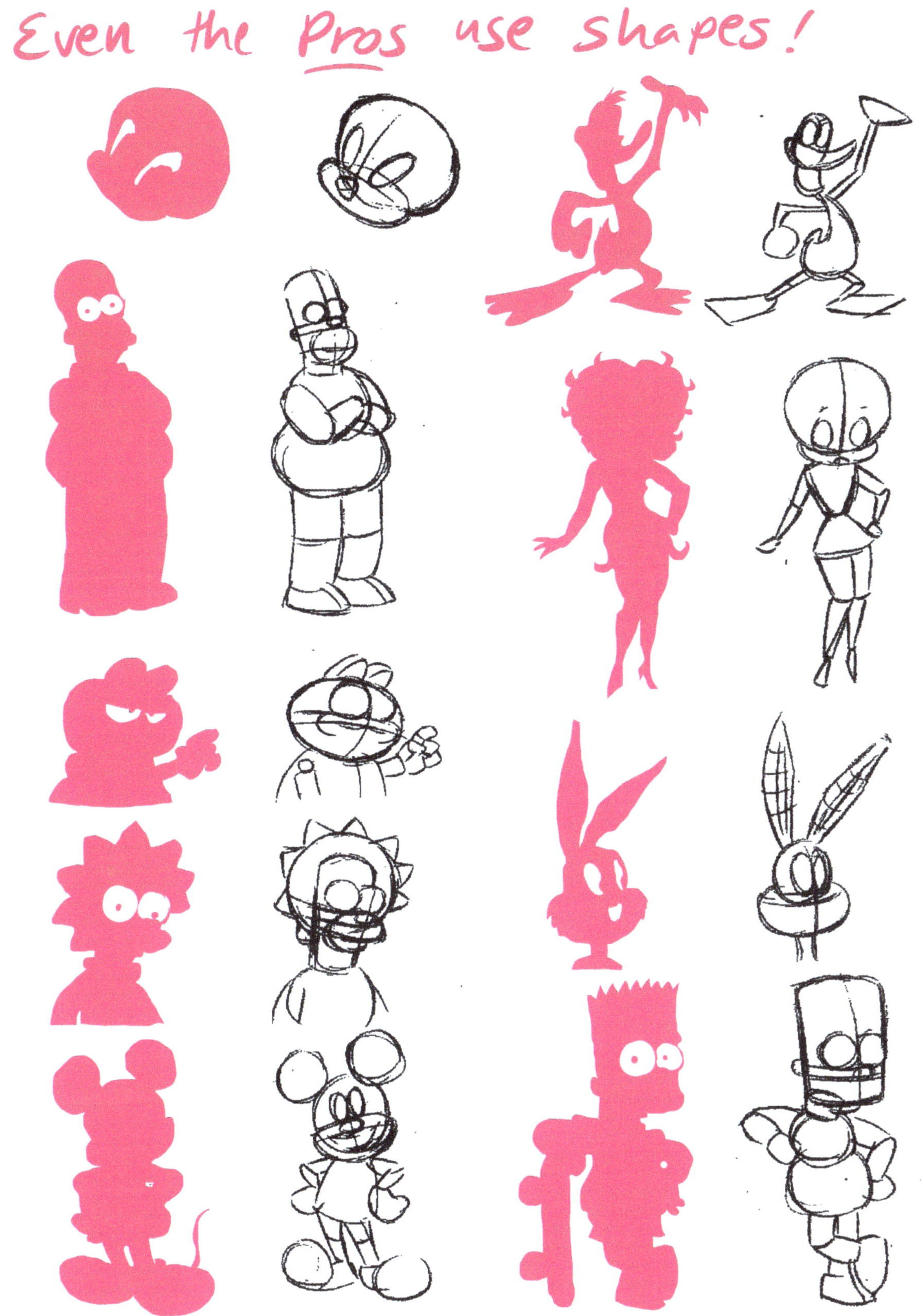

FOR EDUCATIONAL PURPOSES, I'VE ANALYZED THESE FAMOUS CARTOON CHARACTERS, TO SHOW THAT ALL CARTOONISTS CONSTRUCT THEIR CHARACTERS USING SHAPES. HAVING AN EASILY-REPEATABLE METHOD MAKES IT EASIER TO REDRAW ANY CHARACTER OVER AND OVER, IN A COMIC STRIP OR ANIMATION. IT'S AMAZING TO NOTICE HOW FEW SHAPES ARE USED TO DESIGN EACH OF THE ABOVE CARTOONS.

www.MasterpieceArtSchool.com

SHADING

- Hatching
- Cross hatching
- Blending
- Stipple/Dots

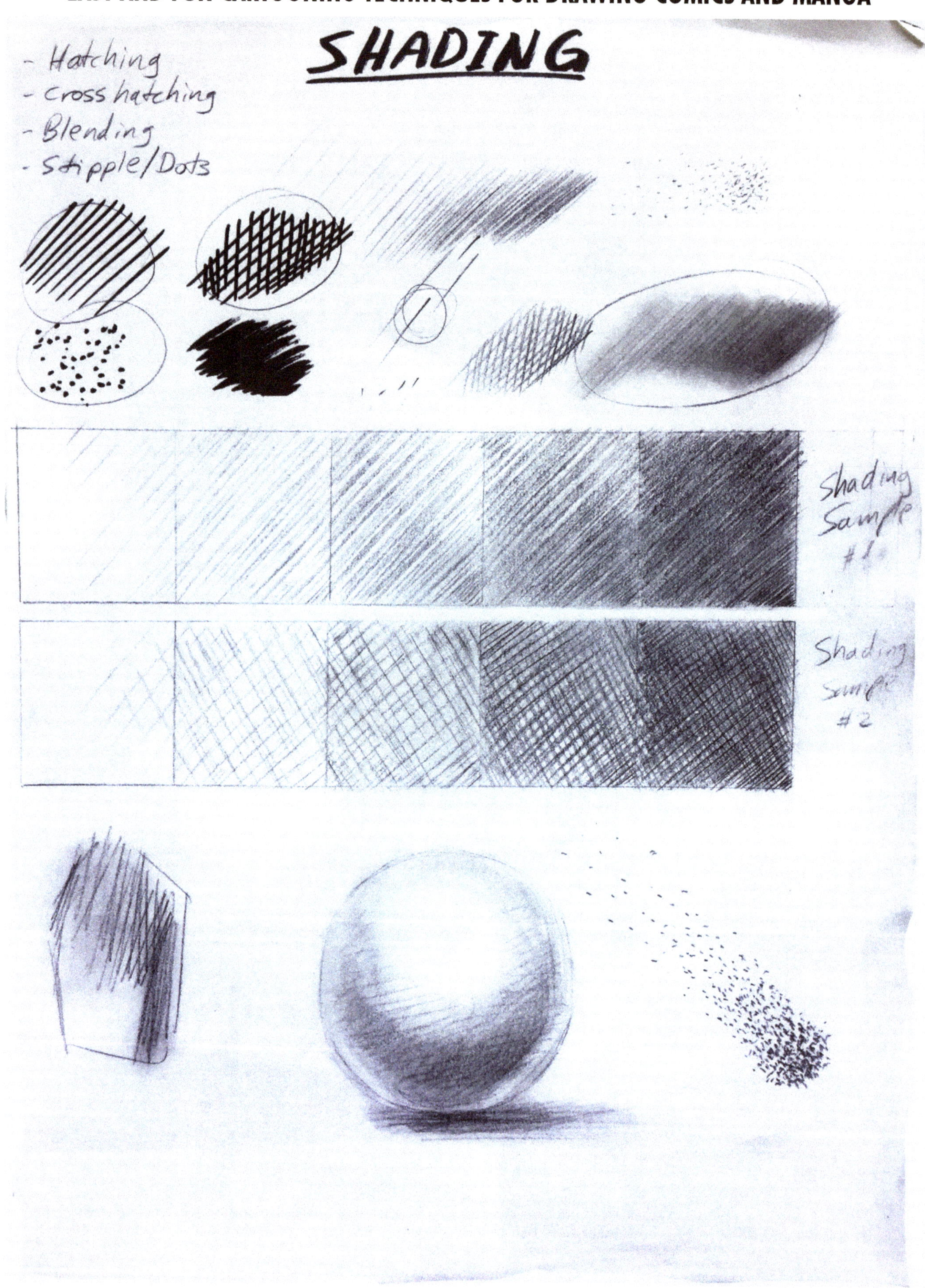

Screentones & Greyscale

OLD SCHOOL COMICS USED TO USE A TYPE OF SHADED PAPER CALLED "DUOTONE" AND SCREENTONES TO DISPLAY VARIATIONS IN SHADING ON COMIC PAGES AND MANGA. NOW, THIS CAN BE SIMULATED WITH GREYSCALE MARKERS OR DIGITAL BRUSHES. ALL TYPES OF TEXTURES ARE AVAILABLE TO SAMPLE AND YOU CAN INK A DRAWING AND USE THE PENCIL TO SHADE TOO. THIS IS USED TO DIFFERENTIATE OR TO SHOW SHADOWS.

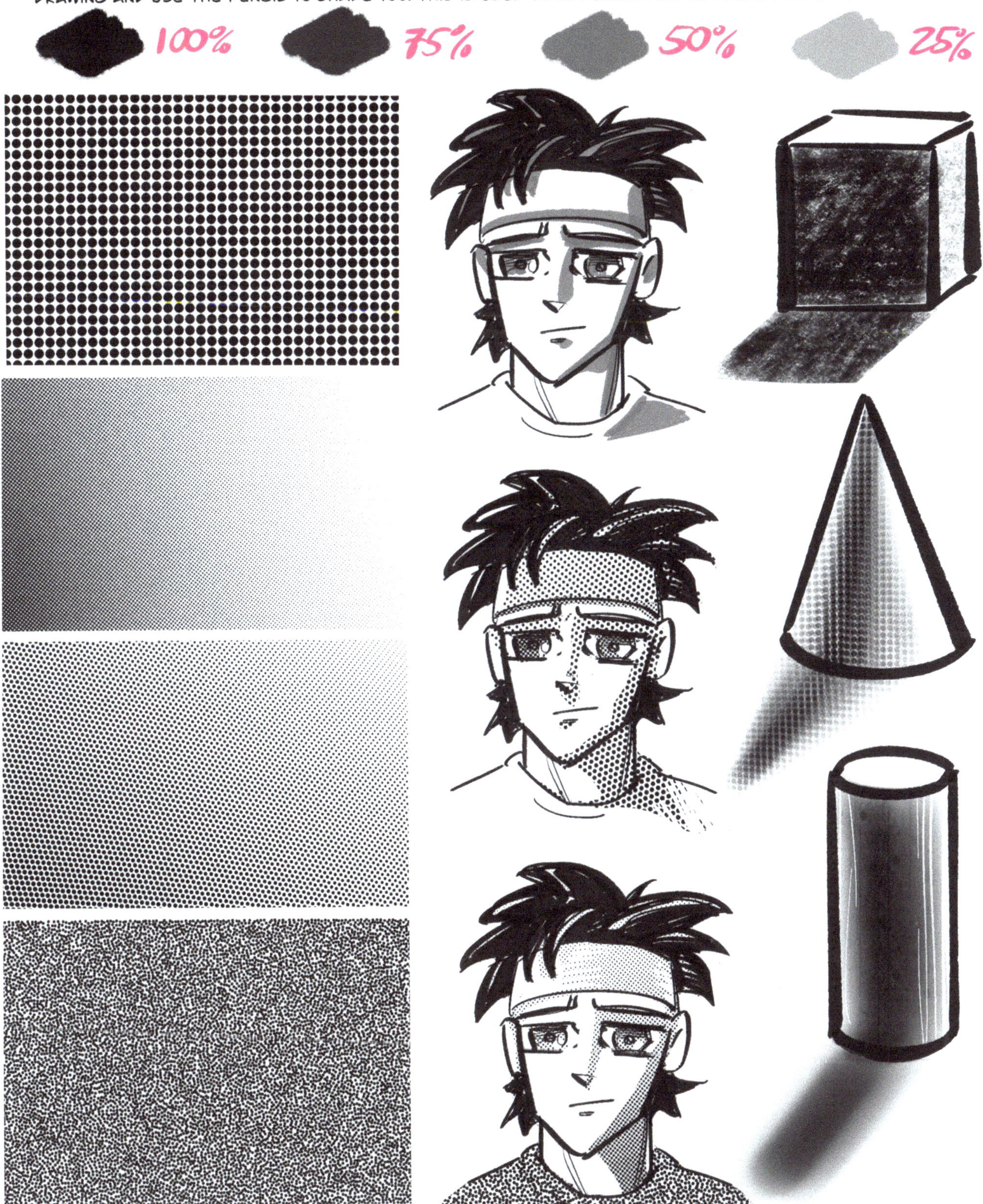

Tech & Mech

Creative machine design

Weapons
multi barrel shot gun
double-edged blades
battle axe
photon rifle
photon gun
incinerator gun

spaceships

robots

futuristic cars

Cars in motion

if the wheels touch the ground it looks like it's parked!

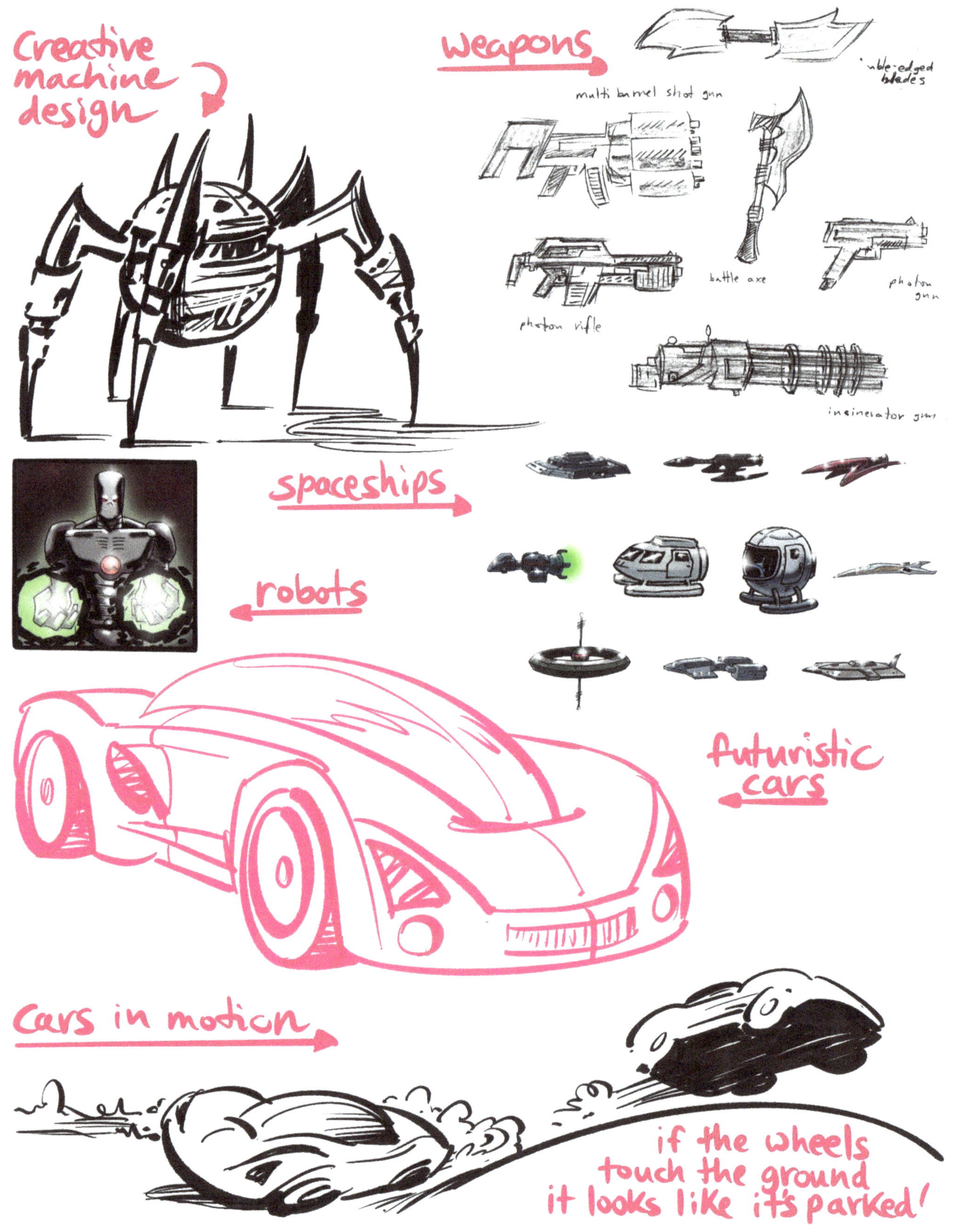

Staging Tips

Stack objects or people

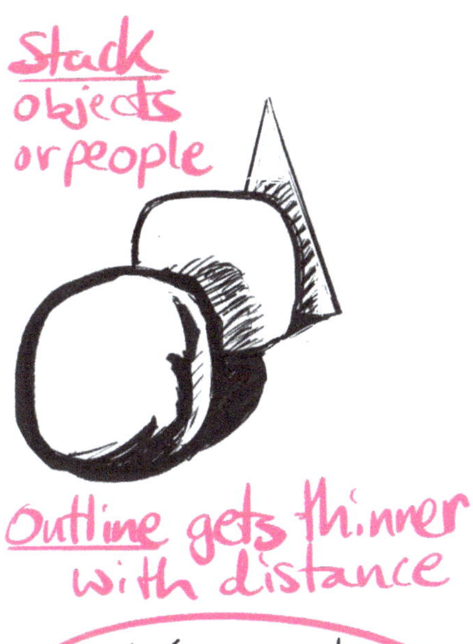

Outline gets thinner with distance

Clichés are okay, just do them in your own way!

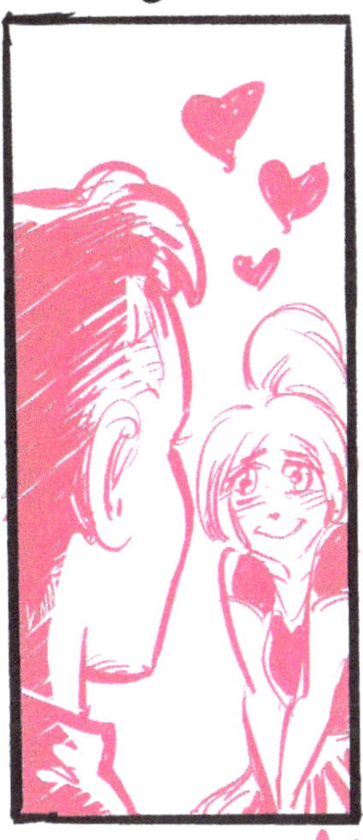

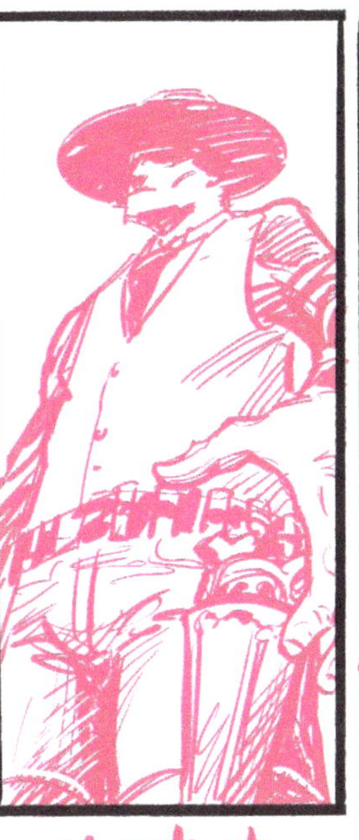

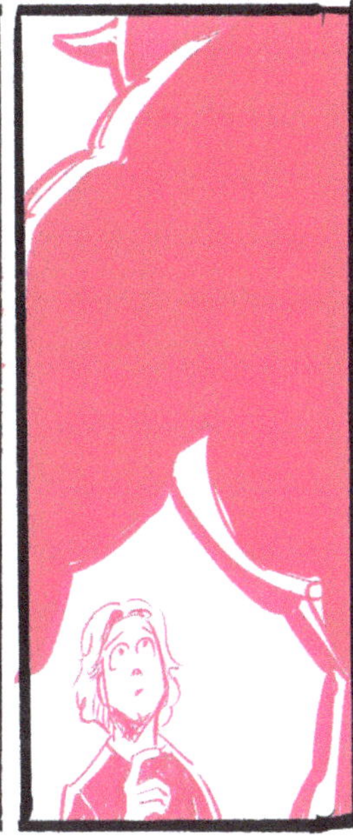

Foreground/ Background

Upshot - for dramatic imposing characters

Down Shot/ Framed Shot - to emphasize or differentiate

Showing **Depth** using **shades**...

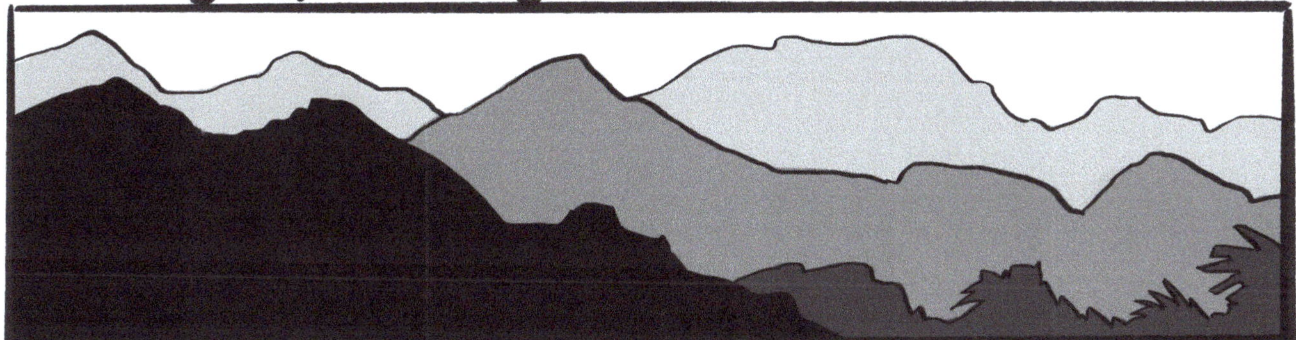

Readability is very important! (Has to be **clear** as a **silhouette**!)

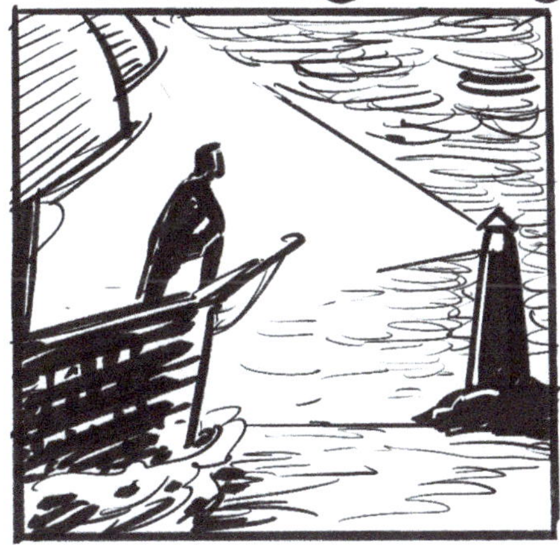

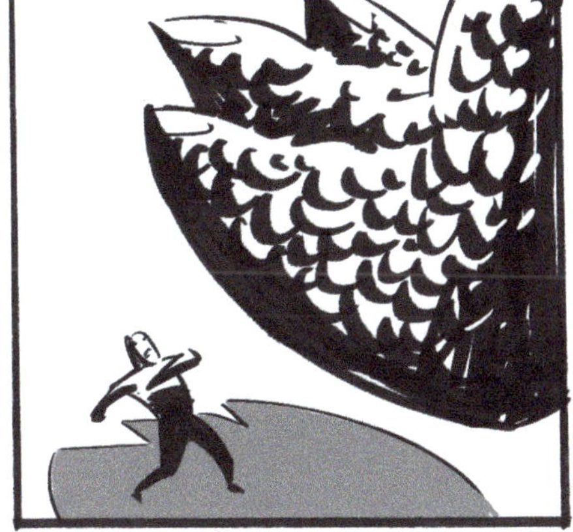

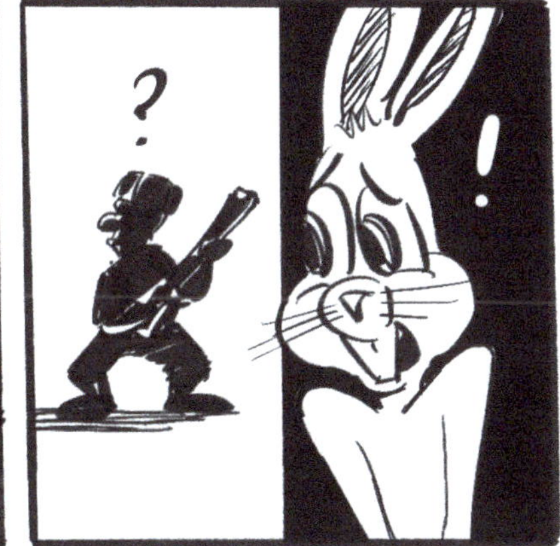

Colour Basics

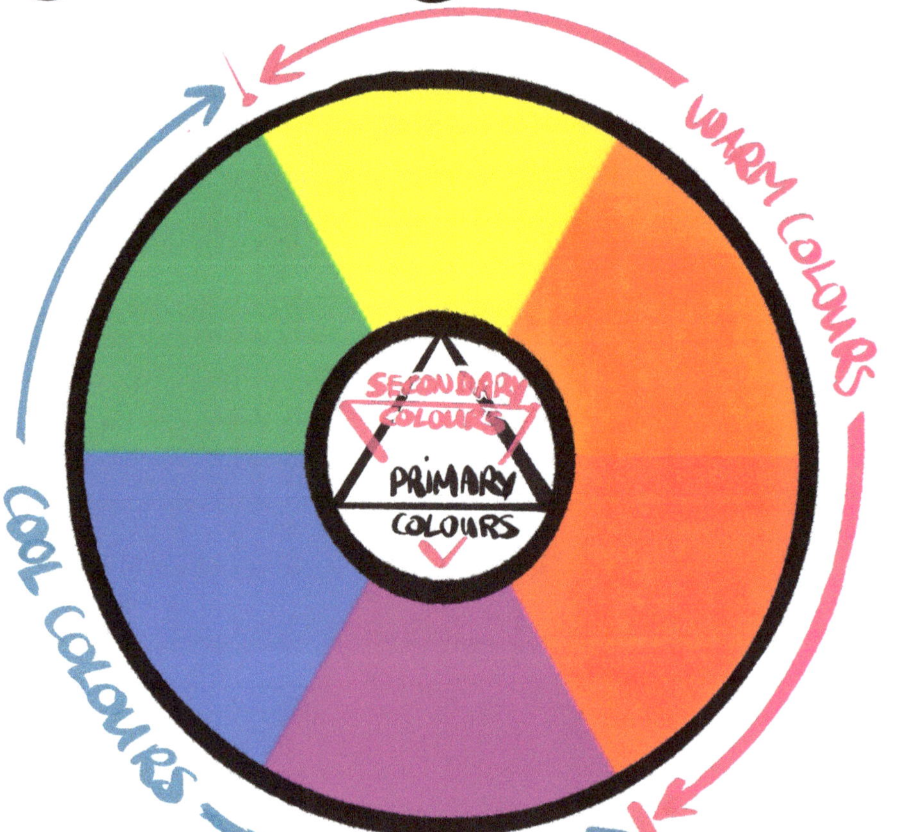

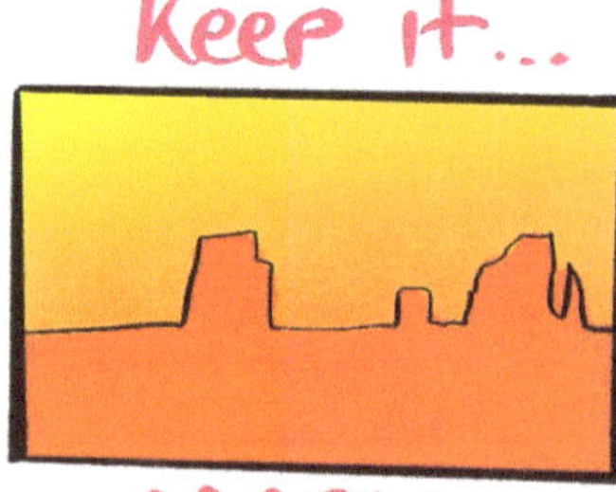

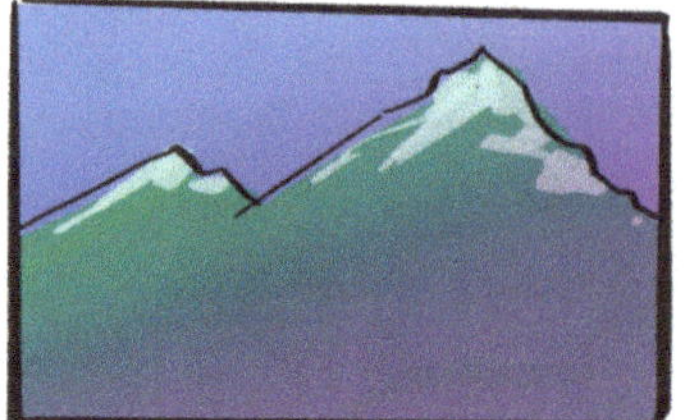

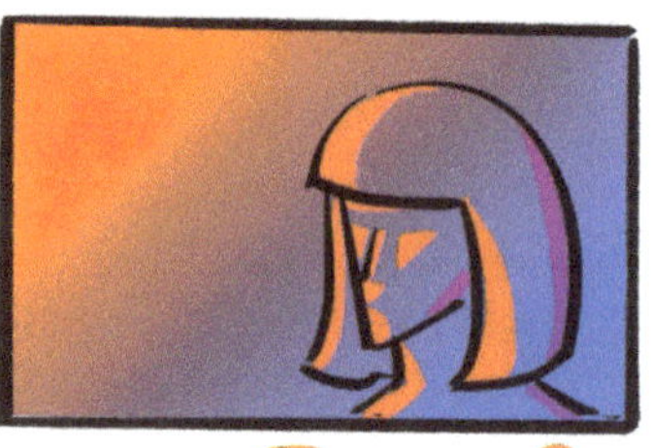

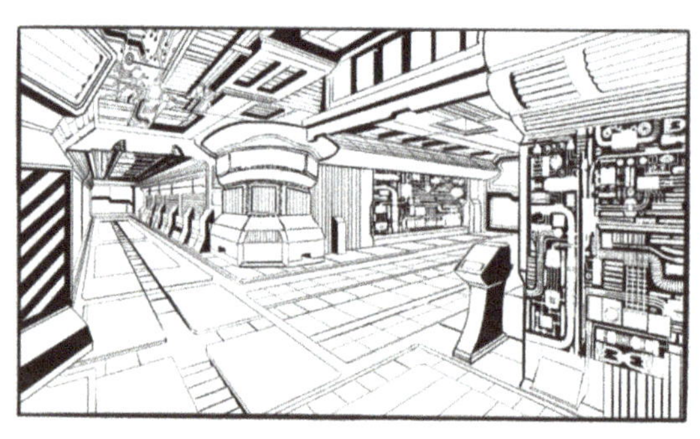

Flat Colours are applied first before the final airbrushing

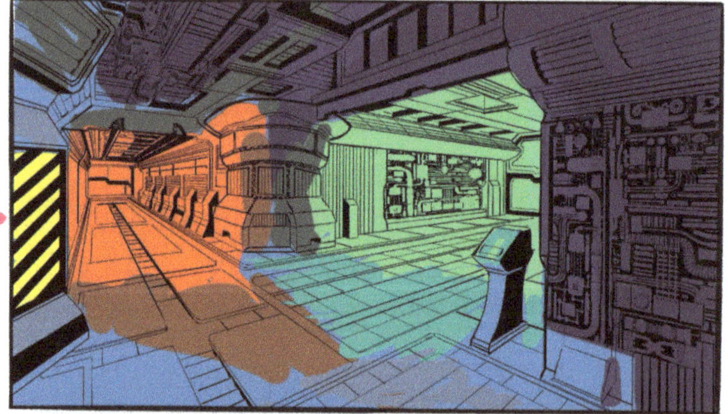

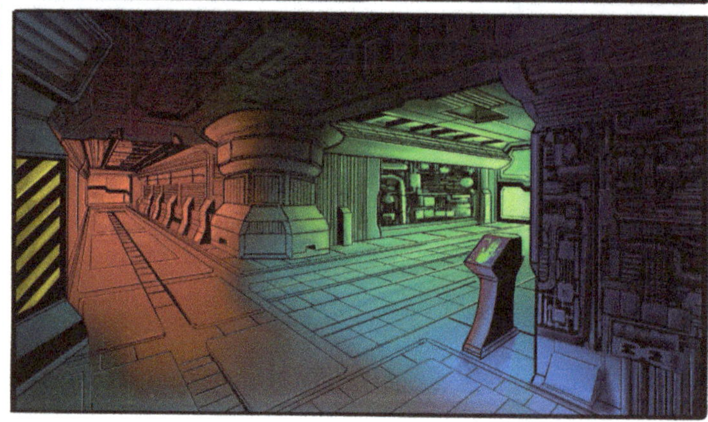

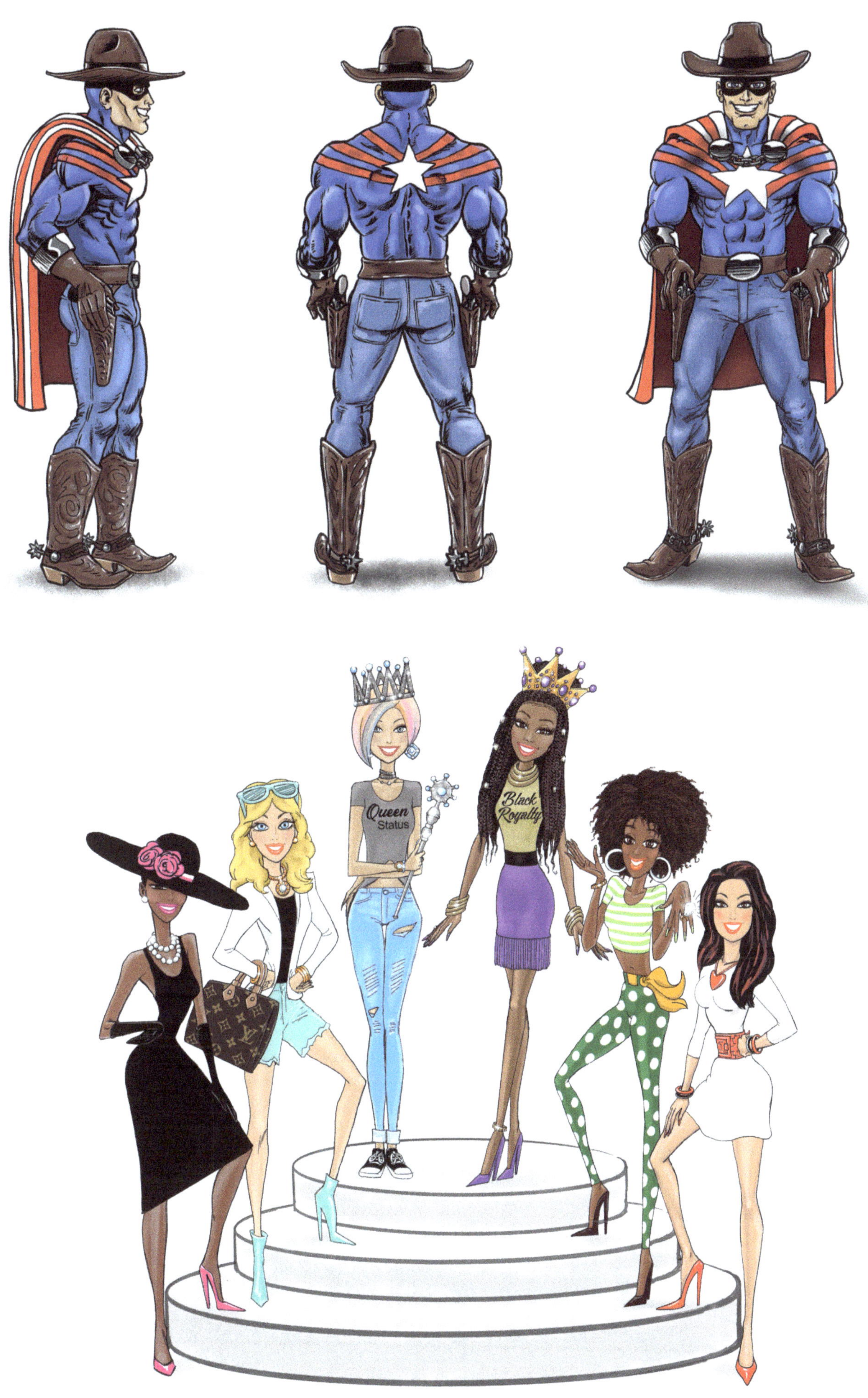

Queen
Status
Black
Royalty

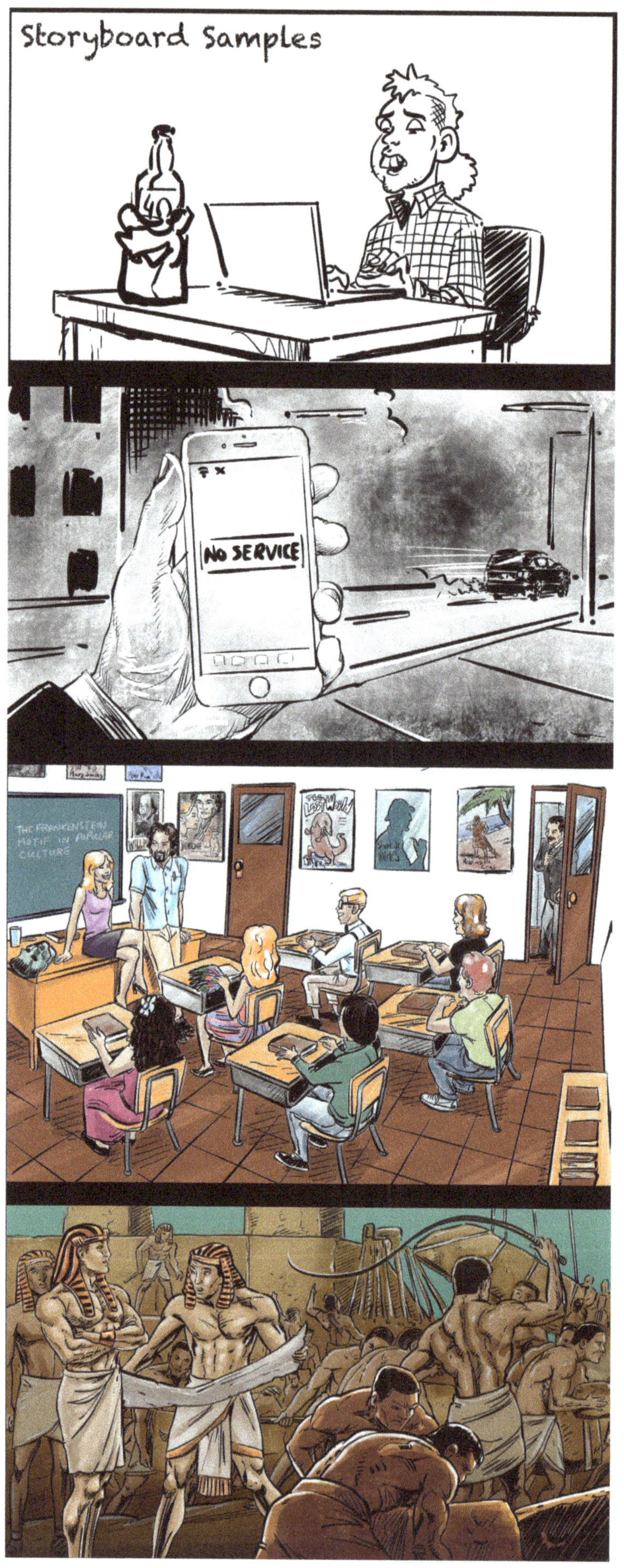
Storyboard Samples
NO SERVICE
THE FRANKENSTEIN
MOTIF IN POPULAR
CULTURE

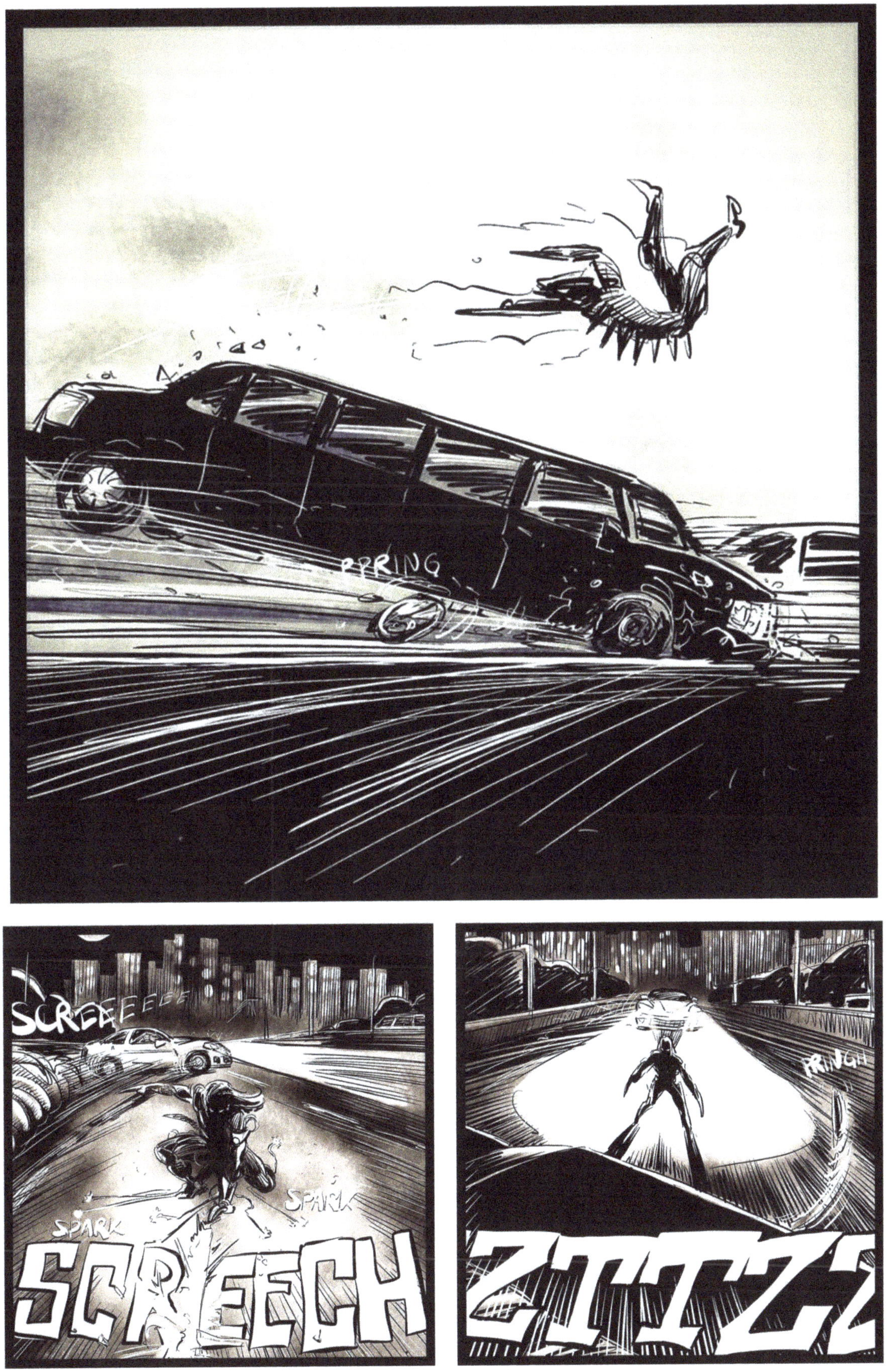

PRRING

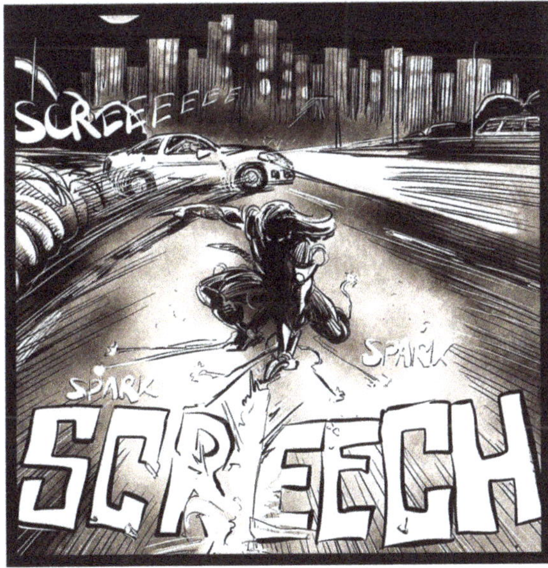

SCREEEEE
SPARK
SPARK
SCREECH

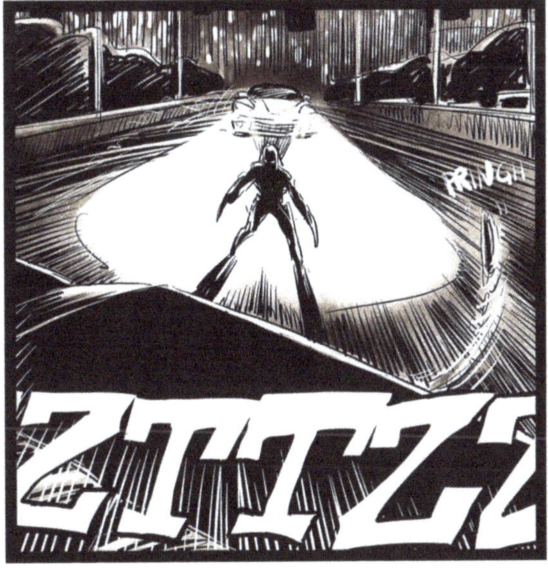

RRINGH
ZTTZZ

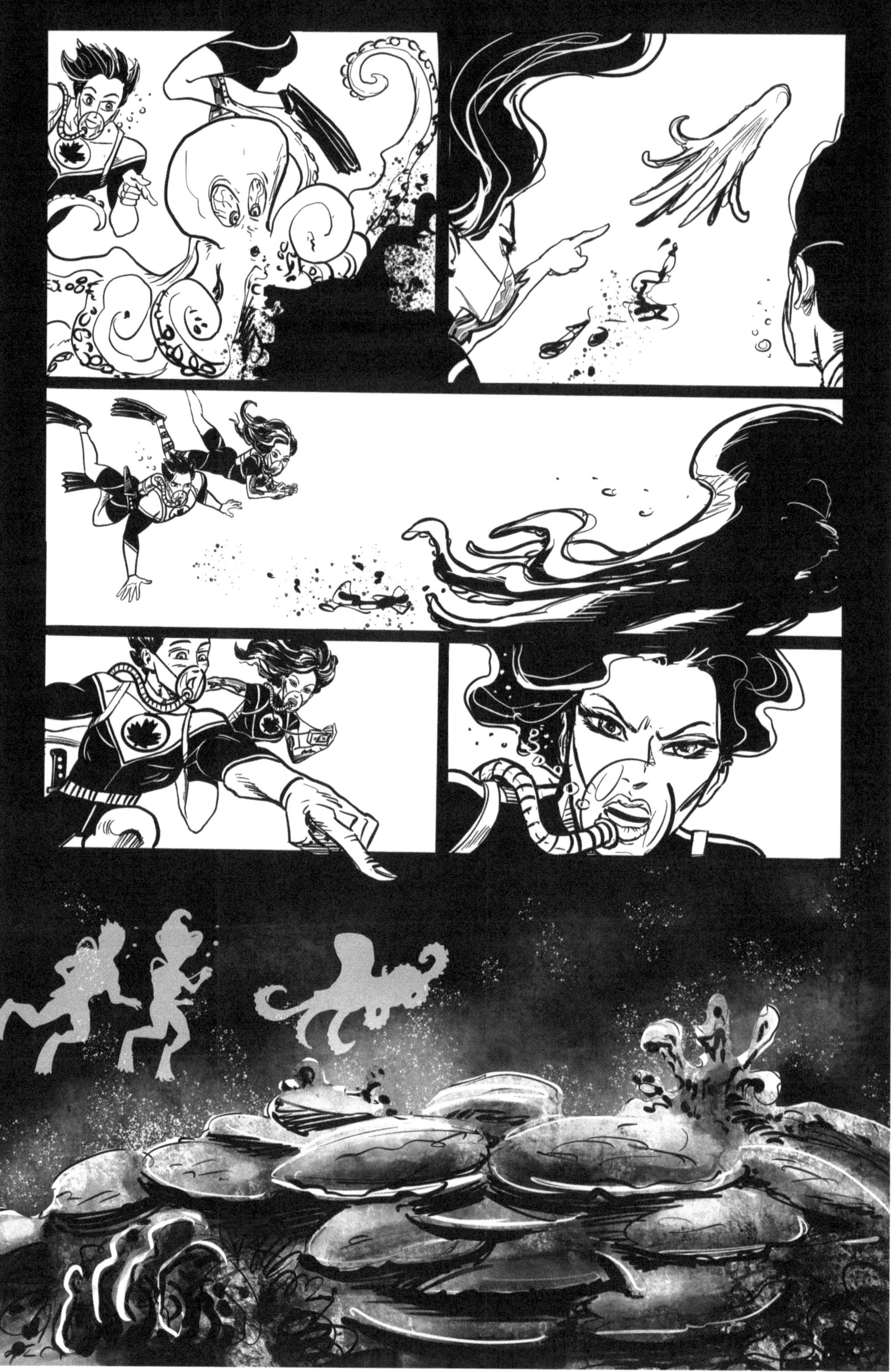

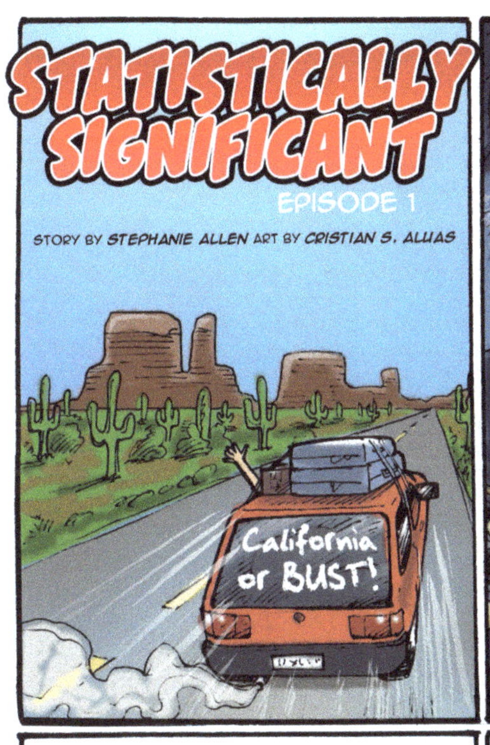

STATISTICALLY SIGNIFICANT
EPISODE 1
STORY BY STEPHANIE ALLEN ART BY CRISTIAN S. ALUAS
California or BUST!

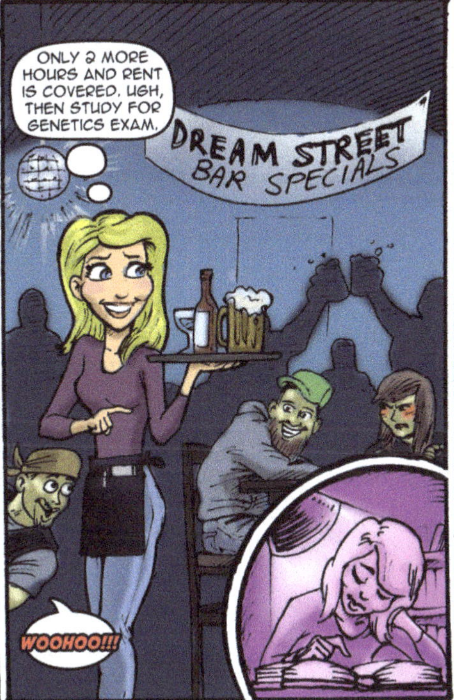

ONLY 2 MORE HOURS AND RENT IS COVERED. UGH, THEN STUDY FOR GENETICS EXAM.
DREAM STREET BAR SPECIALS
WOOHOO!!!

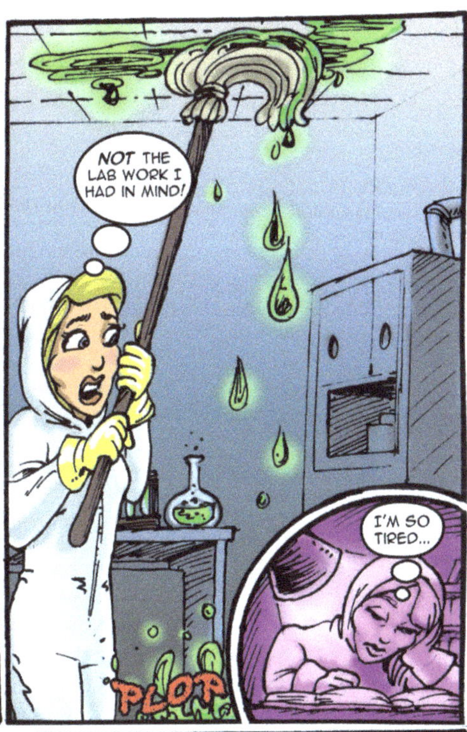

NOT THE LAB WORK I HAD IN MIND!
I'M SO TIRED...
PLOP

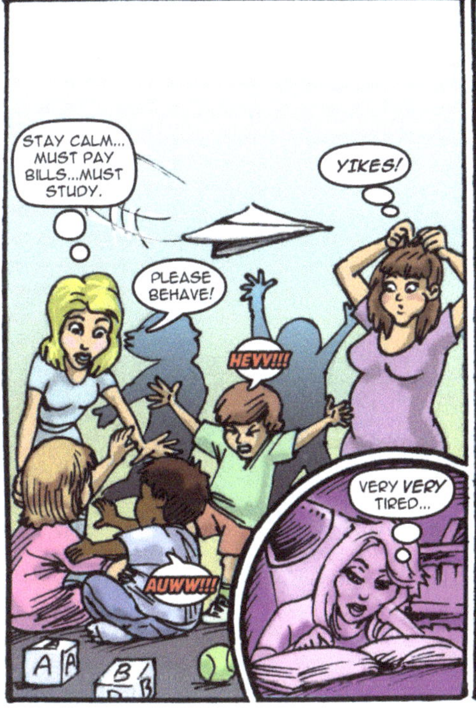

STAY CALM... MUST PAY BILLS...MUST STUDY.
YIKES!
PLEASE BEHAVE!
HEYY!!!
AUWW!!!
VERY VERY TIRED...
A A
B B

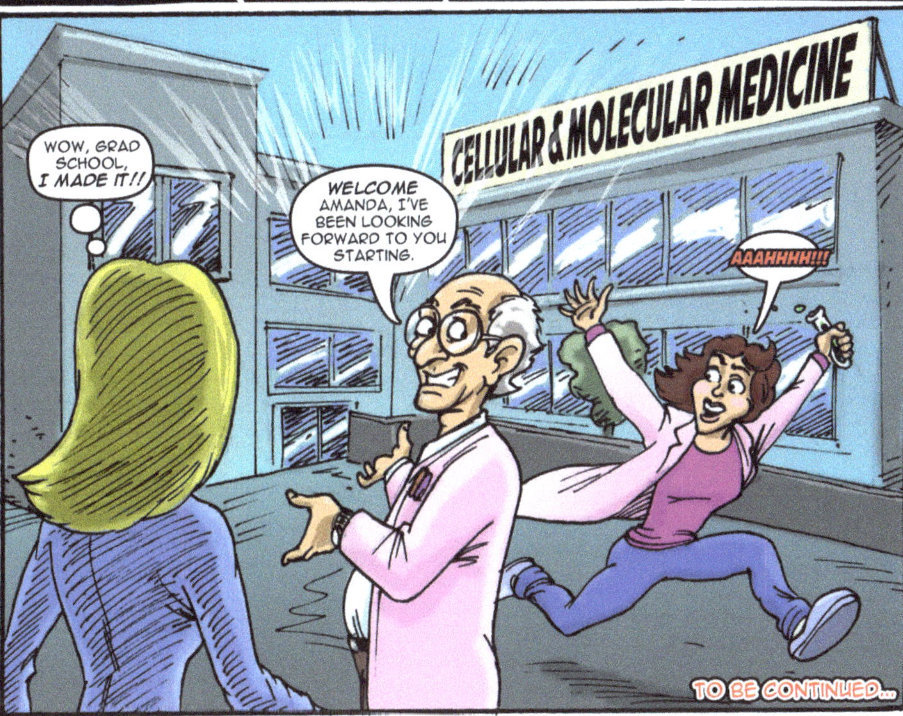

WOW, GRAD SCHOOL, I MADE IT!!
WELCOME AMANDA, I'VE BEEN LOOKING FORWARD TO YOU STARTING.
CELLULAR & MOLECULAR MEDICINE
AAAHHHH!!!
TO BE CONTINUED...

Thank you!

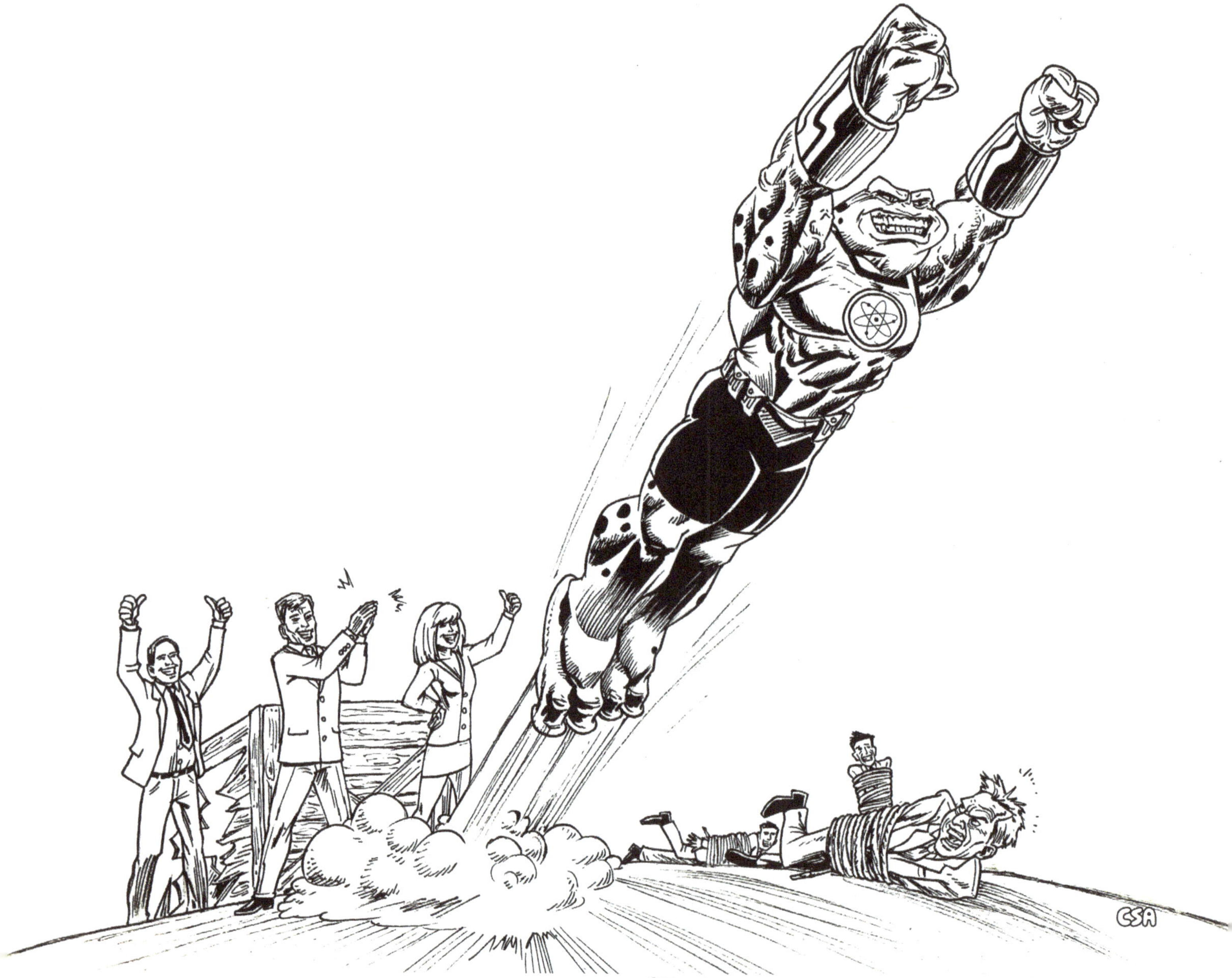

Till Next Time!

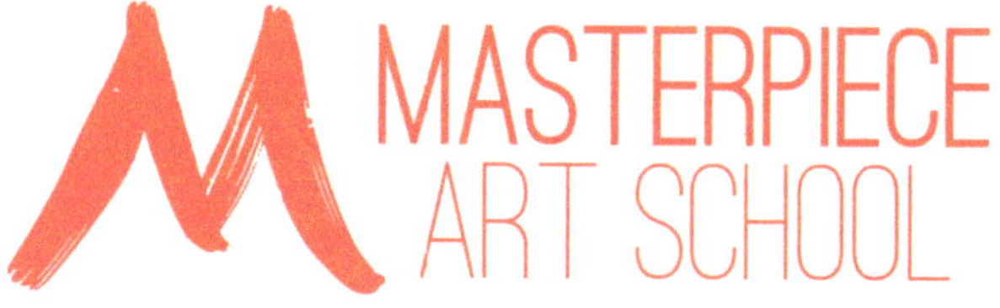